The Michael Jackson

Trial Juror Notebooks

By Vincent F. Amen

The Michael Jackson Trial Juror Notebooks

by

Vincent F. Amen

Author Name: Vincent F. Amen
Publisher Info: Alpha Book Publisher
Publisher Headquarters: Moosic, PA 18507

Printed in the United States of America

Photographs by Bill Shaw of
Bill Shaw Photography

The investigation and Trial of Michael Jackson lasted from November 2003 to June 2005. Leading up to the trial was jury selection. A man named Jeffrey Welbaum was selected as a juror, more specifically an alternate juror. Jeffrey is a controversial juror due to the fact his mother in-law worked at Michael Jackson's Neverland Ranch and he was still selected as a juror. Jeffrey was able to keep his notebooks after the trial since he was an alternate juror. There were only several alternate jurors that had notebooks that fully documented the trial. This book is one of them which is a summary or shortened version of the trial that documents what Jeffrey found meaningful from trial testimony documented witness by witness.

In 2006, Vincent Amen purchased the notebooks from Jeffrey Welbaum and later the rights to publish them as a book. There is a great value to the notebooks with positive implications. What does a juror note from Trial testimony to ultimately render a verdict? This question may have never been explored before prior to publishing these notebooks. For prosecutors and defense attorneys alike, these notebooks can be helpful in determining how to try cases. Based on all evidence shown and witness testimony, what a jury finds meaningful to note can provide a means to being more effective in organizing and trying a case. Enjoy reading the notebooks and based on what is documented, try to come to your own conclusion or verdict.

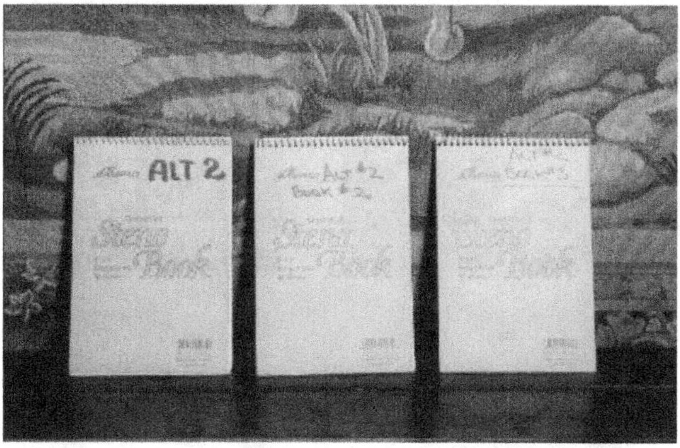
ALT 2

Steno Book
EXP
STENO BOOK

EXP
STENO BOOK
Steno Book
exp
exp

exp
exp

Contents

Chapters	Pages
Juror Notebook 1	1
Juror Notebook 2	74
Juror Notebook 3	146
Juror Notebook 4	210
Juror Notebook 5	268
Juror Notebook 6	331
Index	390

Juror Notebook 1

Chapter 1

2-28-05 Monday

False Imprisonment
Child Abduction

Feb 4 2003
Death Threats

Count 2 – Felony
Lewd Act upon a child under 14

Count 3 – Felony
Feb 20 March 12 2003

Count 4 – Felony
Lewd act upon child under 14
Feb 20-Mar 12 2003

Count 5 – Felony
Feb 20 – Mar 12 2003
Lewd act upon child under 14

Count 6 – Felony
Attempt to commit lewd act upon child under 14
Feb 20-Mar 12

Count 7 – Felony
Adm Intoxicating agent
Feb 20- Mar 12 2003

Count 8 – Felony
Adm Intoxicating agent
Feb 20 – Mar 12 2003

Count 9 – Felony
Adm Intoxicating agent
Feb 20-Mar 12 2003

Count 10 – Felony
Adm Intoxicating agent
Feb 20-Mar 12 2003

March 1st

1st Witness – Martin Bashir

2002 – ITV
1hr – Harold Shipman Serial Killer

1995 Princess Diana 1:45 Minutes

2002 – Jan 14 2003 Shown Feb 3 In G.B.
Current Affairs Team
Program Tonight

Yes knew videographer was there

MJ says

Wasn't allowed to call his dad daddy. Hated his dad for the abuse. Physical and mental.

Says he had a relationship with the 3rd child's mother but later in the documentary says she's a surrogate and didn't really know her.

Didn't want to answer
Drank lots of water
Seemed Nervous

Cross-Examination

3 complaints
1 upheld
Description of story not giving entirety to one party
Teen prodigy
Math genius

Sept 1 2004
ABC Correspondent

Subpoena Jan 2005
Won't answer if he told any journalist he was a witness
Won't answer under shield **law**

2004 Phone Conversation
Det Paul Zellis

Witness #2 Ann Marie Kite (Gabriel)

D Legrand met 2002
Personal Relationship July 2002 – Jan 2003

Worked for Michael Jackson
End Jan-2003

Public Relations (Feb 9 2003 Feb 14)

Signed contract 3:00-4:00 PM

Ronald Konitzer – Leader of team
Schaffel – Head of PR

Backerman – Spokesperson

March 2nd
Says Bashir Documentary was a disaster
Scale 1-10 She says **(25)**

Melanie Riley Belliard
Crisis management
Richard
Mark Geragos – Feb 7 Part of Team

Schaffel became problem negative image
Al Malnik also a problem

Rebuttal on FOX

Schaffel would have creative interest.

Debbie Rowe - Could get her to say whatever he wanted her to say

E-mail Feb 14
R. Konitzer

Feb 10 – Take out MJJ Inc and put in Gabriel Media on Appearance release form

Feb 13 – Schaffel called her to tell her Janet had taken kids off ranch.
Second Call – Schaffel called
Situation had been contained
They had been brought (Arvizo's) back to ranch

LeGrand couldn't discuss it at time.

Schaffel said the situation was taken care of.

Feb 15 – Terminated
Feb 14 – Statement on TV Access Hollywood.
Interview cancelled for call from Geragos
Geragos wanted her to sign agreement, Private
Investigator Confidentiality

Mar 2

Call with LeGrand 10 days after termination. Had Janet Arvizo on tape, make her look like a crack whore

Cross Exam Mrs. Kite
Worked with Webcaster Alliance during same 6 day period
Met with Santa Barbara Sheriffs

March 2004
Didn't tell anybody on the team about her dating Legrand. Stopped dating just before getting hired
Music labels opposed Webcasters
Conflict on interests?

Only represented 1 other so called celebrity
Never met anyone from "Team" other than Legrand.
Phone Calls – Over 50 to Legrand
5-7 to Backerman
Meeting for 2 hours with prosecution

She has talked to Geragos since being terminated.
Never talked to Dieter Wiesner
Learned about the power of attorney for Mr.
Konitzer for Michael Jackson at the end of January.
Konitzer embezzled $980,000 from Jackson.
Discussed about what to do if the story sold in the UK.
Schaffel wanted her to appear on Access Hollywood.
Konitzer and Wiesner had business dealings
Sony may have wanted catalog back
Firemountain Corp getting 3 million for rebuttal video.
She went to work for Legrand after termination
LeGrand afraid of Mr. Branca
LeGrand referred to AL Malnik as uncle AL
Met Jermain Jackson Apr 2003

March 2
She believed the team was detrimental to Michael Jackson. Met with Jermain Jackson 6 weeks after termination. Her work with Legrand ended in April. Her and Legrand are no longer friends. Backerman says he was an official spokesperson for Michael Jackson while and before he was living with Schaffel . She has no knowledge of any molestation or anything about Janet Arvizo. Schaffel trying to make NBC Look bad. Geragos okayed press release. Konitzer wanted a website MJJ Invincible. LeGrand told Michael Jackson about the problems. Fire Mountain set up by Legrand.

March 12 2003

Power of attorney revoked from Konitzer. Schaffel was a gay Pornography Producer. Al Malnik may have been a mobster.
3rd Witness Albert Lafferty

Deputy Sheriff 18 years. Shoot video and photos of the main residence of Michael Jackson's home.

March 2 2004

Aerial Photos for building identification

March 3rd

Arrived at Ranch Nov 18, 2003 9:07 am. Started Video – 9:55 am. After Search Video 8:40 pm. Michael Jackson Bedroom Search 10:38 pm to 10:55 pm
Keypad locks on all children's rooms and Jackson's bedroom
March 3

Did not shoot the first part of the video. 7 forensic specialists. 1 hr Video Pre Search. May 20, 04 Pickup evidence in briefcase **317**. You can see the train station clock from the main house and the guest house.

4th Witness Davellin Arvizo 18 years

Hollywood High 2 years. 5 people living in an

apartment. Comedians at camp at Laugh Factory comedy club. Fritz Coleman, George Lopez. Gavin wanted to meet, she says, Chris Tucker, Adam Sandler and she says Mr. Jackson. First went to Neverland in 2000. Parents argued dad threw soda can at her. **Father was abusive to all family members she says.** Gavin asked to sleep in Jackson's Room. Went with Chris Tucker to Neverland 2 Times. Lived with grandmother during treatment for cancer. Room was made livable for Gavin and paid for by Louise Palanker. Parents separated sophomore year in high school. Father moved. Mom and Kids stayed at East LA Apartment. She was in Police Explorers. Michael Jackson gave them a white bronco. **(She)** has spent the night at Chris Tucker's fiancé Azja house.

Mar 3

She says Gavin and MJ went and talked. MJ asked to talk to Gavin by himself 5-10 min. She says her mother is not with them very often. Met step-father Jay Jackson after Bashir filming. She says her mother taught her to hug people she first meets. Flight to Miami private jet. Chris Tucker, her Mom, and her brothers, Pilot, Flight Attendant. Went to see MJ the next day. She says MJ introduced her to kids Marie Nicole and Aldo, siblings of Frank Tyson. Also met Dieter, Ronald, 2 nannies, MJ's 3 children in the room when they first got there. She says MJ took Gavin into his room by themselves for 15-30 min. She says 2 or 3 times, doors closed every time. She says MJ told them not to watch Bashir's documentary. She says Dieter and MJ would go in the room 2-3 times. Same with Ronald. Frank 1 time she thinks. They all left that night together, mother and her brothers. She lived with her grandparents her senior year in high school. She says Gavin was sipping a Diet Coke can and were whispering to each other. She says Michael Jackson, gave Gavin his watch and a jacket. She says Gavin used his phone once to call a friend.

March 3rd

Her sophomore year after a year of treatment, Gavin was in remission. She says Ronald and Dieter were at the Neverland Ranch 2 day after they arrived. She says they were given a "script" for the Rebuttal video. She didn't remember leaving with Security until he reminded her. She says her mother never came out of her guest room. She says her mother seemed scared. Her mother asked (Security) Jesus to take her and her kids home. Went to Grandmother's. She says her mother seemed upset after being visited in the guesthouse by Dieter and Ronald. She says the family was interviewed by Brad Miller at her step-dads apartment. She says tape was stopped and started and told by Brad Miller some things were not important. She says that Frank had told them there were death threats on them. She says they were told to say nice things and not to say what goes on at Ranch. Rebuttal there till 4 am she says. She says MJ didn't help with homework. They didn't have his phone number. **<u>She considered him a close friend not daddy</u>** but it changed for the worse.

March 3rd

She says they met with social workers the next day after the Rebuttal video. Azja, Mj bodyguard and her family. Social workers asked everybody except the family to leave. She says the bodyguard talked to the mother in the room. She saw a box on the bed and the mother put it in the closet. They were taken back to ranch by Aja instead of MJ bodyguard because they asked her to. She says because they were scared. She met Vinnie at the ranch. She met Jesus at a ranch. She met Brad Miller at Jay Jackson's, her stepdad. Stayed with family in Calabasas. She says Frank and Vinnie were in a room close by and MJ's bodyguard was in the lobby. She says they were told to stay in the room and Frank and Vinnie would get what they needed. **<u>She saw her brothers drink once.</u>** The entrance to the wine cellar was behind the jukebox in the game room. She says she saw MJ, Gavin, Star and Aldo. She says she was offered and drank wine also. She says she was in his bedroom once at the ranch. She followed her brothers into the room because she did not have code. She says she saw bottles that she assumed were alcohol.

March 3rd
She says bottles (alcohol) were on the night stands and other parts of the room. She says she left the

room by herself. She also said maybe MJ's son was in the room also.

While in Calabasas, Vinnie and Ahmed took them shopping and to get passports to go to Brazil because Frank had told them once and Dieter had told them they had death threats. Trip to Laugh Factory mother and Gavin went in first. Then she went in and Starr stayed in the car with Vinnie. Spent 30 min inside with Bill, Jaimie, Gavin and mom. She says she did not sign the document for the passport. She says Vinnie filled out the document. She also says Vinnie filled out both forms from information from his mother. She says they spent 3 or 4 days at Calabasas Inn in 2 different rooms. 1 Room had 1 more bed. Went back to Neverland. Went to Toys R Us with Frank, MJ, Gavin, Starr, (Chris) Bodyguard and picked up some fans. Gavin has to give urine in a big bottle with really (Snug top). She says her relationship changed with her brother Gavin. She says she became distant and didn't want to be around anybody.

March 4

Watching Rebuttal Video Gavin asked to sleep in the room. The mom seems to me to be on something. Janet says she had to make sure they were safe. But she didn't seem like she was with them a lot. He refers back to 1993. Gavin, when he was (3), that he heard stuff about MJ, but didn't listen to it? Janet talks about being poor and how

MJ ended all that. When they didn't know if the camera was on, they seemed playful and Gavin says he doesn't like Martin Bashir. Janet says they had full access to Mj 24 hrs a day. They talked about MJ like he is their real father and Janet talks about him like she loves him. Janet seemed to cut off her kids a lot, couldn't wait to reply. Davellin says she or her mother never saw Bashir Documentary. She has a conversation before the rebuttal video with Frank and Dieter about death threats. She says Frank called her mom a bitch and was being difficult after the rebuttal video. She said faggot yesterday but wouldn't say bitch today? She says she was videotaped and the same person threw rocks at her grandmother's house. She says she saw MJ hugging and kissing Gavin on the cheek and head in his bedroom one time, then laying together, and MJ hugging and kissing him on the cheek she thought that was inappropriate.

March 4

Cross Examination of Davellin Arvizo

Vinnie drove them after the Rebuttal video to Jay Jackson's home. She seems not to remember a lot of things on cross but it seems she remembered more on direct. Det Robel's wife picked her up for meetings with Sneddon. Talks to her family everyday but she says they never talked about testimony. She says she never had attorneys or her family has never had attorneys. She told the Dr at Hospital she was told not to say anything by the attorney._ Witness seems emotional and agitated. She's been to Neverland about 5 times? She says her mom was told by Dieter to hold hands with Gavin, like in the Bashir Documentary. Chris Tucker – Close Friend, Fritz Coleman – Close Friend, Kobe Bryant – not close friend. She says Louise gave them $10,000 but Mesereau says 2 checks for $10,000. She says her father asked for money and the mother would get mad at him. She says she's never discussed anything with anybody? She does not want to see the social worker report at all?!!! She says she would lie about some things during social worker meetings.

Mar 4

She says mother never asked the newspaper for anything. Once again, she says they have never discussed anything. Stayed with Carol Lemure she says 1 week at a time. She says she never complained about her mother at all to anyone. She says Carol Lemure was making faces at her and mother during testimony about abuse. She said Gavin never made allegations of molestation against parents or anybody. She says they were abused multiple times of day by their father. She never told police her father molested her. She found out, she says, from her mother and father arguing. Gavin, Starr, David and mother involved in JC Penney suit. Gavin's treatments for cancer cost $12,000 each. She says LAPD didn't raise money, just donated a Christmas Tree. Doesn't know anything about Chris Tucker giving mother $2,000.00 or Fritz Coleman giving anything or having fundraisers. She says the car was given for Gavin. Close with Chris Tucker, went to a house, Raider game, brother's wedding. Spent night at Chris Tucker's girlfriend. She says they spent a couple of days in Miami. Couldn't describe Mj Kids rooms but she did describe Mj bedroom? Gavin got in a lot of trouble in school. Disruptive.

Mar 4

For such a close knit family, she says they sure don't talk about too many things about each other. Aldo, Marie Nicole, Starr would switch seats on plane from Miami. Mother gave all credit to God for Gavin's recovery on tape. She also said MJ. After they got back from Miami, went to Neverland 3 times maybe. Never told social workers. Mother never tried to call the police at Jay Jackson's house. Never discussed mother's testimony in pre-trial hearing. She never used a computer a Mj but She did at Carol Lemure. Mj gave Gavin a computer. Asked July 2003 how she knew it was wine. She did not tell police Mj poured wine. She says she doesn't like Rio or Simone. She says she doesn't remember ever going anywhere at the Ranch with her mother except the first visit. Vinnie took them to her grandmother's house after the Brazil Incident. Overall the Arvizo's had plenty of opportunity to tell people they were being restrained against their will. She says her dad, David, says he has a brother that can have people killed. She says Gavin had a trust fund, doesn't know who set it up.

Mar 4

She says George Lopez was close to the family and father David ruined the relationship. She knows Bret Ratner, director of Rush Hour 2. Gavin did talk and play with Bret Ratner. Gavin shot his sister and mother with BB Gun. She says that Gavin and Starr were always with Michael.

March 7

Last week she said she wasn't present for any deposition for the JC Penney case but she was present at Gavin's and Starr's. Mj rushes out for a supposed bathroom break with brother and Messereau and bodyguard. Assistant DA says this is not a bathroom break. She told the Sheriffs she had been in the wine cellar many times but here she says she's only been there once. She says she hung out with her brothers when Mj wasn't there, but she says they didn't hang out at all together, if he was. Brad Miller Tape 9:47 am Feb 16, 2003 for Geragos. Starr 12, Gavin 13, Davellin 16. (David) Husband arrested for domestic violence Oct 2001. Mother says. Starr has a cyst on his brain. Restraining order was for 5 years. She remembers all of his (David) vital information SS#, DL#, DOB, etc…

March 7

Michael Jackson and her danced on their 1st visit with David. On tape they say David was at Neverland more than 10. Neverland happiest place on earth Starr says on tape. On tape they all say Mj never acted inappropriately. (Davellin on the witness stand during the playing of tape shows no emotion, is not looking at anybody) Says father, David, did a lot of drugs and was very abusive on the tape. Janet says no amount of money would make them sell a story. Interview ends at 10:25 pm. She says she met with Bill Dickerman once. Met with attorney Larry Feldman after meeting with Dickerman. She says she met with Feldman once. She says she did not drink on the plane.

Re Direct

She seems to answer these questions a lot better than any "I Don't Remembers." For a girl in college she doesn't seem to know some simple terms.

Mesereau Cross-Examination

I don't remember.

5th Witness Starr Arvizo 14 years old

Went to a lot of different schools. He says Jamie Masada, George Lopez and Louise don't remember their last names. Starr was present twice when Mj called. He says him, his brother, MJ and Frank went on carts around the ranch. He says he, his brother and his dad slept in the same room.
March 7
His mother and sister slept in the same room. He

says he went to Mj bedroom. First time on second visit. He says there is a bell that goes off in the hallway. He says he got bedroom code from Mj and got master code for all doors from the security guard. Got both codes after the trip to Miami. He says he, his brother, Mj, Frank and Mj's kids were in the room. He says they went to pornography sites of females only without clothes and saw breasts and Mj said "got milk" and he says that Mj whispered in Prince's ear that he was missing some pussy. He says Mj told them not to tell what they did. You don't need a code to get in the hallway door that leads to Mj room or the door to the hallway through the library. Says he's been in the video library lots of times. He says that him and his brother and father went to the ranch mostly. He says he and his brother went with Chris Tucker, 4 times. He was introduced, brother and sister introduced to Martin Bashir. Mj took Gavin for about 20 minutes before Bashir taping and Starr and Sister stayed in Kitchen. He is currently in the Infantry Program. Was in 2 Naval programs. They stayed the night after Bashir's video but didn't see Mj.

March 7

They first went to Chris Tucker's room when first arriving in Florida. Next day got up at 2:00 approximately and went to Chris Tucker's room then went to Mj room. He says he went into the room where Gavin and MJ were. He says "cussing" and he was asked to join in by Mj. The nanny walks in and they stop. He says he left the bedroom, but his brother stayed. He says he only saw his brother once go into the room with Michael Jackson. He says he saw his brother staggering and saying weird things and he saw red on the top of his 7 up can. He was told not to watch TV show. In Miami he says his mother left the room at night and then was sent for to come back. He says he first met Dieter and Ronald in room and he says MJ bedroom for Aldo and Marie Nicole in his room. He says he saw Mj with diet coke can and his brother with a Sprite can. Says his brother seemed to be acting different. Says he saw Mj licking the top of Gavin's head. He said Mj made crank calls and says one of them involved Mj asking a girl "how big her pussy is." He says back at Neverland he, Mj, Gavin, Aldo all slept in MJ bed.

March 7

First I met Jesus after the Miami trip. He says that Aldo slept next to him, he slept next to his brother, slept next to Michael. He says he drank alcohol with Mj, Aldo, Gavin (a lot) in the bedroom, office and wine cellar. He said Mj called the wine "Jesus Juice." He says he saw Mj intoxicated 2 times. He says he was never in the wine cellar without Mj. He says Mj would make crank calls with Aldo, Gavin and him from Mj bedroom. If no one picked up the phone he says Mj made them drink wine. He says wine in the bedroom was on the floor and tables. He said they made maybe 7 crank calls. He says he typically went to bed at 2:00 or 3:00

am. He says he saw Dieter and Ronald with Mj in his office, bedroom and guest units. He says he saw stuff written down (script maybe) when Dieter met with him and his family. He says he was told by Frank that his grandparents could disappear. He doesn't remember who was there then he does remember? He says his family was told by Dieter to say only good things about Michael. They arrived at 1:00 am, left at 3:00 am to step-dad's house. He says the bodyguard had a tape recorder and tried to tell his mother something.

March 7

Mj called Starr blowhole and Gavin dodo. He says Gavin called Mj daddy twice. At Calabasas Inn Hotel with Family and Johnny, Frank, Vinnie. First met Vinnie at Hamid's house. Shopped at Levi Club Banana and Luggage store. He says they never had time to go to the pool. Frank took them back to the Ranch, he says. He says Mj showed them how to listen in on phone calls. He says he saw Mj do it twice. Phone is located on the dresser near the piano. Different phones used to make prank calls. Movie called "The Devil's Backbone". He says he doesn't know what clitoris means then or now when Mj said it. He says Mj came into the bedroom naked and said it was natural. Gavin and Starr did not say anything to him. He says Mj had an erection. Starr's version of the left side of the bed varies from Davellin's. Says he does not recognize documents that have his picture or were written on. Briefcase was first seen by Starr, Gavin,

Aldo and Mj by the tub in the bathroom. It was open when they saw it and he says Mj handed out the adult material. Saw it for the 1st time after Calabasas hotel. He saw it for the 2nd time upstairs in MJ bedroom with Gavin, Aldo, Mj.

March 7

He says Mj opened it and gave out magazines to them. A few days in between showing of adult material, he says that Mj was acting like he was humping a small girl mannequin on his bed with Gavin, Aldo and him in the room. He says they had a conversation about masturbation with Rio, Gavin and Starr. Starr was only one he asked, he says. He says most of the drinking was done by Gavin and Mj. Rio and him drank some. He says he was on right, Gavin in middle, Mj on left in Mj bed. He went to the theater to get chocolate, said he came back, saw his brother facing away from Mj and Mj had his left hand down Gavin's pants and Mj had his right hand down his own pants. He says Mj was masturbating himself with his eyes closed and Starr says his brother was asleep. Stairway lit light over the bed. Says he didn't see any alcohol. He says 2 days passed he says he went up to room and he says the same thing was happening but they were on their backs. First person he told was Dr. Katz.

March 7

He was not with Gavin the night before he gave a urine sample. Says he doesn't know how long it

was after Gavin's doctor visit did they leave the ranch for the last time.
March 8

Starr says they were told not to tell their sister because she might tell mom. He says the comforter was rolled down and on the floor, both times. He says his brother was on the bed with Michael Jackson. He said he was told by MJ with Gavin and Aldo not to tell anyone anything even if they put a gun to your head.

Cross Examination

Testified under oath 3 times, 2 times at grand jury and yesterday. But actually 1 more time in the JCPenney thing. He says every time he entered the hallway alarm went off. He had the master code to get in every door at Neverland. There is no alarm to enter the upstairs room. Spoke to DA at 7:00 am this morning. Says he's only discussed this case with prosecution. Met with Larry Feldman twice but said just before that once and couldn't remember. Says not really when using cuss words before meeting MJ and didn't know what they mean.

March 8

Deposition for JC Penney Dec 2000. He says he didn't discuss that case with anybody. First he says he didn't model at JCPenney. Then after shown paper he says he did model but it was way before that incident at JC Penney and at a different JCPenney. Every time he's asked a question about JC Penney, he doesn't recall, then when he is shown paper he remembers? He thinks the 1st time he discussed what MJ did to him was with DR. Katz. He says his Mom and Dad never fight in deposition. His dad never hit him. He says he was lying. He says he doesn't cuss at all right now. He says on the police transcript that the rim of the can was red and looked in and saw white wine. He says the court reporter must have made a mistake. A LOT OF I DON'T KNOW LIKE SISTER. They referred to their father as the biological father or dad. Couldn't really describe Prince and Paris even though he saw them many times. Went over a picture of the inside of an airplane with the DA. He says he first drew a picture of the plane before he testified in front of the grand jury. He says he never discussed seating on a plane.

March 8

He doesn't know exactly when they left Neverland for good. He says he slept in the guest unit the 1st time at Neverland. Never returned to Neverland after meeting with Katz and Feldman. 7 locks, 1 keypad, and 6 locks you have to open manually. He says he or his brother were never caught trying to get in the room when code wouldn't work or didn't know the code. The Security Guard he says gave them the master code. He said he used the code 100 times maybe at the house. Then he says he never used code when Mj wasn't there. He says he and

Gavin were never caught drinking wine at any time. He's giving a very detailed description of the downstairs rooms in Mj's bedroom. He says they were never caught in there and asked to leave. The Barely Legal magazine has a date of Aug 2003. He says he and his brother were never caught trying to get into a briefcase. He says he never saw an adult magazine before he got to Neverland. A Transcript of Santa Barbara Sheriff was sent to him a month ago. He says he didn't read it till towards the end. He says he told the Santa Barbara Sheriff MJ and Frank showed them a site like AOL on a report but he said he didn't know how to use the internet.

March 8

He says that he and his brother did not know how to use computers. He says in a report that they may have looked at www.pussy.com and www.teenpussy.com. Now he says he doesn't remember saying that. He says there were never caught looking at adult websites at Neverland. He says there were no computers at Neverland. He says they didn't know the exact time or date because they were kept away from clocks. He says clocks at Neverland were wrong. Says he wrote a card but from another card. He says he wrote the card, his mother never asked him to write it. He says the rest of the family wrote on the card after he did the card. He said yesterday he got red and white wine but today he said he had vodka also. **He says that he never said that MJ was masturbating his brother. He says that he never told Katz that**

MJ was rubbing his penis on Gavin's buttocks. He went to several dance classes and comedy classes but says he never told anybody he wanted to be an actor or comedian. He says Frank threatened him before rebuttal tape. It says the molestation began Feb 20.

March 8

He says they, Gavin and him used to look through the telescope into his mom's guest unit. He said and Davellin said that the mother never left the guest cottage. Says they never saw their mother when looking through the telescope into the guest cottage. He says they have seen rides, trees, hills, guest cottage but couldn't see any clocks because of the trees. He says he and Gavin were only at the telescope 2 times.

March 9

Brother and Dad have been to George Lopez house, he thinks. He says his father had a dispute with George Lopez. He says his mother went to Neverland only once before the Miami trip. He says he doesn't have a cyst on his brain but says it won't need medical treatment. He said the 1st time he tasted alcohol was on the plane. He says he knew it was wine just by looking in a soda can. He says they kept on drinking at Neverland when they got back. Told the Grand Jury he knew where the key was and knew how to get into the wine cellar. Lines from Grand Jury 1578-1579. Got a

DNA swab in 2003. He says there was a camera looking at who walked into Mj bedroom.
March 9

He says there's 7 locks on the door into Mj bedroom. He says they did go through the dresser and closet in Mj room. He says in a police interview a second inappropriate act that he was on the couch faking sleeping and that his brother was sleepy from all the alcohol Mj made him drink. His versions of inappropriate actions by Mj vary a lot from police interview to testimony. He said in a police interview that he did not get a good look at Mj penis when he walked in front of him and Gavin naked with an erection. He says in a police interview everybody was going to be killed but today says it was just his grandparents who were threatened by Frank. He says the computer at top of steps didn't have internet access, no phone line plugged in and was covered up. He says he's never been in the room with chalkboards and books. He says that he said whatever came to his head on rebuttal video. When Gavin was ill and visiting Neverland, he was not in school. He says Prince and Paris often stayed in MJ's room. He thought they were going to Florida for a press conference. He says he saw 7 security guards at the hotel for Mj and that he played with Prince and Paris.

March 9

He says there was no security on the plane back

from Miami. He doesn't know when Mj gave Gavin watch. In Miami or on plane. **He says Michael Jackson gave his sister vodka in the Kitchen not in the wine cellar.** He says they went to an ice cream shop once in the plaza when in Calabasas. First he says his mother never had a cell phone, then he says she had a cellphone in her back pocket at JCPenney. He and Gavin were taken to the dentist with their mother by a Neverland employee. He says he saw vodka in Mj room when he says he caught Mj inappropriately touching his brother but he says all the lights in the room are out except in the hallway and he only looked for a few seconds. **First he says he heard his mother say she wanted to leave Neverland and then on transcript he says no.** He says both times Mj touched his brother, his brother never moved. He has slept in Mj room with father there the first time he visited Neverland. He says that Mj would touch his brother a lot, like fixing his shirt. **He says on the transcript not his genitals. He says he saw it in the paper.** First time he saw the video he made at Neverland was at Hamid's house.

March 9

He says he wasn't excited about narrating the video on the Neverland channel. He has seen the Mj and Gavin video. He says he never heard the Pac Man analogy. He says on rebuttal video that he was talking about his step dad not Mj when he was talking about a father figure and said Michael. He says so far on rebuttal video he has been lying in every comment he made. Asked if he thought his mother was lying in a rebuttal video he says **he wasn't paying attention.** Then he says she was just doing what Dieter told her to do. Doesn't answer a lot of questions, just keeps responding by saying he was sleepy and just wanted to go to sleep. Still in touch with Louise Palanker. He says he knows Louise Palanker gave his dad $20,000 to fix up a room for Gavin at his grandma's house. Alarm goes off when you go through the 1st set of double doors. The sensors are at the next set of double doors. He says there were 3 incidents, 2 he saw from the stairs and 1 in the bedroom. He said there were 17 stairs to the upstairs bedroom. Never mentioned it before to the grand jury or police.

March 9

He says they were never caught in Los Olivos on the ATVs

March 9th

6th Witness Gavin Arvizo

15 years old 12-2-1989

First lived with grandparents. Then moved to Soto Apartment. He says they fought everyday about bills and each parent's family. He says all the kids and mother were abused by Father. His comedy coach at camp was George Lopez. He admired Jay

Leno as a comedian. Went to hospital with stomach pain and bulge on Monday and had surgery on Thursday. George Lopez, Jaime Masada and Louise Palanker would visit him in the hospital Always refers to dad as his biological father. Got Jay Leno's phone # from Jamie and Louise. Got Chris Tucker's phone # from Chris Tucker at benefit. Chris Tucker spent New Year's Eve with Gavin, took him to a Raider game and to a Laker game and the Nickelodeon Awards. First time he met Kobe was in the hallway at the Laker Game. Met Chris Tucker at graduation of comedy camp. There were 2 Benefits at Laugh Factory. He says it was either Jamie or Caroline Muir that got Mj to call him in the hospital.

March 9

He says that he had maybe 20 phone calls with Mj. He says that Mj had a bib on because he was eating when they got to Neverland for the 1st time. He says parents fought, mom had makeup on, dad said she looked like a clown and threw soda in her face. He says it was Mj idea for him and Starr to sleep in his room. But that they wanted too. He doesn't know if it was his computer or Frank's. He said Frank was doing all the typing Mj was just commenting. They looked for 15 to 30 min. He says Mj said "got milk" when the girl had her shirt up and whispered in Prince's ear while he was sleeping that he's missing all the pussy. Went back to Neverland 7-10 times with my father. He says they made the video of Starr and Gavin in wheelchairs just so Mj would have a video of him. Mj at ranch 2 of the 7 times he went to Neverland. But he says sometimes Mj was there and they said he wasn't. Got most of Mj phone numbers from Frank or Mj. Spent 1 day at Neverland for Chris Tucker's son's birthday, no Mj. Then I went back with Chris and Mj was there.

March 9

Introduced to Martin Bashir by Mj. He was told by Mj to say how he called him dad on Bashir video and how Mj helped him beat cancer. He says that when doing the marching sequence, he didn't know they were taping it.

March 10

Started 1 ½ hrs late because Mj was sick. Mj gave him a laptop computer. He says that he needed help setting up an internet account because he didn't know how Mj paid for it. His screen name was Whitehawk and his password varied. He says he visited Mj in the hotel 1 time for 2 hours. He says he saw his part in Bashir video at home on VH1 after he left Neverland for the last time. He says Mj told him to hold hands but he put his head on Mj's shoulder. Mj called him after news of Bashir video and wanted him to go to Miami. He says Mj got angry that his mother was coming to Miami. He says they left in the day and arrived at night. He first met Dieter, Ronald, Marie Nicole, Aldo in Mj hotel room in Miami. He says Mj and Gavin had a meeting for 5 minutes and he says they did an improv of Mj as principal and Gavin as a student in trouble for doing something to

March 10

a female student. He says Mj gave him wine he called Jesus Juice in a Diet Coke can in the hotel room. He says that Mj told him to keep drinking the wine when they were in the living room of the hotel. He says it was white wine. He says his head hurt and he just wanted to lay down the next morning but he says not sure it was from wine. He says on flight back that Mj gave him white wine in a Diet Coke can. He says Mj said it was Jesus Juice and it would relax him. He says the can was refilled and he always drank out of Mj's can. He says Mj gave him a jacket and EA games, which Aldo didn't like in the hotel. He says Mj gave him a watch on the plane and he says Mj said it was so they would always be friends. He says Mj said the watch was $75,000. He says no one at Neverland ever asked for the watch back. He says Mj offered the wine to Starr as Jesus Juice also and he didn't like it. He says he doesn't know if he felt intoxicated on the plane. But he says he knows what intoxicated means. He says he and his brother spent the night in Mj room the night they got back from Miami.

March 10

He says he had alcohol every time Michael was there at Neverland. He says they never went to drink in the cellar without Mj. He says he drank Bacardi, Vodka and **Jim Beam.** He says he told Mj 3 times that alcohol was bad for him because he only has 1 kidney. He says he and Mj went to the wine cellar 5 times. He says they would take alcohol to Mj room. He says they all made crank calls from Mj room. He says they made up a game to drink a gulp of wine if the call didn't get answered. He says he didn't want to leave Neverland. He says mother was scared every time he went there. He says his mom said she was afraid they were going to kill them. He says he didn't see Dieter or Ronald at the Ranch until after the trip to grandma's house. He says Frank called him and told him he wanted them to come back to Ranch. He says that Frank told him they would never have to see Dieter or Ronald. He did see Dieter when they got back and Dieter told him he wanted them to go to Austria or Brazil on vacation. He says the alarm in the hallway goes off 3 times. He says he **got code from Mj and other codes from Mj or Maids.**

March 10

He says Mj gave him vodka in the wine cellar. He says he drank it in one shot because he thought it was water.

Sgt Robel

Brought up to lay the foundation for an alarm in the hallway. To authenticate bell sound.

Re-Direct
He says the microphone on the camera from search.

Back to Gavin

He says that was the alarm. He says he slept hard but doesn't think he passed out. Says he got sick but never threw up. He says he would call him dad sometimes. Saw a video of Mj carrying him across the bridge when they showed it to Chris Tucker. He says the first time he met Vinnie was at Hamid's house. He says rebuttal video started at 10:00 pm-12:00 am. He says Dieter told them what to say in the Rebuttal Video. He still considered Mj his best friend in the world. He says the meeting with social workers was after a rebuttal video. He says the guy in the blue shirt was (Gavin) his size but bigger. He says the tape recorder was in mom's hand when talking in the bedroom with the guy in the blue shirt. Then he asked Sneddon "wasn't that Brad Miller" and Sneddon says I'm not the one testifying.

March 10

He says that nothing bad happens in Mj bed to social workers and says it was the truth at the time. He says they bought clothes at Anchor Blue because they didn't want them to go back to their apartment. He thinks just Vinnie took them to get their passports. He says Mj told him he would go to Brazil a week later after they got there. He says he didn't know or see anybody in the lobby but didn't feel free to come and go because Frank and Vinnie had their key cards. He says no one told him about Italy or France. He says he went to Brazilian Consulate with his family and Vinnie. He says Vinnie and Frank bought the suitcase. He says that when Mj was there, he slept in the room sometimes with Starr and Aldo. He says every time Mj was there they would drink. He says the computer was at the end of the bed by railing. He says nobody used it because it was bad. He says Mj was pretending to hump the female little girl mannequin on his bed. He says he first saw the briefcase in Mj's jacuzzi tub room. He says Mj said that it was Frank's and all the adult material.

March 10

in it. He says the second time he looked at it in the Mj room with Mj, Starr for 30 min to 1hr. He says there were cut out pictures of naked girls in briefcases. He says Mj showed him how to listen in on telephone conversations. He says Frank told him about listening to conversations about mom and Jay Jackson. He says he saw a movie twice about ghosts and orphanages and kids getting killed. **He says Mj was naked and he doesn't recall him saying anything.** Where's the question about the erection? Blue bag is the cover for Starr's sleeping bag. Items inside were Gavin's jr high school books. He did have them at Neverland. First book is a workbook for English, 2nd thing was also from English about black history, the next thing is assignments from school and the last thing is an airman manual for his cadets. He says there were times he had to pee in the bottle at Neverland. He says he has had a conversation with Mj about the alcohol showing up in his urine specimen. He says Mj told him not to take the test. Then in the wine cellar he says Gavin and Mj drank after that conversation.

March 10

He says after conversation with his mother he went to bed nothing happened. He did take a bottle to Dr's appointment. It was full of urine. Vinnie was driving mother in the front passenger and Gavin in the back. Stopped at Denny's so Gavin could pee and mom went in with him. Bottle was empty when they got to the hospital. He says he can't remember grand jury testimony about the naked thing. After reading it he says Mj said it was natural after they said (gross) or something like that. He says Mj did help him with a little homework and then they started playing around. He says he put wine bottles on the floor next to the bed nightstand, and wasn't too good because of stuff on there. He says the crib and computer weren't in there and the desk with the computer that didn't work is not there. He says Mj touched him inappropriately 2 times but he feels maybe more. He says Starr stopped sleeping in Mj room before the 1st incident. He says Mj told him a story about a boy who didn't masturbate, the boy had sex with a dog. He says that he and Mj were under the covers and Mj was masturbating

March 10

him and he did ejaculate. One day later in his bedroom, this time, they were on top of the covers and Mj masturbating him and Mj grabbed Gavin's hand to do it to him (Mj) and he pulled his hand away. He says he thinks he ejaculated again. He says Mj told him both times that it was natural.

Cross Examination

He said the incidents happened about a week before they left for good. Larry Feldman sent him to psychologist Katz. Went to 2 Lawyers and a psychologist before going to any police. Says he did not lie on JC Penney deposition. He says he felt bad because he felt Mj was trying to avoid him when he had cancer. He says he (escaped) Neverland with Jesus, but went back twice after that. They had a blood drive at Neverland he says he doesn't really remember. He **seems very bitter** that he feels Mj didn't treat him well when he had cancer. He says he doesn't remember what happened the last time he left. **He looks at the clock** . He says he never discussed.

March 14

He said Mj told him about masturbation and he says he told him if he didn't do it he might rape a women. **On the police report he says his grandma told him that.** After Mj told him. The words used are almost identical. Gavin seemed very combative, non responsive today. His chemo was once every 3 weeks. Ended June 2001. He talked to Mr. Sneddon over the weekend for 15 minutes. They talked about a teacher witness, maybe named Mr. Gerralt. He was a detention teacher. He says Mr. Gerralt put him against the wall for not having a pencil. He says he would go outside and smoke. He says the teacher asked if he was on drugs. Said he (Gerralt) was going to call cops but he didn't he just called campus security. Also talked about Mr. Alpert (Dean of the school). **He (Gavin) says he told Mr. Alpert that Mj never did anything to him of a sexual nature.** He met with all prosecutors and Det. Robel, last night. He says it wasn't recorded and no one took notes. He doesn't remember if he told Mr. Alpert 2 times that Mj never did anything sexual to him. He said he had a lot of disciplinary problems and got into a few fights.

March 14

He said he may have called a few cadets stupid. He says Mr. Gerralt asked him if he was on drugs in a way of trying to make fun of him. **He stood up to Mr. Gerralt. He says he didn't like how Mr. Murphy taught his class.** He says he was disruptive in his class. He refused to sign a detention paper. He says Mr. Parker was Mr. Alpert's replacement and he did apologize to him for the way he acted in school. Argued with Mrs. Slaughter over going to the restroom. He says the other students were dancing around like retarded people. Had problems in Mr. Finkelstein's class with his conduct. **He didn't like the way he taught either.** He says he doesn't remember Mr. Moon but then he says it was his homeroom teacher. Says he never had problems in that class. He says he does not remember being asked to apologize to a student. Couldn't read the paper that the attorney showed him. He said Mr. Davie was vice principal and was cool. He says he had a conversation with Mr. Davie about his problems with another teacher. Ms. Bender was his history teacher. He says he got complaints from everyone of his teachers. He doesn't recall her saying he had good acting skills. He said he never did his homework.

March 14

He said he was probably accused of being disruptive in Martinez drama class. Agreed to do independent study at the end of 8th grade. **Had the same problems at Le Conte Middle School.** He says he was a disciplinary problem. He says he told Mr. Alpert that nothing bad happened with Mj. He says he kind of remembers the card to Mj assistant Evvy. He used to call Mj Daddy and call himself son. He sent many cards and letters to Mj. He asked for phone numbers from Mj that worked. He doesn't remember writing to Prince and Paris. **He says that Mj told him that he keeps every promise he makes.** He has been in a music studio with Mj. He usually only went in the studio with

MJ there in the afternoon and stayed 1-2 hours. Been in there 1 time he says without Mj in there but the door was open because he didn't know the code. He says he and Starr have been in theatre without Mj a lot and the door was open. Learned cancer was in remission **June 2001.** He says Mj wasn't talking to him anymore Aug-Sept 2000. Surgery was June 2000. Did not go to Neverland in 2001. He does play football.

March 14

Called Evvy assistant quite often. Evvy setup internet account on the computer Mj gave him. Says he learned how to use a computer in 1st grade. He says he saw an alarm system in place where Mj keeps his awards and gloves. He didn't learn code to Mj room until he got back from Miami. He says he has been in the main house theater, his unit train station, library without Mj. He says he never went into the Prince and Paris room. Other than maybe just to play with kids. Helped Grace with schooling of MJ kids in a playroom place after he came back from Miami. He says he introduced Chris Tucker to Mj. Heard hall alarm to Mj room after Miami. He says mom didn't ask for security after the Bashir video. Prosecutor asked him about Jay Leno. Never mentioned Jay Leno in a Grand Jury or police report. Says he never spoke to Jay Leno but did call his phone. He says no one ever tried to get a hold of Jay Leno. Says he never had conversation with anybody about Jay Leno testifying in this case. He says he or Starr never went into Mj room when Mj wasn't there.

March 14

He says it was Frank's computer that they looked at naked girls in Mj room the 1st night. He says that was the only time they looked on the internet. He says Mj showed him Hustler and Playboy. He visited Mj at Hilton Hotel for 2 hours. Father drove him in an SUV Mj gave to the family. Gary Hearn told them Mj gave them an SUV. He said they asked Mj to repair the SUV after it got wrecked. Never got it back. He was sad. He says he was sad he never got a vehicle from Chris Tucker. He never got the computer back after they sent it to Mj to pay to get it fixed. His mother asked to get it fixed. Says he knew how to use email a little bit. He says the only phone number that never changed was Evvy's. He says Mj phone numbers didn't work and he was upset after the 3rd or 4th round of chemotherapy. He said dad for the 1st time when referring to (biological father). He complained to his biological dad about Mj numbers being changed. He says he went with Chris Tucker for Destin's birthday. He was in remission when Bashir's documentary was filmed. He went to Neverland in 2000 mostly with his biological father.

March 14

Both parents approved of Gavin and Starr staying in Mj room the first night. Sometimes I slept in the train house. Mother didn't visit Neverland again until after the Miami trip. He says they mentioned his name on newscasts about Bashir video. He says his mom talked to Dickerman about Gavin's legal rights about Bashir video and that she didn't give ok for Bashir video. He says he was not upset about no press conference in Miami. He says he never stayed in Mj's room overnight in Miami at Turnberry Resort. He says he was wearing Mj pajamas when he was masturbated. He says after his escapes and return to Neverland is when he was inappropriately touched. He says that he and his brother drank every time Mj was there. **Says (Gavin and Starr) they were never caught by employees drinking in the wine cellar by themselves. Says** he and Starr never got caught taking alcohol out of the fridge in the kitchen. First saw black briefcase the first night back from Miami. Frank wanted him to give the watch back to Mj, but did not. He still thinks the watch is worth $75,000. Wasn't allowed to have a dog but got a vacation from Make a Wish Foundation. He asked Mj if he donated to Make A Wish. He says he was supposed to be in video with the burn victim.

March 14

He was never threatened personally by anyone associated with Mj. He says in a police report that they didn't drink a lot in the wine cellar with Mj. He never discussed drinking with his mother. **After their "escapes" they never called police, never screamed help.** He says the inappropriate touching didn't happen till after they "escaped" and came back and when he knew Frank said he could have killed his mother. And after the meeting with social workers. Never told anybody he was inappropriately touched by Mj. Hasn't talked to any prosecutor or sheriff about meeting with Larry Feldman. He told Dr. Katz he had memory problems and it messed his head up from the medicine. He feels his other friends helped during his cancer more than Michael Jackson. He says he was not caught masturbating at Neverland in the guest cottage. Says in rebuttal video that he lied about how his parents were asked to stay in Mj room the first time and that there was no cure for his cancer and the part about no one else was helping them. He says on other testimony that the touching happened before the rebuttal video now he says it was after.

March 14

He says she lied on rebuttal about being spit on, turned away and could have stayed at any relative's house. He says he never tried to call Mj when on ranch because he said he could just get in the cart and go see him. He says he felt and Starr felt they were part of Mj family. Can't speak for his mother. Says he considered Paris and Prince as a brother and sister. **He says he felt Mj was dishonest but loving** because he had phone #s that were disconnected. **He says he didn't want to be in movies and Starr also and he says they told Mj that.** He says that it was his mother's idea to hold hands like in the Bashir video. Says he did not make any gang sign and he isn't or was not in a gang. He says he didn't want to live and be with Mj forever. He says he just considered him like a dad for guidance. Says they did pray at the dinner table with Mj. He says he wasn't upset about leaving Mj, the father figure. He says he never heard Mj was going to get them a house in Hollywood Hills. Lived at Jay Jackson's Apt for 2 months before rebuttal video. He says Mj was still his father figure even when mom was dating Jay.

March 14

He says his mother was not trying to look like Janet Jackson. He says Dieter told them what to say. He says they only got in trouble at Neverland for crashing the carts. Doesn't remember seeing any news crew or anything the day after they got back from Miami. Saw "Old School" the movie March 1, 03. Went to eat, no one ever screamed for help. Says he doesn't think he ever watched tv with Rio in guest rooms. Says he never stole the $1,000 bill that was laminated. Says he never masturbated in front of Rio. Says he never wanted to watch adult movies with Rio in guest cottages. March 15th He was given a DNA swab, but doesn't know the results. Says it was a joke when he said he wanted to have a press conference when he was doing the grand jury testimony. He says he just went to the movies with Barbara Schroeder of Fox News. He says they never asked Gary Hearn to stop so they could shop. Met Andrew Lasik LAPD after he finished his chemo. Never complained to him about being held against their will. He says Shane Meredith did catch him with an open bottle of alcohol.

March 15

Doesn't remember asking to go to Florida when in a room with Mj and Brett Ratner. He says he never saw Starr cook in the kitchen. He says he never told Chris Tucker that they didn't make any money at the fundraiser. Met Rene Watson through a dance studio, he thinks, and says they did not ask her for money. Went to the dentist, Dr. Seamont, in Solvang to have braces removed 2-24-03, and was in town for 5 ½ hours. Says he doesn't know who paid for it. Says he loved being at Neverland and it was his mother that was always worried but she kept going back to Neverland. He says they never complained at the dentist of being held against their will. He says his brother wrote on the cover of a guest book, not him. He said he didn't know the mannequin that he says Mj simulated sex with was actually custom made to be of Mj cousin. He says he or his brother didn't deface the vaginal area of the mannequin. He says he didn't discuss with an attorney about how he could sue Mj till he was 18 and if Mj convicted he could automatically win a civil suit.

<u>Redirect</u>
He says he has followed directions not to discuss

the case with anybody involved.

March 15

He says Mj never visited him in the hospital. He says Mj told him Frank was like a cousin and would change his diaper when Frank was a baby. Says he's not seen Bashir video just heard about it on the news. He says he was angry at Martin Bashir. He says Mj called and wanted him in Miami. He says Aldo was there in the beginning. He says he doesn't think there was a code to get into Mj office. He says he's on honor roll and not a discipline problem in high school. He says when he went back to school, the kids would make fun of him saying there's the kid who got raped by Mj. So he says he got into fights. He says Frank and Vinnie brought suitcases to their house and he says some of his underwear and pants were missing and someone else's pants were in there. He says he was told by Mj when he went to take a shower to put his stinky underwear in the clothes hamper. He did and he says he never got them back.

<u>Re Cross</u>

He says he showed up at all detentions.
7th Witness Terry Flaa SMPD

Was a Sheriff for 8 ½ years. 1st referral was assigned to him 2-20-03, 2nd Referral was because of Bashir Video.

March 15

Mrs. Blackburn read a report to him on 3-10-03 of an interview with the Arvizo family. Interview with Mrs. Arvizo 3-13-03.

Cross Exam

Terminated his time with Sheriffs Jan 2004. He filed report 4-16 that no criminal activity went on. Ended being detective March 2003. Went undercover work. Det Zellis started his investigation in June 2003. The first report was generated by Carol Leiberman. He was not aware that she had never met Mj or his children. He just read the 1st report. Did nothing else.

2nd referral generated by someone in the LA School District. Attorney Gloria Allred wanted investigation over Bashir Video. Talked to LT Klapakis about the case. Actually had a conversation with SGT Legalt. LT Klapakis called DCFS supervisor and told them not to interview children but they had already done it. He, Terry Flaa, was the lead investigator. **He did not at that time make a conclusion to investigate further.**

Re Direct

The 1st report he received was a copy of the report. March 13, 2003 interview they decided not to investigate further.

March 15

Re – Cross

Just Established timeline

8th Witness Lt- Jeff Klapakis Santa Barbara Sheriff

He contacted the Lompoc office of CPS first. He told Lompoc CPS to try and get a hold of someone to not interview children. He decided not to pursue an investigation after the Blackburn Report. Decided to re-open the case after talking with Larry Feldman.

Cross Examination

Did discuss referrals with Lompoc CPS. Carol Lieberman was a psychologist and TV personality. She (Mrs. Lieberman) intended the next day after the report to have a news conference. He agrees that a reporting party can have an agenda. He agrees nobody from reports had **personal** knowledge of Mj or his children. They LT Klapakis, SGT Legalt, and Det Flaa had a meeting and decided not to pursue the case any further after the report from Blackburn and after meeting with David Arvizo. He spoke with Larry Feldman after Mr. Sneddon and then spoke with Dr. Katz. **Then he reopened the investigation.** He says sometimes they bring back former investigators. New team Him, Det Robel and Det Zellis.

March 15

9th Witness Sgt. Robel

Worked in sexual assault and child cases for 5 years. Assigned to Mj case 6-20-03. 1st interviewed Arvizo family 7-7-03 Janet, Starr, Gavin, Davellin. He was familiar with the Det Flaa Report and Dr. Katz interviews. Starr's interview was videotaped. He says he was told of 2 incidents that he saw and a 3rd. Starr, the 3rd was an incident where Starr was faking sleeping and says he saw Mj get in bed with Gavin and start moving back and forth. Gavin interviewed the same day at the same place. He says Gavin told him the molestations happened towards the end of his stay at Neverland. Said the same thing in an August interview. Search warrant at Neverland Nov 18, 2003. His request was to be on ranch for 2-3 days. He was denied by Mr. Sneddon. They could only be on the ranch till midnight of that day. Jerry Franklin, Deputy DA spent 4-5 hours at the ranch. Mr. Sneddon left at 1:30-2:00 in the afternoon. He personally seized evidence in Mj bedroom. Picture an open cardboard box with magazines in it at the foot of Mj bed. Other things in the box. Box was closed and he opened it. the 15-20 magazines in box 1 they showed were a nude teenage girl magazine, a nude picture of a woman over a fountain and a picture of a guy with a finger to his mouth and it said chop suey club. #280 In the nightstand in Mj's bedroom. #281 is Starr Arvizo's fingerprints and palm print. #282 Gavin Arvizo's finger and palm prints. Gavin's on 9-14-04, Starr's on different days.

Cross Examination

He is not a certified finger printer. He does not know if anybody looked in the box before him. There were officers who wrote down numbers of things seized and officers who seized things. The Box was folded not sealed with tape. Teenage nude magazine he says is not illegal to possess, the nude woman over fountain Defense attorney says is a collector item, the picture of the guy with finger in mouth that says Bruce Weber on it he was the guy who photographed the Jackson 5 and it was sent to Mj unsolicited. He was first assigned to the case June 15-20th 2003. Det Zellis was already assigned to the case. He says he was brought in to supervise and conduct interviews.

March 15

Feb 7, 2003 got back from Florida. March 12 2003 when Arvizo's left for the last time. Feldman contacted the DA. June 13, 2003 Det Zellis interviewed Dr. Katz the same day. First date he interviewed Arvizo children 7-7-2003. Next time 8-13-2003. Mr. Sneddon did have a meeting alone with Janet Arvizo before Search Warrant 11-18-03. Next Interview with Arvizo's at 11-25-03 for swabs. They showed Arvizo's rebuttal video and said Mr. Zonen asked the kids questions while he and Mr. Sneddon were outside the room. Now after looking at the report he says Mr. Sneddon did in fact help with interviews on 1-19-04. Grand Jury end of March and April 2004. 11-18-03 they also searched Brad Miller's office and Hamid's house. None of the kids mentioned rebuttal video in interviews before the search warrant. He had not seen rebuttal video before 11-18-03. First time Davellin said anything about the rebuttal video was 1-19-04. In previous interviews the Services were not asked about Miller interviews or rebuttal videos. Seized Brad Miller tape 11-18-03 couldn't listen to it till Feb 2004. Davellin says she did not observe any molestations. Gavin and Starr talked

March 15

about how Mj talked about masturbation and if white stuff came out. Defense says mother told Davellin about urine bottle story. Davellin says that Gavin tells the story and Starr just agrees with it. In an 8-13-03 interview she said Gavin was becoming violent as a result of these events. In court was the 1st time he heard Gavin put the statement towards Mj about masturbation. He says that statement came from Gavin's grandmother. Gavin said he called Michael and then on transcript it says he thinks Mj called him. On 7-7-03 Interview, **Gavin said Mj masturbated him 5 times. On 8-13-03 Interview, Gavin said Mj masturbated him 5 times and he ejaculated 5 times. In the 11-25-03 interview of Gavin, he says molestations**

<u>happened before and after the CPS Interview. In the Grand Jury he said it was after Calabasas trip 3-2-03—3-12-03 the molestations and he says there are 3 days in there that they can prove Mj wasn't there.</u> On 7-7-03 Interview, Starr said Gavin had pajama bottoms on but said Mj had his hand in his underwear. In an 8-13 Interview, Starr said Mj put his hand in boxers. On 11-25

March 15

He says Gavin has underwear on because Mj told him to wear them and Mj had his hand in his underwear. It was 5 days to a week after 2-20. In an 8-13 interview Starr says boxers on transcripts.

March 16

He was not present during Jan 19 interviews. Just while watching the video. He says that is true what Davellin said about her brothers telling her stories. He says he didn't see on transcripts where it said that Davellin said she was not allowed to see her mother while they were at Neverland.
2-16-30 Brad Miller Interview
2-19, 2-20-03 Rebuttal
2-20-03 DCFS Interview
2-3-03 Bashir video shown in UK
2-7 Return to Neverland after Miami
He needs to review for timeline transcripts

Re Direct
Prior to this case. He and Mr. Sneddon had never met. 11-18-03 day of search warrant there was also an arrest warrant for Mj. He was present for a warrant for Schaffel. He says Gavin became quite folded his arms and sunk in his chair when talking about alleged molestations to Det. Robel.

Re Cross

He knew nothing of rebuttal tape before 11-18-03

March 16

Det Bonner showed him the DVD on computer for the 1st time. Before 11-18-03 they made some inquiries and also kept quiet to keep anything from leaking. He says they are still investigating this case during trial.

10th Witness Det Paul Zelis

With Sheriff 8 years, Det 4 years. Assigned 6-13-03 Friday to case. He was assigned during the search to collect evidence mainly from the upstairs part of Mj bedroom. First located a briefcase with adult material in a closet at the bottom of the stairs in MJ bedroom. After opening the briefcase he had forensics take a picture of it, they closed it, sealed it and booked into evidence. He says a photo of children was found in the nightstand bottom drawer next to MJ bed on the right side. He says he found several adult magazines in the drawer in the bottom of the same nightstand. He says a mannequin was found in the upstairs bedroom on the floor. Says futon or something like that, next to the nightstand where magazines and pictures were found. Found 2 books next to futon in Mj room on top of boxes. He participated in interviews with Arvizo boys before the 11-18-03 search for Neverland. He says he took a briefcase to the grand jury and wore gloves and no one else touched it.

March 16

Cross Examination

Briefcase and contents were never examined for fingerprints. After the grand jury it remained with the clerk of court. **The briefcase was finally examined for fingerprints in 2004 Spring after it was possible that many people could have touched it.** He was detective for 2 years before this case and he says there were other detectives with a lot more experience with sex crimes. **The 2nd Book that was supposed to be in the bag was actually found in the courtroom.** 1st book by Robert Maxwell. He says there were hundreds of books not thousands. He says that nothing that he saw or seized was illegal to possess. He says there were a lot of pictures throughout the house of adults and children. **Picture a mannequin with what looks like black marker scribbled on the vaginal area. He says he never asked Arvizo's children if they did that.** He was at the Administration Office on the last search warrant in Dec 2004. Friday arrived at 9:00-10:00 am. He says no one searched the office on that day and he didn't see the pile of stuff sent to Mj from all over the world. He says there were magazines, books and all sorts of reading material throughout the house.

March 16

He participated in 7-7-03 and 8-13-03 interviews. He does not recall interviews from 11-25-03. He doesn't think he was there. He was at 1-19-04 meeting with children. He never saw a rebuttal video before this date. He says they were instructed not to talk to each other during the rebuttal video. He says he doesn't know if they were asked about the video before they watched it on 1-19-04. **He says the 99.9% comment from Gavin saying what was said on rebuttal was not true. He says it was the things that Dieter told them to say. And on transcript that what was said and he says that's what Dieter told them to say.** He says Gavin told him he wasn't sure when molestations occurred. Gavin said he thought they could have occurred before the DCFS interview. **He did not ask about cards sent in 2001 to Mj with the same kind of language or words that were used in rebuttal video.** He says it was refreshing when he read transcripts of the exchange of words between Gavin and Mr. Sneddon. Gavin tells them molestation happened at the end of stay but then he says he doesn't know if it happened before or after the DCFS interview.

March 16

He never talked to Det Flaa about the case. He does not recall when Robel was brought in. Now after break he says he may have spoken with Det Flaa.

Re Direct

Comment that preceded the exchange of Gavin and Sneddon.

Re Cross

Defense says those comments came after the exchange between Gavin and Sneddon and they were.

11th Witness Det Victor Alvarez

Deputy 25 ½ years
Detective 5 ½ years

Assigned Nov 2003. Fingerprinted Arvizo's Boys 3 to 4 months ago. Got fingerprints at Arvizo's home from boys. Assigned to interview on Nov 18, 2003 same day as search warrant to interview Jesus Salas with Det Bonner at sheriff station. Then he and Det Bonner went to Neverland. His job was to interview employees and help with search of Mj bedroom. He found books with adult material near the bathtub in the master bath. Found a computer bag with adult material on the floor in the bath next to the sink. #565 contents inside black computer bag. Contents. 2 Adult videos #566, Is Adult material #567, Is adult material
March 16

#562 Contents found in master bath in between sink and tub book of adult material (Genetically Manipulated), #564 Adult Material, #563 Adult Material. He says he went through everything in black computer bag. #294 Document out of bag addressed to Mj with his initials on all 12 pages.

Cross Examination

Became Det Nov 99. Became involved in case Nov 11, 2003. He was one of the lead investigators. These molestations are said to have occurred Feb March 2003. Date of Penthouse magazine if Jul-Aug 2003. Date on Hustler Barely Legal is July 2003. He did not put the magazines in binders. He is not a certified fingerprint examiner. He started to assist in the search around 11:00 am. He says there were 2 or 3 officers in the MJ room when he started assisting. He says quite a few officers and others went through the entire area throughout search. Letter from bag is addressed to 3 different people, not just Mj and its care of a company in L.A. No DVD in one of the adult video cases. On the DVD it says it was released 3-21-03.

March 16

Date on the letter is May 1 2003.

12th Witness Karen Shepherd
7 ½ years with the Sheriff. Current Detective

before that. Scientific Research. She got to Neverland early. She was 1st assigned to search the master bedroom and master bath. Det Padilla in charge of packaging evidence. She started her search at 10:00 am in the master bath. #59 Picture of master bathroom. #569 5 DVDs #570-574. They were found on top of the TV next to the jacuzzi tub, she says. She also found 2 magazines and 3 books in the master bath that contained adult material. #576 Contains 3 books. #577-579 are the books. The 1st book looks like adult nude photos of men. Next book adult material, Next book looks like kids dress up book. #575 Found in stack of books and magazines. It is adult material. #580 Found in a metal briefcase next to the jacuzzi tub. #65 Picture of adults DVDs. #64 Picture of adult mag. #63 Picture of adult mag. #62 Picture of where she found #575. #633 Found inside the master bath closet inside the suitcase inside the manila envelope.

March 16

Cross Examination

She doesn't know how many people searched Neverland. She was just in the master suite area and Mj office. **She says she didn't see anything about 3 Stooges and there was something that said 3 Stooges right under one of the DVDs she photographed and seized.** One of the DVDs seized had been shown on HBO. Mannequins in Mj office and memorabilia. She says she didn't notice anything in the office. She says she was just a scribe. She did notice the memorabilia in the upstairs part of the bedroom and other rooms. She noticed the memorabilia. She says she noticed a lot of books of art entertainment and photography. She thinks there were 100s of books in the areas she searched.

March 17

13th Witness Fritz Coleman

Weatherman Ch 4. 23 years. Summer camp at Laugh Factory has been going on 5-6 years. He says the Arvizo's were polite and personable. He visited the Arvizo home once during Christmas and bought them gifts and dropped them off at their house and spent 20 minutes there. This was before the cancer.

March 17

He says mother and children are very thankful. Next time he saw one of the Arvizo's was Gavin and his dad at hospital. He says the dad wasn't working because he spent every night at hospital with Gavin. Fundraiser started at 8:00 pm. He says he saw David Arvizo at a Fundraiser. He heard talk that they raised a couple thousand dollars. He thinks Chris Tucker and Bob Sagat were there, not sure though. He says he only saw Janet Arvizo 3 times and he says she never solicited money from him.

<u>Cross Examination</u>

First met Arvizo's Summer of 1999. He thinks

Gavin became sick 6 months to 1 year later. He learned his name was used from a reporter from NY Daily News. Never authorized Janet to use his name for any lawsuit. He has never been to El Monte house. He says there were stories that **David** did anger George Lopez and became problem asking for money. He thought he was raising money not for any reason. He was told Janet was working that's why they never saw her. He says he knew nothing of their personal life. He did know Louise Palanker was giving the Arvizo's money. He says he heard that Chris Tucker was very generous to the Arvizo's.

March 17

There was advertising for a fundraiser. He had known Jamie Masada for 10 years. He did not see Kobe Bryant at a fundraiser. He says he did not see Arvizo's after the fundraiser. He says they had to be impoverished to be in comedy camp. He saw Janet at Laugh Factory 1 time. Brought them at Christmas time $350 worth of gifts from Best Buy. Every time he saw Gavin in hospital David was there. He only saw Janet 1 time at the hospital.

Re Direct

Nothing inappropriate written on the thank you card. He says he didn't see anything at the apartment that made him think they weren't poor.

14th Witness Kiki Fournier

Housekeeper at Neverland. Left Sep 2003. Her duties were to clean the main house, guest quarters, theater and serve food. She worked mostly at night. Joe Marcus managers, Jesus Salas, Violet Silva. Joe Marcus oversaw all of them. She did have interaction with Mj. He, **Mj,** was there a lot she said in 2003. She never saw him personally fire somebody. She was aware that people got fired. She says Mj is very detail oriented and he wanted things a certain way.

March 17

Frank Tyson was first a guest of Neverland in 1991. She thinks Frank was MJ's assistant. She says Frank and Mj were close. She worked off and on for 10 years for Mj. Frank was there early 2003 and he stayed a while she says. She knows Vinnie Amen. He worked with Frank Tyson. She knows Dieter Wiesner, he worked for Mj. He was there early 2003. Ronald Konitzer associate Mj. Mark Schaffel was a guest at the ranch and he worked a party for Mj. She was there for the party. Party had DJ, tents, artwork and it cost to be there, she says. She thinks 800-1000 attended. She says children were guests quite a bit when Mj there. She says they were quite a bit without parents. She says that there aren't really rules. She says Mj would discipline sometimes. She says the kids got pretty rowdy. Children got assigned somewhere to sleep and sometimes stayed with Mj. She says children became more wild and destructive the longer they were at Neverland. Frank Cascio, Aldo Cascio, Dominic Cascio, Brett Barnes, Gavin Arvizo, Macaulay Culkin, Jimmy Safechuck, Elijah, Little Michael "Omar", Robson.

March 17

She says most of the boys were 10-15. She says 4-5 boys from Los Olivos could be in 7th - 9th grade. She says she saw Mj drink alcohol. She says he drank wine and sometimes vodka. She said children appeared to be intoxicated a couple of times. **She doesn't know if the children were intoxicated when around Mj, then she says to her they seemed to be intoxicated and she says Sep 2003 while serving dinner 4 or 5 children with Mj. She says at least 3 seemed intoxicated.** Pinocchio's Pleasure Island is what she called Neverland. Dec 2002 till Sep 2003 key to wine cellar was supposed to be safe in the Break room.

Cross Examination

She went to college full time 90-91. 2-3 days a week away from Neverland. 2-3 hour class, 45 min commute each way and spent 10-15 hours a week on homework. She remembers Frank's whole family would visit but not as much as kids. Frank told her he worked for Mj but doesn't know who was paying him. She says there were a lot of weirdos etc, that would try and get in with Mj. She says Mj never supervised the groups of kids that show up. She says it's not unusual for kids to go wild at Neverland.

March 17

She says Dieter told her he was manufacturing dolls of Mj. She says Ronald seemed much nicer than Dieter. **She thinks Schaffel was an opportunist. She says she met a lot of those kinds of people.** She says you never could predict when all these characters would show up she says. She says Mj would leave for weeks or months at a time. She knows of a tree where Mj liked to climb and sit-on. She says maybe 50-60 employees. 5 employees assigned to the main house. She would watch children sometimes. She says towards the end that Gavin and Starr room were a mess towards the end. She says she felt the Arvizo kids showed no respect. She says she didn't know about being caught with adult material or masturbating in the guest quarter. She says Janet stayed in her guest cottage but she was in the main house a lot also. **She says Starr pulled a knife on her in Feb 2003** in the kitchen when she was doing dishes. **She doesn't know if the key was not in safe all the time.** Hard liquor in the cabinet in the kitchen in the wine cellar. **She says she found a wine cellar open sometimes.** 7-8 security people at Neverland. She says it was about 2 weeks before they left for good.
March 17
was very messy. She says they really trashed it. She complained to Jesus Salas. She also

discussed it with Maria, another housekeeper. She remembers the blood drive for Gavin but does not remember when it was. Her supervisor was Gail Goforth. She says to the sheriff how hard it is to leave, just walk. **She says Arvizo children were destructive.** She says Mj was a close friend to the entire family, not just to children. **She says Mj allowed a lot of people to go through the main house. She says alcohol was in the cabinet in the kitchen by the sink, not locked up and in the refrigerator**. **She never saw Mj give any kids alcohol.** She says that she felt it was somewhat up to employees to watch children when Mj wasn't there. She described Mj as a big kid. **She doesn't remember Arvizo kids being intoxicated in her mind.** She says there was a LA radio station at a party that Schaffel organized. The birthday party she talked about. She says she thinks Arvizo kids were there when Ed Bradley came to Neverland. She says Janet Arvizo usually had her dinner in the main house. She says Janet mostly ate in the kitchen bar area. She says Mj spent more time with

March 17

Cascio children than the Arvizo children when they were both there. Met with Assistant DA Auchincloss and Det Alvarez for 2 hours yesterday. She's had 2 meetings with him, the other in January that also lasted 2 hours. Employees and certain guests have stayed at Ranch House.

Re Direct

Joey, 2 other kids were in ranch house with Mj and she says they seemed intoxicated. She says Mj has appeared intoxicated by any substance. She says once Mj seemed intoxicated at dinner table when she says the 3 kids seemed intoxicated. She says it's about 1 to 1 ½ miles from the front gate to the main house. And 5 miles to closest town. She thinks Mj was aware of some of the destruction at Neverland. Brett Barnes, Elijah, Little Michael, Frank, Aldo, Los Olivos Boys and Jimmy Safechuck all spent time without parents. She says Frank and Vinnie had desks in video library. They were there when Arvizo's were there. She says employees would act on their best behavior when Mj was there. She says **she though Starr was joking when he pulled knife on her but she said she thought he was trying to display authority over her.**

March 17

15th Witness Det Wolff

6 years sheriff. She seized card in master bath in dresser next to sink #712 card.

Cross Examination

She did read the card after she found it. Then she gave it to Det Padilla. Read Operations Plan before search. She says approximately. 69 people were involved in the search. She says she can only remember Det Pierce being in the master bath and she can't remember other detectives that were in there. She says she saw 1 camera and helicopters on the way in and on the way out she saw news vans. She also searched the Paris room. She doesn't remember what else she saw in the dresser with the card.

16 Witness Shawn O'Grady

Sheriff Deputy since 1997. He was assigned to search the bedroom and bathroom of Mj room. He seized an adult material book on the border of the bathtub. #588 The adult material book. #711 A photograph of Front of Book

Cross Examination

He didn't know the book was sent to Mj by the photographer.

March 17

17th Witness Jeffrey Ellis

Works for DA as investigator. Seized item in lower part of Mj bedroom by fireplace in B Dalton bookbag on floor. #589 The book that he seized. #710 A photograph of the front page of the book. Book (Naked as a jaybird).

Cross Examination

You can get that book on amazon.com not illegal.

18th Witness Con Abel

Deputy Sheriff 30 years. One area he was assigned to search was the arcade. He did see alcohol in the cellar. Bottles of red and white wine and a variety of different Liquors and Sky, Grey Goose, Smirnoff Vodkas. #581 1 Book. #583 1 Book, #581 Books located in the wine cellar in the wine rack without wine in it. #582 in cardboard box upstairs in upstairs library. #583 in a cardboard box within the library doesn't know if it was in same box as #582. #714 Adult Magazines, Found in the restroom of the office. #713 Photo of 716 Adult Magazine. #584 Brown Bags. #715 Photo of 714 Adult Magazine. #585 Binder contains Adult Magazine. #716 Found in restroom of office, Adult Magazine, #586 Brown Bags. #587 Binder contain Adult Material.

March 17

He was also required to search museums and offices. Seized #581 Books because of nude or semi nude men and women and some young people. #582 seized because it showed young female and male nude and semi nude. #583 Seized because youthful to elderly nude and semi nude. #717 Black case found in closet storage area of museum/office. It was closed when he found it. It contains a large tape recorder for monitoring phone calls with adaptors for headphones and used to monitor non-phone conversations. Instructions on how to use equipment in case.

Cross Examination

He doesn't know for sure if the item in black case has ever been used. **He doesn't know if anybody can just buy that equipment at the "store".** Card in case has the name of James Lupari P.I. from Culver City. **Never checked name on card or if phone # worked. Never asked for equipment to be tested. He didn't check if it was part of the security system at Neverland. Didn't ask anybody.** Does not know if equipment fingerprinted. March 21. He met with all the prosecutors this morning to discuss hist testimony from

March 21

Last week, he said they met for only 5 minutes. He says that the prosecutors did not tell him anything about security equipment. He says he doesn't think internal security systems have hidden cameras and he's not aware that they exist. He's done no investigation since his testimony Thursday. He was undercover narcotics for 10 years. He says he is not an expert on security systems. He says there were a lot of books in the library area (not the main house). He says they could not go through all the books with the time that they had. He says somebody opened all the boxes of books. He says there were boxes of books that were never opened. He says that he means they were none that were sealed, he says that it was just closed with the flaps of the box. 2 Books were seized in the boxes from a search of the library area. Books that were seized were given to Det Cooley. He estimates the library area is 50-60 yards from the main house. He says he saw no cameras and he doesn't know if the door had a code box to get in but the door was unlocked when he got to it. He was told there was heavy security at Neverland. He says it was not his responsibility to call the name on the card found in equipment.

March 21

He says the door to the library was locked. An employee had to open it. He says the door to the wine cellar was locked and an employee had to open it. **He says there was a bottle of vodka in the library. They did not fingerprint anything??** He says museums and offices are the same thing. He says the area he searched was videotaped but not by him.

Re Direct

He says most cases deal with telephone monitoring. He has dealt with 3 wiretap investigations during his time with narcotics.

Re Cross

He does not know about any threats against Mj or his kids. He says he discussed it with prosecutors during a meeting this morning with alligator clips. He says he's never used or installed the kind of equipment in that black case. He did not say this morning that he did some investigating on the internet whether you could buy the contents of black box at any store, if it's legal. He says that the contents are only for telephone monitoring not at all for video monitoring. **He says he assumed it was bought by Mj for his use.**

19th Witness Dr. Anthony Urquizo

A Licensed Psychologist. Assoc Prof UC Davis. Works at an abuse center for children.

March 21

Started in position Jan 1990. Been Psychologist since 1988. Been working with children since the 1970s, focused on abuse since 1982. He stopped his treatment of children a few years ago. He's done 35 to 45 publications on child abuse. He says of the children he's seen at least 1/3 or 1000 kids are sexually abused. He has testified in juvenile court on his evaluations. He been used in 85 sexual abuse cases and has of the those testified for defense 5 times. Child Sexual Accommodation Syndrome, (1) Secrecy, (2) Helplessness, Special attention, special favors, retraction, (3) Entrapment Accommodation. He says by far most children are sexually abused by someone they know. (4) Delaying unconvincing disclosure. He says it is common for disclosure not to happen right away. He says 30-50 percent wait till adulthood to disclose. He says most perpetrators are male and that's why boys don't disclose because of being called a homosexual. Children look to disclose to people who would believe them and support them. He thinks it's more difficult for boys to disclose than girls. Early adolescents 10-14 years of age. He says when a child discloses for the 1st time, they don't very often give every detail. He says they may just say that they

March 21

were touched in a weird way or made them uncomfortable. He says most children go through a process according to him and all the research. He says research says that each time a kid is interviewed their story may vary, with times and dates but he says they should be able to tell what they see or what happened. He says often love or like is involved in relationship of a sexual abuse case. He says children may enjoy molestation if they think there is a boyfriend or oral copulation. He says it is not unusual for ejaculation in molestation. He says some minor off center comments of sexual nature can be used in molestation. He says adult material introduced to 10-13 year old boys could be sexually exciting. He says boys usually show aggression externally from sexual abuse also from physical abuse or neglect. He says children feel relief from disclosure if they get a positive response.

Cross Examination

90% of his testimony in criminal court for prosecution. He is not involved in juvenile prosecutions. He makes $175 per hour. He says he's put in 10 hours so far. First contacted 1-2 months ago. I had a conversation with Mr. Zonen. He says UC Faculty is research (30-40%), teach (30-40%) and clinical activities (50-60%). He has not done therapy on children for 3-4 years.

March 21

Less than 52 percent deal with forensics. He says false claims of sexual abuse are made by children. He does not do research of false claims of sexual abuse by children. He says he knows a little about the McMartin case that contained false allegations. **He says it's very difficult to research false allegations.** He knows personally of 2 cases of false allegations but says more could be out there but he doesn't know about it. **He says his testimony would be the same if he thought the allegations were false. He says reasons for false allegations could be because marital disillusion, husband and wife break up other reasons.** He says it could be case specific. His main job is research and to evaluate their mental health. **He says it is possible for parents to put their child up to saying false allegations. He says 2-6**

percent of kids make allegations that are false. He does not know of any research for false allegations for financial gain. He says it is possible for the child to exaggerate the way he was touched from appropriate to inappropriate. He says you can be aggressive for a lot of different reasons. He says children who have been sexually abused react in different ways. He says some will tell right away and some will never tell.

March 21

All of his testimony is based on research not what he has seen. He says 4-7% of children who are molested are by strangers. Some children have very accurate accounts of their abuse. He does not know anything about "auto suggestion". He says it's hard to look at a child and determine he has been sexually abused. He says a child's view on lying could be changed if he or she sees parents lying quite often. He says it is possible that when things are added every time, they tell a story about their alleged abuse that it could be they are making it up or it could be true. **He says it is difficult for him to answer if you can just interview a child and tell if they were sexually abused.** He has never read any research about false accusations against celebrities. He is an acquaintance and is known and has an ongoing relationship. He says most of the time the perpetrator and victim know each other.

Re-Direct

He says a person who supplies alcohol and adult material and things that kids like could be considered to be grooming for molestation. He says he has no knowledge of false accusations for financial gain.

Re-Cross

Juror Notebook 2

Chapter 2

March 21

20th Witness Lauren Wallace

Was a flight attendant for ExtraJet. Ended June 2004. They flew 4 aircrafts. She supervised 2 flight attendants Cindy Bell and Jamie Crow. Her boss was Jim Duggan. The jets carried approximately 12 people. Gulf Streams can go coast to coast. 5 to 5 ½ hours from CA to Florida. She's been on 15 to 25 flights with Mj. She was the one who prepared the plane. Last flight 11-22-03. She did not fly with Arvizo's. She says Mj had special catering orders. KFC, Subway sandwiches, chicken breast with rice pilaf. **She says Mj, his request for alcohol was not on the trip sheet. She says he drank on 9 or 10 of the flights. She says sometimes he had liquor and she says he drank out of glass and sometimes white wine out of a diet coke can.** She prepared the cans for him. **Never had mixed drinks in diet coke can. She says other people would drink wine out of coke cans. She doesn't remember her name but she thinks it was a 22 year old family member.** She hid bottles of Tanqueray, vodka and tequila in the bathroom. She says it was rare that he drank them.

Cross Examination

Her understanding was that he didn't want children seeing him drink alcohol. He wanted white wine in the can because he also gets nervous on flights. **She says she never saw intoxicated children on a flight with Mj.** White wine in diet coke cans was prepared for every flight. She brought little bottles of alcohol because she knew he didn't like for his children to see him drinking. That's why she hid them in the bathroom. She met Mj March 2003 and last saw him 11-2003. 6 out of 10, all the seats were taken on flights. She says Mj would sleep on 7 of 10 flights.

Re-Direct

4 or 5 without his children and he still drank wine out of cans and a couple of the little bottles were gone. Dieter 3 or 4 flights with Mj. Schaffel on 4 out of 10 flights.

21st Witness Louise Palanker

She's a comedian, writer, teacher, and producer. She helped Jaime Masada with comedy camp. Camp would meet every Saturday for 4 to 5 hours. Jamie always took the entire family, not just one sibling. March 22. She says all the children arrived and left the comedy camp on the bus with their mom.

March 22

Her and Fritz and Fritz 2 sons delivered gifts from Best Buy on Dec 20. Fritz kids made the Arvizo's cards. She had never met the father. Father was not at the graduation party for comedy camp. She visited Gavin in hospital 2-3 times a week. She pulled her father aside to offer financial assistance. #718 Copy of check (6-15-2000) to Janet Arvizo for $10,000. David told her to write the check to Janet. She says David told her they didn't need the money for hospital bills. She says Janet was seldom at the hospital. She says at that point no Arvizo's had ever asked her for money. She had no demands on what they had to use the money for. She says David after the first check started asking her for money. She says she knew him 2 weeks before he started asking her for money. **Benefit for Gavin was Oct 2000.** She told him she could give him $10,000 but that would be it. 2nd check 7-10-2000. Given to David at Laugh Factory. She says **David** kept telling her that they had no money to live on. She says David never paid contractors for fixing the room for Gavin at grandma's house. She says David continuously asked her for money.

March 22

She says David told her his brothers were gangsters. Benefit was to raise money for family to live on. She says the 1st benefit she thinks will raise $800-$1,000 dollars. Janet was not at 1st benefit. She says she thinks Gavin had 9 rounds of chemo, started in July and ended June the following year. Some people thought the second benefit was purely David's idea just to raise money. He, David, was insistent that George Lopez host the 2nd benefit. George Lopez did not perform because he was angry with David about a wallet that Gavin had left at George Lopez house. She was present when money from 2nd benefit was given to David from Jamie \$800-\$1,000 dollars. Ann and George Lopez became irate over the wallet because David said there was 300 dollars in it but there was only 3 dollars in it. David went to where George Lopez was and George started screaming at him in front of everybody. She says when Gavin wouldn't say which wallet his father became infuriated and threw the money from benefit at Jamie and then gathered it back up and took it. After viewing Bashir Video she couldn't contact Arvizo's because all the numbers had been disconnected. Phone call with Janet

March 22

was late Feb early March. She says Janet was very scared and fearful and agitated. Janet told her it's not a safe line because they are monitoring it. She was concerned after the phone call she called her lawyer. She told Janet to call her at noon next day to meet at a location. She never got a phone call. She says she called a lawyer because she felt they were being held against their will. She says she is friends with Mother and kids. She says Janet has never asked her for money and she says Janet, she thinks, was not interested in her finances. She says Gavin has been honest in the face of people pushing him not to be.

Cross Examination

She did not know that Gavin tried to trick his father into buying clothes at JCPenney. She says she doesn't know much about the JC Penney case because they told her they weren't allowed to talk about it. She says she learned that the checks were deposited into Janet's mother's account. She doesn't know which one called Lopez's wallet, Gavin or David. She met Arvizo's 1999 at Laugh Factory. Spoke to Sheriff Jan 7, 2005. She says that family can be as wacky as they want to be.

March 22

She says she thinks Janet is bi-polar. She says she was exaggerating because she didn't know she was being taped. She never knew she was recorded. She says she didn't say Janet would sell them at the hospital and Laugh Factory. She says she meant (seldom). She feels the kids were being coached at times. She says she doesn't remember saying Janet always put him to it and he had to do it. She says she doesn't remember saying that these people are teaching their kids to lie. **She says she thinks Jamie Masada is a pathological liar, but** she says she was exaggerating. She says David's made up committee thing to get more money from her. That's what Jaime told her. She thought Janet needed to see a psychologist because she was never with her son in the hospital. She says the Arvizo's loved to call people who's phone # they had. She was asked to tell Arvizo's to stop calling Jay Leno. **She says there are mistypes in the transcript? She thought they were trying to latch on to anyone that could help them.** She says she was afraid of David and didn't want the Arvizo's at her house. She says Janet said to her she was David's Sweetheart.

March 22

David did talk to her about Gavin having erections. She says she didn't know what was going on with them. She says they were strange as a family. **She believed Janet wanted her kids to be in show business.** She says she may have done a lot of assuming regarding the Arvizo's and how poor they were. **Janet had led her to believe that David had wrecked the car, possibly that Mj had given them. She says there are inconsistent statements to things that Janet told her. She says she thought Janet had a hostage syndrome.** She said she was impressed with the basket Mj sent Gavin to hospital. **Gavin would ask Jamie to meet Adam Sandler and other stars, Quincy Jones, to get a hold of Mj. She never called police over anything Janet told her.**

Re-Direct

She says the contractor intended to work for free but expected to get paid for material. **She says**

Janet was very emotional. She says she understands more now because she was told that David would tell Janet he would kill her if she came down and that she was abused. She says they, kids, were much more affectionate with their mother. She says she never thought Janet was teaching her kids to lie.

March 22

She says David left 3 years ago. She says the family is much happier. She says she does not think Jamie is a pathological liar. She says Jamie cares deeply for them and he wants to do the right thing. She says she never saw Janet ask for money from anybody.

Re-Cross

She says Janet didn't use the words but she said she had been held hostage since she was 16. Janet didn't tell her she had been held hostage at any time. She says her conversation with David was short. She says the Arvizo's called her guardian angel on cards she was sent. The fundraiser was approximately 6 months apart. She says she had a red flag with them coming to her house. She never drove or had the Arvizo's at her house.

March 23

22nd Witness Robert Cooley
Sheriff 25 years. Det. Santa Ynez/Solvang. Scribe

at arcade building. Scribe takes, seizes, packages and marks things that are seized. He's the one that bagged #581 3 books. #582 He bagged 1 book. #583 He bagged 1 book. They were turned **over to forensic detectives.**

Cross-Examination

As a scribe the search sometimes.

March 23

He did some searching the day of the search of Mj house. He says he did package those items so they could be fingerprinted. He says it could have been possible to do DNA also. **Lead investigators decide what gets fingerprinted and DNA tested. He was not told that the 3 items were going to be fingerprinted or DNA tested. If he wanted to know who gave him those items he would have to ask each officer if they remember. He says there was no procedure on keeping track of who was turning in seized items to the scribe. He does not know why that procedure was not done.** He does not recall how much time he spent in the library.

Re-Direct

He said things are photographed in the place it was found.

<u>Re-Cross</u>

23rd Witness Deputy Freddy Padilla

11 years with the Sheriff. Det Persons Crimes. Package seized items from main house in Mj Bedroom. #580 In front of the bag. **<u>Given to him by Det Sheppard Magazines.</u>** He says he tried to keep all items in numerical order and in his view. #576 **<u>Not on the package who gave it to him. He had to look on another sheet given to him by Det Sheppard.</u>** #575 Given to him by Det Sheppard. #569 Given to him by Det Sheppard.

March 23

He says he stored all items in his view in the master bedroom area. #633 Given to him by Det Sheppard. #588 Given to him by Det O'Grady. On his sheet SH451 it says a different Det gave it to him. #589 Given to him by DA Inv Ellis. #712 Given to him by Det Wolff. #562 Given to him by Det Alvarez. # 288 Given to him by Det Alvarez. **<u>#565 didn't ask any questions about appearing to be repackaged.</u>** #470 **<u>He does not remember the briefcase. He had to refer to his SH451. He doesn't recognize writing on his SH451, it says Det. Zellis gave</u>** that to him. **<u>He says sometimes Detectives were backed up so the Detective would help him seize things.</u>** #561 Given to him by Det Zellis. #552 In the master bedroom Given to him by Det Robel. He does not recall what was placed in the bag. Check SH451. He says it is magazines he didn't put a number of magazines in. It contains 1 item right now and that's a book. Item he marked as #364 given to him by Det Robel. He says #553 couldn't find it.

Cross Examine

He performed his duties as a scribe downstairs of Mj Bedroom.

March 23

He was a scribe the whole day he did no searching. He was relieved of duties for lunch and bathroom breaks by Det Klapakis but he does not recall ever using the sign out sheet. He says Det Klepakis did not package anything. He says he thinks he saw 15-20 people searching the bedroom of Mj. He says he doesn't know how many bedrooms are searched. He thought they were talking about the entire house. **He does not remember all the detectives he just talked about 10 min ago.** He had no role in determining if things had to be fingerprinted. He says there were several items to be held for prints that he was told. **He makes no record on anything of something to be held for prints.** He has noted in his cases to hold for prints but not in this case. **Anything to hold for prints was not separated from any other item.** Sgt Cintron.

24th Witness Det Craig Bonne
11 years Sheriff. Detective 5 years. His job after

the search was to look at all items seized and make sure and document them related to the case. #321 Opened bag. 11-26-03 photo documented. Wrote a report.

March 23

After that he sealed them back and initialed bag. #554-560 In box contained in item #321. He documented on 11-26. #682-688 Photographs of front cover of magazines in box #554-560. All adult material magazines. #309 Dec 2 2003 Opened inventory and checked there were 2 adult material DVDs. #363 Adult magazines 11-26-03. Followed same procedure as with #321. #530-551 He was wearing gloves during all these events he says. #689-709 Photo of front covers of magazines. #565 in Item #309. #470 Briefcases handled the same items as before. #471-529 Magazines out of briefcase. #295, #632, #634-681 Photos in front of magazines found in briefcase. **Some magazines and just some pages.** All adult material. July 20,2004 went to superior court to pick up from grand jury evidence and photographed every page. Oct 20, 2004 brought to have forensically processed. He, Det Lafferty and Det Spinner. Some items were removed before going to the grand jury. #720 Envelope with writing on upstairs of Mj bedroom, found in briefcase. #721 **Found on furniture in bathroom of Mj room. Picture of Macaulay Culkin**. #151 Found in Mj bottle of wine. Locked closet in bathroom bottle of whiskey.

March 23

Cross Examine

Those bottles he does not know if they were fingerprinted. He does know they were DNA swabbed and there were no results. #317 Materials were tested to see if there were any DNA. No DNA found. Lt Klepakis, Sgt Robel, Him, Det Zellis, Prosecution and others in meetings. Have not made any effort to see where you can buy these adult materials. He was initially with Det Alvarez to interview witnesses not search houses. Forensics separated all magazines. Prosecution and Lt Klepakis decided what got forensically tested. Certain items in #317 were tested before a grand jury. They have not found any DNA on anything from any ARVIZO. #317 had ALS Test Alternative Light Source. He says he had gloves on during search of #470 Black briefcase. **No testing was done for at least 1 year.**

Re-Direct

#470 sent for fingerprint analysis 11/04

25th Witness Dr. Antonio Cantu

US Secret Service. Chief Scientist of Forensic Duties. 20 years in areas. Degree in Chemical Forensics. Protective Research for threats of chemical or biological. Published 26 papers, 7 on fingerprints.

March 23

Is involved in developing new techniques to look at fingerprints, Latent Fingerprint that is not noticeable by the human eye. Every time you touch something you leave some kind of fingerprint behind. Water Soluble – Amino Acids, Salts, Proteins. Water Insoluble – Lipids Fats Oils. There are no oil glands in your fingertips. Oil gets on your finger by touching something that has oil on it. 4 Optical methods. Ultraviolet Light, Reflective mode. **He says textured objects don't absorb prints very well.** Ridge is raised with a portion of fingerprint. One of the lines. Fuming with a gas vapor (Super glue), forms around the fingerprint. It hardens fingerprints and makes it bigger. This treatment will enhance the ultraviolet technique. Heat the vapor in like an aquarium. Super glue fuming enhances both Water Soluble and Water Insoluble. The scene scope is a Ruvus. Ninhydrin to look for fingerprints on porous like paper and the print comes out purple. You do optical methods first, then super glue fuming then the ninhydrin. Spex Industries makes the scene scope. He is not being paid extra.

March 23

Cross Examination

He helped develop scenescope. Electro Optical

Systems, Inc before they were bought by French Company. He is not a latent print examiner. Visible Prints – Paint. Plastic Prints – Puddy, clay. Latent Print – Can't see unaided. March 24 . He has testified in court in front of a jury 40 times and he says most of them for the prosecution. He has seen evidence in this case but he says he hasn't evaluated any of it. The IND advancement for the amino acids of prints was not used in this case and that's an advancement that he helped develop.

Re-Direct

He has not reviewed photographs of fingerprints taken with a digital camera.

Re-Cross

Fingerprints are evidence you want to preserve at a crime scene. Part of the protocol he agreed to was the right protocol so you should try and pressure fingerprints. **He says fingerprinting should be done first before being booked into evidence. He was not aware that the fingerprinting process wasn't done for a year.**

Re- Direct (2)

He would not expect fingerprints to disappear if handled correctly.

March 24
He says chemicals of the fingerprint can change but not the pattern.

Re-Cross (2)

It is possible he says that you can lose detail of print over a period of time. You would want to know if one of the subjects did handle the evidence within that year.

26th Witness Lisa Susan Roote Hemmen

Senior Identification Technician 8 years. She was at Search. She was assigned to the arcade/cellar and security office. She did not seize anything, she just photographed. Jan 2004 #316, #317, #321, #363, #364. She was asked to examine. She examined all items with a light source. **Body fluids will fluoresce under UV light but it could be other things also.** She packaged items in separate evidence bags to go to the Dept of Justice. She was 1st person to use bag that was del to Dept of Justice with evidence from #317 Feb 5, 2004. **She says you search for DNA first before fingerprints because the fingerprinting process could ruin the DNA.** Started examination 1-20-04 completed 2-5-04. When she went home at night everything was in a secured lab.

March 24

LSHR 2696 is her initials on evidence tape. Hawk

magazine published Feb 2003. #687 Finally Legal published Feb 2003. #689, #690, #691, #692, #693, #694, #695, #696, #697, #698, #699 – She processed all these magazines. #518 Barely Legal magazine with Yellow Stickers because she wanted them to specifically look at those pages because some things showed up under Ultraviolet light. #700, #701, #702, #703, #704, #705, #706, #707, #708, #709 – Not taken by her. She took all these photos.

Cross Examination

She did fingerprint comparisons in this case. She did not photo document anything from the main house. Next time she saw evidence in this case was 1-20-04. After the 11-18-03 search, she says you never cut somebody else's seal on evidence. She doesn't know if anybody did anything with evidence from 11-18-03 - 1-20-04. #470 last seal 12-03-04. Yellow seal from 11-18-03 search. She sealed it back up 1-26-04. She delivered 2-5-04.

March 24

She says she put the contents of the briefcase back in order but she doesn't remember which magazine was on top. She went page by page examining with UV Light and her orange goggles. She says that is not destructive to evidence. She says you are likely to find more latent prints than visible or plastic. **She did not use a scenescope in 1-2004.** She doesn't know if anybody else looked at Briefcase between 1-26-04 and the grand jury. She says she had nothing to do with #470 after the grand jury. She did look at photos of latent prints, late summer early fall. She says when she sent off for DNA it was for Mj DNA. She doesn't know if that was superseded to look for Gavin or Starr DNA. No DNA of Starr or Gavin was found.

Re-Direct

It would be illegal for a minor to possess or look at this material according to the penal code book.

Re-Cross

Mj is not charged with a code section. She was asked to look at it in a penal code book. She's not licensed or certified by any fingerprinting organization. You can add fingerprints such as scars, warts etc but prints don't change.

March 24

She says fingerprints are unique to an individual. She does know about the Madrid bombing case of finding a lawyer in Oregon print but it was not him. She says validation studies are tests for competency. She is aware of proficiency tests that came back false positive and false negative. **A print has to be 100% positive if its 99.9 is inconclusive.** #317, #1 A print on page 31. She was deemed inconclusive. Was found to be positive and print belonging to Starr Arvizo. Field report Fall 2004, Jan 2005 her and

Det Spinner concurred on all inconclusive. They had to do 21,000 comparisons. #3170 Print #1 Page 7 was a positive Mj print, but Det Spinner put it as inconclusive because he couldn't agree. Most latents on a magazine you won't get to edgeoscopy or proscopy.

Re-Direct (2)

She says she thought it was Starr Arvizo's print even when she labeled it inconclusive. She says fingerprint comparison is an applied science.

Re-Cross (2)

SWIG Fast says it unethical to come to court and give your opinion on an inconclusive print.

March 24

27th Witness Charlene Marie

CA Dept of Justice. Senior Criminalist 15 years. They accept evidence delivered directly or by UPS, mail or they may go to the scene and help collect. **#317, #529 and various subsets of that 15 total items on 2-4-04.** First examined the contents on 7-27-04. Bag was PU 5-20 by Lafferty and returned 5-21. She says it remained in her evidence locker in lockup. #766 Photos of front covers of what was in a brown paper bag released to the sheriff for good on 7-29-04.

<u>Cross Examination</u>

She never saw a briefcase. She was looking for biologicals (body fluids). **<u>She found no bodily fluids on anything she examined.</u>**

28th Witness Heriberto Martinez Jr.

Sheriff Dept. He took fingerprints on card #767 exhibit. On Nov 20 2003, he said they were Mj. Done on a lifescan machine shows up on screen when being done.

<u>Cross Examination</u>

He is sworn only when on duty. He is a correctional officer at the jail. He is not trained as a latent print examiner. He had 15 hour class on how to

March 24

book people and fingerprint them and it was on the job using the lifescan machine.

29th Witness Alicia Romero

Not Prosecution ready for Witnesses.

30th Witness Det Tim Sutcliffe

Det Forensics Unit. Law Enforcement 16 years. He has had training in latent fingerprinting. Uses all the techniques mentioned already in finding latent fingerprints. He is an ID Technician. Torres and Det Lafferty. Used super gluing technique followed by scenescope followed by ninhydrin. #723 Slideshow of how everything was done. Fuming was done in a lab at Santa Barbara Sheriff Station. Used 2 Scene Scopes. 1 in Santa Barbara, 1 in Santa Maria. Grid is used to mark the location of prints if any are found. Images photographed with a digital camera 4 megapixels. Midrange for resolution. Can't scan from monitor with regular camera. Ninhydrin reacts with your amino acids. The ninhydrin prints were scanned and not photographed. Started processing at the end of August. Sheriff had to bring in extra help. Det Spinner, Det Wittenbrock, Technician Shelley.

March 24

All photos of fingerprint on Magazines

Finally Legal
#725 – A photo of #3172 fingerprint
#728 - #317R fingerprint Barely Legal, Hustler
#729 – #317R Hustler Barely Legal
#730 - #317R Hustler Barely Legal
#731 - #317R Hustler Barely Legal
#732 - #317S Penthouse
#733 - #317S Penthouse
#734 - #317T Visions of Fantasy
#735 - #317U Visions of Fantasy
#736 - #317YY Best Adult Videos

#737 - #321A Playboy
#738 - #321A Playboy
#739 - #321E Barely Legal
#740 - #321E Barely Legal
#741 - #321F Finally Legal

All items were already superglued when they got them. #768 Example of quadrant grid. Error on #321F sticker says #321D. He found the error and went back and checked the rest of the labels.

Cross Examine

Ninhydrin makes prints purple. **If you overfume you can lose a lot of the definition of print. Used a digital camera as a matter of convenience. A digital camera will not capture all of the area that a 35mm will.** Downloaded to the hard drive then onto the disc. **He is not a certified latent print examiner. He does comparisons.**

March 25

Never had meeting with 2 from Santa Barbara, Det Wittenbrock, Tech Shelley. 700 total prints. 600 from Santa Maria.

March 25

19 Total usable prints out of 700. He says they did a few test pages with just scenescope **before doing superglue test.**

Re-Direct

He says the superglue does not alter fingerprints. **He says the scenescope company Spex has told him that a 4 megapixel camera is sufficient to photograph fingerprints found with a scenescope.** #769 Notebook with 19 pages in it pictures of Adult Magazine pages with the fingerprints on them.

Re-Cross

#741 Print was originally put as #321D but that was wrong. **No way to determine the age of a fingerprint.** He says if the superglue process is done too long it can obscure some of the print.

Re-Direct (2)

#321D was actually #321F. He says #321D was associated with Hawk magazine, not the Finally Legal they were checking.

Re-Cross (2)

He says that evidence should not be mis-labeled

31st Witness Alicia Romero

Supervises courtroom Clerks. Handles exhibits also. They were locked in a vault , the exhibits that were for the grand jury. Only 2 other people had access to the vault.

March 25

All exhibits that were accessed had a record kept. The 1st time the exhibits were viewed other than the Clerks, Steven Dunkel and Amy Cassell. They work for the defense 6-9-04 at 2:53-3:45. She put that they viewed most of them and that they used gloves. 7-20-04 next time they were viewed by Det Craig Bonner. He took pictures of items. She was present the entire time while Det Bonner took pictures of everything in #470 black briefcase. He wore gloves, she says. She says he may have not placed them back in the same order as he took them out. She put it back in the vault. 7-21-04 Mr. Sanger and S Dunkel examined and opened black briefcase and she doesn't know if they looked through all of it; she says maybe just some of it. 7-27-04 S Dunkel and S Watts looked at all of the exhibits for 1:30 hrs they had gloves on. To release the item you had to have a stipulated order from the judge. Removed by Det Craig Bonner 10-1-04 #770 is a disc of exhibits that were released.

Cross Examination

Grand jury process was complete when Mr. Sanger and Mr. Dunkel went to look at it.

March 25

They all the defense people took all precautions according to her to not contaminate evidence. **Nobody was wearing gloves the first**

time the boxes of exhibits were put in the vault and when the inventor logged all the exhibits they did not wear gloves. She takes her directions from Gary Blair, Court Director. **She says if she were told they were going to be fingerprinted she would have acted appropriately.**

32nd Witness Nancy Torres

Santa Barbara Sheriff. ID Tech Forensics Unit. 5 years. She says everyday they do fingerprint comparisons. She was Det Sutcliffe's partner in fingerprint search of magazine pages. **Why do they just list one date Sept 1993 of the magazines?**

Cross Examination

She's not a deputy or sworn peace officer. She is a latent print examiner in training for 4 years. Only had a scenescope for 5 months prior to this case. Began processing Sept 16, 2004. They had 1 training day on it. The Santa Barbara Office got their scenescope at the same time. **They got training before they got a scenescope. They had not used it prior to this case.**

33rd Witness Michelle Shelley

Santa Barbara Sheriff 2004. ID Tech on job training for latent fingerprinting. **None so far are certified latent fingerprints.** She has **had training in ninhydrin.**

Cross Examination

Previously ID Tech Delaware State Police. Trying to return to that job. She worked in records in Santa Barbara Sheriff when 1st started. **She is not a latent print examiner. The first time she used scenescope was in this case.** She did not receive training on scenescope from Spex company.

34th Witness Det Jim Wittenbrock

Retired Santa Barbara Sheriff 28 years. He has had training in Superglue and ninhydrin and a little on the scenescope. **His assignment was to use scenescope to search magazines for latent fingerprints.** 1 mag from 3/1998. 2 mag from 7 and 8/ 2003.

Cross Examination

4 years in forensics. He had no training on scenescope, he was just shown how to use it by ID Tech Torres. He has not heard of a digital camera being a problem in photographing latent prints.

March 25

He says he told the people doing the superglue process to not overfume.

Re-Direct

He says the 3 he spoke about were not overfumed.

35th Witness Robert Spinner

P/T Employee Santa Barbara Sheriff. Spent 32 years as Sheriff. From 1986 to retirement 2003 in the forensics department. Sgt and supervisor of forensics when he retired. 80,000 Fingerprint comparisons over his career. 21,000 just in this case. Testified in court 10-15 times. He is not a certified examiner.

#744 – Starr Arvizo fingerprints
#745 – Gavin Arvizo fingerprint
#743 – Mj fingerprints

He says no 2 persons have ever been found to have the same fingerprint pattern. Level (1) Loops arches or swirls. Level (2) Friction Ridges. Last part of July 2003 is when I started helping in this case. They were told they had to be done by 12-17-04. 706 Latent Prints provided. 178 were found to be used. Some were palm prints. They used the print cards. They were able to identify 19 of the 178. 7 they did not come to a conclusion about. Some parents would get a first look and then later a more thorough look.

March 25

He and ID Tech would look at latents separately and then compare to see if they agreed.

#735 Picture latent print. Came to conclusion.
#757 Charted comparison of Gavin's right middle

finger on #317U Page 10, positive identification found (20 points)
#772 PowerPoint Presentation
#726 Picture of latent #317L #126 fingerprint
Finally Legal Magazine
#748 Charted Comparison of latent #317L #126 and right index finger of Starr Arvizo, positive (25 points)
#773 PowerPoint Presentation. There were 25 points that matched on Starr Arvizo print
#727 Mj latent fingerprint #317O #2
#749 Chart comparison of latent and Mj known print, Left thumb (17 total points found)
#774 PowerPoint Presentation
#746 Chart latent #304D #52. Left little finger Mj. Positive
#747 Chart #317L #31 Latent positive (20 points) left middle Starr Arvizo (ninhydrin)
#750 Latent #317R #54 (18 Point) left thumb of Mj positive
#751 Latent #317R #92 (21 Points) left little finger Gavin positive
#752 Latent #313R #92 (13 Points) left ring of Gavin positive
#753 Latent #317R #92 (14 Points) left index Gavin positive
#754 Latent #317S #63 (16 Points) right thumb Mj positive
#755 Latent #317S #87 (21 Points) left ring of Mj positive

March 25
#756 Latent #317T #3 (21 Points) left thumb Mj

positive
#758 Latent #317 #A (18 Points) left index Gavin positive
#759 Latent #321A #3 (26 Points) right thumb Mj positive
#760 Latent #321A #29 (30 Points) right thumb Mj positive
#761 Latent #321E #1 (24 Points) left thumb Mj positive
#762 Latent #321E #7 (19 Points) right thumb Mj positive
#763 Latent #321F #11 (16 Points) right thumb Mj positive
#764 Latent #363 #57 (19 Points) right thumb Mj positive

These are all 1 Charted Comparisons. He says he reviewed these findings several times. He says if there is a problem he would correct it. #317O Thumb print of MJ, he had a problem with, he changed from positive to inconclusive. Putting all binders and loose pages of adult material magazines found at Mj search into evidence. #775 Paper with pictures of various fingerprint patterns 8 class 1 types.

March 28

#317 series of items. He was told when he got #306 the #317 was not available. He got 1 portion of #317 in August. #622 is a timeline. #529 is the bag that had #317 evidence. He 1st got 8-3-04. Dec 2000 Finally, Barely Legal, Penthouse, 100 Best

Adult Legal. #317L, #317R, #317S, #317YY positive fingerprints.

March 28

Started processing items in #317 on 8-11-04. #317S, #317yy were started on 8-12-04. Got black briefcase #470 on 10-5-04

#317O Barely Legal (Mj) Prints Processed on 10-5 – 10-12 05
#317T Visions of Fantasy (Mj) Prints 10-5 – 10-12 05
#317U Visions of Fantasy (G.A.) Prints 10-5 – 10-12 05

He says he didn't process **much at all in September**.

36th Witness George Lopez

Nov 99 Aug 2000. Radio show host. Performed at Laugh Factory last 15 years. Fall 99 participated in 1 comedy camp for 7 weeks. Worked with Arvizo's for a month in 1999. He says they were 2 hrs a week sessions. Janet Arvizo was at the Laugh Factory every time her kids were there. He says Janet never asked him for money. He met David for the 1st time at the hospital. He visited him at his grandparent's home in El Monte. He says the house was modest at best except for Gavin's room.

March 28

He says he never saw mother again after Gavin got sick. Feb-Mar 2000, father David asked him for (assistance) money etc.... He says these requests were on occasion but mostly 20 dollars here or 30 dollars here. He says David was more interested in money than Gavin. He was going to use the radio and do it at the Icehouse in Pasadena. He says he got behind the radio and David became aggressive in trying to get the fundraiser started. He says David did talk to him about a blood drive. May 5, 2000 in El Monte at Acapulco Restaurant outside David approached him and they had words and he never heard from David again. Before that incident he took kids to the mall. George and David weren't around when kids were asking for things. He says he found Gavin's wallet at his house with a $50 bill in it and they mailed it to them and David accused him of taking $300 dollars out of it. He thinks he was at a fundraiser that Fritz Coleman hosted.

Cross Examination

He interviewed with Mr. Zonen on Friday for 25 minutes. He did not want it recorded. He only went shopping once with David and Kids.

March 28

He didn't buy everything that Gavin asked for. **Feb 16 he says he didn't give Arvizo's any money in his statements under penalty of perjury. Jan 18 2005 he says he wasn't involved in any**

<u>fundraiser. He says now that he was.</u> He says he saw David 10 times at hospital when he went to see Gavin. He says he thought the family lived in El Monte because that's where he always went to visit Gavin. He says Janet asked him not directly to go spend time with Gavin in hospital. He just assumed Janet was working. Every time he spoke with David it was about money. He doesn't know if he gave any money to Janet. He thought David's attitude changed after he talked about Neverland. He says he became angered. Jamie Masada helped to fix up the room. He arranged visits to El Monte house with David. He says nobody was allowed in the room where the wallet was found. He says the mantle was shoulder high and possibly too tall for Gavin to reach. He called David an extortionist. He says he never talked to Arvizo's again after May 5. Janet gave him a keychain 6 months after he cut ties with them. He never thought about if they had addresses.

March 28

<u>Re-Direct</u>

Nobody ever took him to Soto Street Apartment. Janet told him a story about kids diving into a fountain for coins, but he says she told him they put coins back. He says Gavin was a great kid. He says it was David was the reason he cut ties with them.

37th Witness Ann Lopez

She met Gavin in the hospital. She has never met Janet Arvizo in person. Just phone conversations. She says she went to the hospital 6 or 7 times. She says David was always at the hospital. She says David told her Janet was distraught and couldn't handle the situation. She says David told her they lived in a studio apartment and didn't know what they were going to do. She told him (David) to go back to work to keep his insurance benefits. **<u>She says there was no closeness between Arvizo kids and their dad.</u>** She says Gavin would ask for 3 or 4 toys at every store and David wouldn't say anything. She says she thought it was odd the wallet had a crisp 50 dollar bill. She says Jaimie told her about the claim of money missing from the wallet found at their house.

March 28

She says David was calling her every other day about fundraising and how much money they could make. She says David called her a fucking bitch and motherfucking whore when she told him how the money would be handled from fundraiser, how they would pay there bills and he would not just get the money.

<u>Cross Examination</u>

<u>She thought it was odd Janet was never at</u>

hospital. She never visited Arvizo's home. She says the mantle was probably 5 feet. She says she thought both parent's behavior was odd. She says she thought David used his kids to get money. She says they went into 4 or 5 shops at the mall. He never asked his (Gavin's) father to buy him anything. Knew nothing about $20,000 from Louise Palanker. She says they talked about Neverland a lot after they first went there. She noticed a change in all of the Arvizo's except Janet when they went to Neverland. She never talked to Janet about her Neverland experience. She says Janet said it was more spiritual of them being with Gavin than financial. She says David told her they did have insurance.

March 28

She never knew about any civil settlement or any $150,000 dollars. She didn't know till recently that the Arvizo's divorced.

Re-Direct

She says the keychain given to her husband George from Janet meant a great deal to him.

Cross-Examination of Witness 35 Robert Spinner

He says it's his opinion who's fingerprints match is a subjective opinion. Items in #470 when he received them were not in separate bags they were just in briefcase. 1 print was inconclusive in 2004 and then put as positive in 2005 and 1 was positive on Mj and then switched to inconclusive. He says now it's 100,000 – 120,000 prints he's examined in his career. 21,000 from this case. 165 fingerprints and 13 palm prints. He says he just had fingerprints for Mj no palm print to compare. They had 2 sets of each, Gavin and Starr's fingerprints. 1 set of Gavin's were no good, he says. So he had their prints, Starr and Gavin's redone. He says Mj prints were ok but could have been better. He says there should be more detail in Mj prints. He says ink prints are better than Lifescan prints.

March 29

It is very important to have a good known print and it's also very important to have a good latent to compare it to. **There is no way to tell when a print was made on something.** He had no training on the
scenescope other than 10 minutes from Det Lafferty. **They decided the superglue was too long so they cut back a minute on the time. #748 does not depict what's in #723.** Started working on latent prints in 1987. **They have access to all the known fingerprints in the country. He was never subject to proficiency testing nor is the Santa Barbara Sheriff's office.** He knows there was a problem with some proficiency testing from other places, but he can't remember if they were false positives. **The FBI admitted making a mistake in the Madrid bombing case and blamed**

it on digital imaging. Sgt Ashbaugh coined the phrase ridgology.

Analysis
Comparison
Evaluation
Verification

All these comparisons were done (in house) no prints were sent out. They could have sent them to the DOJ or FBI. There were 12 magazines out of all the magazines that he got positive prints from.

March 29

They used adobe photoshop in this process. **They did not print out the layer comparisons from computers that were made by him and the ID Tech.** He did not review reports of other officers. **He did not see a forensic request form that was dated before July 2004.**

#743 – Mj known prints
#744 Starr Arvizo know prints
#745 Gavin Arvizo known prints

65% of the population has looped fingerprints. There's distortion in the #317YY print page A Al Goldstein's 100 Best Adult Videos. #321E Page 7 has a marker through the print. #363M page 57 he says has slippage.

Re-Direct

He did not testify on Friday about #723 comparison to #748. You do DNA testing first before fingerprinting. **Depending on what lab was used, a turnaround on DNA testing can take some time, he says.** He sent prints to Pat Warheim. He says that's his mentor and a teacher.

Re-Cross

He does not know what DNA testing was done in this case and how long any of it took.

March 29

All fingerprints found to be Arvizo's came from black briefcase.

38th Witness Jamie Masada

Opened LA Laugh Factory in 1979. He was 16. He was 14 when he came from Iran and then Israel. Most kids at comedy camp are underprivileged. He says he keeps in contact with 90% of kids. Takes 30 to 45 kids per camp. They meet on Saturdays and they provide lunch. He believes that laughter helps heal the children. They were recommended to him by Eric Sight for comedy camp when he first met the Arvizo's. He says one was 8 (Starr), 9 (Gavin) and 13 (Davellin) years when they went to comedy camp. The mother called him to tell him Gavin had cancer. Janet asked him to pray for Gavin. George Lopez was the main comic to work with Arvizo's. He says he gave Gavin a 50 dollar bill about 7 times. He encouraged people to give blood and offered free admission and food if they did. The fundraisers, the charity or person it's for, they keep the door money. He met David Arvizo in the hospital. He says the money raised was never more than $2,000.00.

March 29

David Arvizo asked him for money many times. He told him he wasn't working (David). He says he saw Janet at hospital several times early in the morning. He never gave Janet Arvizo money. He says David told him Mj gave them the car to go back and forth to Neverland. He says David did something to Gavin when he was explaining the wallet story. #622 Date 10-13-00 of $350 copy of check. #623 copies of a check for $800. To David Arvizo for his rent. Because Gavin wouldn't confirm the story about the wallet again David became angry and threw money from the fundraiser at him. David told him Mj invited them to Neverland. Janet called him and told him that Gavin was in the Bashir Documentary. He was asked to talk on TV about Mj in Laugh Factory in LA about Bashir Documentary. He was encouraged to talk about who helped Gavin. He believed he was to talk about Martin Bashir. He says Janet called him from Neverland upset and crying. He introduced Janet to attorney Bill Dickerman, to get Gavin off television. He was present for 4 occasions. He participated in them. 1 at Dickerman office, 2 at Laugh Factory and

1 time at a baseball game. He offered Janet money. He told Janet that somebody had offered to give any amount of money she needed. She told him she didn't need money, just a friend and prayer. He saw Janet with bruises on her neck, 1 time on her face.

Cross Examination

He didn't know his phone conversation was being recorded with Santa Barbara DA in Dec 2003 where he says his parents asked him for money. He says he meant the father? He says on phone conversation that Janet wanted a watch so he bought her watch but he says now he bought Davellin a watch. He did know Louise Palanker wrote a $10,000 check to Janet Arvizo. He offered money for Judo and for him to switch schools after they told him some story. Janet did discuss JC Penney Lawsuit with him after he heard it on the news. He has discussed **this** case with Janet 7-8 months ago. He last saw Janet and Jay at the apartment. He has Janet's cell phone #. He introduced Gavin to Adam Sandler. He introduced Philip Palmer KABC to Gavin. Patrick Press Fox TV, PBS, Lady from FOX, Fritz Coleman. Mj Press did story on

March 29

Arvizo's for FOX TV 1999 (Just Arvizo's) at

comedy camp. PBS did a documentary 2000 on Laugh Factory comedy camp, the entire camp. The PBS one only showed Jamie going to hospital to visit Gavin. It was Gavin's idea to meet Mj, he said Mj was his idol. He introduced Arvizo's to Chris Tucker. He introduced Gavin to Rob Schneider. He says he paid Arvizo's rent twice. He just wanted to stop the abuse of Gavin that is why he introduced Janet to Bill Dickerman. He says Bashir got rich and Arvizo's got nothing. He testified before today 3 times under oath. He doesn't think he ever spoke to Larry Feldman, but he has been to his Office (waiting room). He did financially help send Gavin to private school. He says he just gave them 1 check for it. **Nobody called the police at any of the meetings with Bill Dickerman, Arvizo's or Jamie Masada.** He says a bank account was set up for Arvizo's from something Fritz Coleman did. He says he never told the press that he paid some of Gavin's medical bills. He has issued checks to all the Arvizo children for performing in his club. He wrote a check to Shayna Tranfeld for a bed for Arvizo children.

March 29

He says he told his office to give prosecutors whatever they needed. He last talked to Jay Jackson 3-4 months ago. **He didn't know how to tell David ``No," he says.** He says he doesn't remember telling Santa Barbara Sheriff he wrote a check to Janet for Christmas. He met Louise

Palanker a few years ago. **He knew she wrote 2 checks to the Arvizo's. She called him after her appearance in court and complained about Attorney Messereau. He doesn't remember telling DA T Rooney Investigator about talking to Starr Arvizo about what he experienced with Mj at Neverland. He says Starr mentioned sleeping pills not alcohol.**

Re-Direct

He paid the money directly to Karate school. He gave David a check for rent he offered to make it out to the landlord but David said no. He bought the bed after learning the kids were sleeping on the floor. Not Patrick Press, Patrick Perez.

Re-Cross

He told them those books were gone because they raised a computer virus.

39th Witness Cynthia Bell

Corporate Flight Attendant. Extra Jet Intl 2003.

March 29

Feb or March. From Miami to Santa Barbara. She says all the seats were full. 12-13 people. 2 Pilots. She did serve Mj alcohol on that flight in a diet coke can. She's flown with Mj 3 times, 1 time with Pacific Jet. **She says she served other clients**

that way. It was her idea to use a diet coke can. Mj never told her to serve him wine in a coke can. She says Gavin sat next to him most of the flight. She says he drank 1 or 2 bottles of wine. Mj was the only 1 drinking white wine. Now she says she doesn't remember if he had red wine. **She never saw Mj share his can of wine with anybody else.**

Cross Examination

3 no more than 6 flights with Mj now. She's never seen him share any drink with any children. She never saw Arvizo children drinking on flights. She knowingly served Davellin on flight. She's never seen any inappropriate actions by Mj with any children. She says one of the boys threw food and she described him as rude. She's talking about Gavin.

March 29

She perceived Mj as a touchy feely person, even with her. She says Mj was not rude nor were his children. Everyone else who had wine had it in a glass. She says Mj is a very nervous flyer. She told the grand jury Gavin was a weird kid. She says she could see everything that went on. She says Mj did not sleep on flight. His vodka drinks were always in diet coke cans. She says he didn't want children to see him drinking alcohol. She says Mj drank more with turbulence.

Re-Direct

Always concerned with the lead passenger. There were 2 girls on flight. She only ID 1 of them. She served them in a crystal glass. She says the doctor slept and Mj youngest child on flight from Miami. The only time the seat divider moved was when MJ went to the bathroom. She says Gavin spent most of the flight next to Mj. She says he was secretive even when he didn't drink out of diet coke can on her 1st flight with him on Pacific Jet. She told other flight attendants how Mj liked to be served his alcohol drinks out of diet coke can

March 30

Never talked about on flights that he was drinking wine from diet coke cans. She says she served him 1 mixed drink rum and coke not vodka because that's what the girls ordered. She says he showed physical signs that he had been drinking and intoxicated. She says Gavin was rude from the start of flight. She says behavior stayed the same throughout the flight. She has no idea how Gavin normally acted. Mj did nothing to stop Gavin's behavior. **She says he was not drunk but in the grand jury she said he was.** She says Mj did have his arm around Gavin at times. She says she thought it was strange that Mj didn't stop Gavin from being rude.

Re-Cross

Janet never tried to stop his rude behavior; she found that very odd. She sat on the blue couch with the girls that were drinking. Briefly she says. She says Gavin was the only rude passenger on flight. She says the aircraft is small inside compact and everybody on board could see Mj. She says he wasn't drunk, just more calm. She says she served Janet a glass of white wine. She met with Mr. Robel yesterday. She met with Sgt. Alvarez and Mr. Auchincloss before the grand jury.

March 30

Re-Direct (2)

She says the girls weren't specific about what they shopped for in Ny. No movies were shown on this flight.

40th Witness Stan Katz
Licensed Psychologist. 60-70% seeing patients. He consults on a TV Show called "Starting Over" and he's on camera sometimes. Been Psychologist since 1978. 1 of his specialties is with abused children. He has testified as an expert witness. He deals with all aspects of abuse of children. He has worked with Larry Feldman twice besides this one. He was to interview the 3 children about allegations of molestation, being on a TV Show. May 15, 16 and June 11 2003 Janet Arvizo. May 29 June 11 2003 Starr and Gavin. May 29 2003 Davellin Arvizo. He went

June 12 2003 to give a report to Social workers. He was contacted June 13 2003 by the Sheriff's office.

<u>Cross Examination</u>

He doesn't think Mr. Feldman ever referred any patient to him. He knows Feldman's current Firm is with K Sholer, Leonora Housner therapist. He thinks one of her kids is married to one of Feldman's kids. He's known that for about 2 years.

March 30

He billed $4,800.00 to Mr. Feldman's office for interviews of Arvizo's. He was retained on the Jordan Chandler lawsuit against Mj in 1992 with Larry Feldman. He says he has no personal relationship with Larry Feldman. He had 1 meeting with Larry Feldman June 5, 2003. Then he had phone conversation June 11, 2003 with Feldman on phone. Phone conversation with Det Paul Zellis 6-13-04. Mr. Zonen gave him a copy of transcript of phone conversation with Det Zellis. He says he thought Feldman was going to file a lawsuit against Mj. Feldman called him yesterday about this case. Before that it was a couple of weeks ago at Feldman's office for ½ hour. He's talked to him 2 or 3 times on phone about this case since 6-5-03. He's testified in less than 6 criminal cases all in LA. He's written 3 or 4 articles on child abuse. He says 40% of child molestation allegations are false. He did not investigate anything about Arvizo's before he interviewed them. He says he was talking about children under 5 years of age about how children can be influenced by their parents. He says it's possible to complicate evaluation of molestation of child if the family has physical

March 30

or mental abuse in it already. Over 10 years on dependency court panel. He was an advisor on TV movies about child abuse and so on. He never interviewed the Arvizo father. May 15,16 Jun 11 – Interviews Mother. May 29, June 11 Gavin and Starr. May 29 Davellin. Meeting on 6-12-03 at family welfare with Larry Feldman. Bill Dickerman was at meeting with him and Feldman on 6-5-03. First time he ever met Mr. Dickerman. He thinks it was a month or 2 before he interviewed the Arvizo's is when the Arvizo's met Larry Feldman. He says he thinks the first notification to Authorities wasn't till after DCFS Report. No criminal case was ever filed in 1993 case.

<u>Re-Direct</u>

<u>**He says there are very few false allegations against someone outside the family on someone over 5 years old. He says children can't maintain consistent allegations.**</u>

<u>Re-Cross</u>
<u>**He says children who make false allegations**</u>

sound scripted, they exaggerate. **He says children who can't remember or get mixed up is a true sign of abuse.**

March 30

He says adolescent teenagers don't often make up false allegations according to research he has read.

41st Witness William Dickerman

Attorney since 1977. Civil litigation/trial lawyer. Met Janet Arvizo Feb 21, 2003. Introduced by Jamie Masada 3 or 4 meetings with Mrs. Arvizo where Jamie Masada was present. One was Feb 25th at Laugh Factory. He wrote letters to Mark Geragos, various media outlets. Wrote a letter on March 26th to Mark Geragos to stop Mj people from harassment. He later asked for passports, Birth certificates etc. Clothing of Gavin's. #625 Letters to Mr. Geragos and 1 from him. #630 Letters from him to attorneys and various media outlets regarding Bashir video. He was not successful in getting Arvizo's things returned to them. Mr. Geragos told him that there were 2 vaults of stuff. The day the things were delivered he was off for a religious holiday and nothing was accepted. Mr. Geragos never acknowledged that the passports and other things ever existed. He did not file a lawsuit. He referred it to Larry Feldman because he thought he's

March 30

the go to guy regarding Mj. He has a fee sharing agreement with Mr. Feldman in case of any further lawsuit.

Cross-Examination

His fee sharing agreement is not restricted to a referral fee. He and Feldman would get parts of the money. He represented Jamie Masada for 12 years before he met Arvizo's. He represented him in 5 civil lawsuits. He represented the Arvizo's and Masada at the same time. Mar 27 letter to Disney. He never witnessed any harassment of Arvizo's by Mj or his people. He says Jay Jackson was harassed but he was not his client. Arvizo's signed agreement with him on 3-24. He says 3-26 Mj was illegally eavesdropping on there phone conversations. **No mention of molestation to Geragos on 3-26 Letter. No mention of alcohol. No mention of false imprisonment or kidnapping or extortion. He never called police about any of this.** He said he wanted the keys to all places there stuff had been stored. He wanted all tapes and films of Arvizo's. He wanted all releases signed by Arvizo's regarding Bashir Video. **3 years from fraud reported is the limitation.** He threatens Mj, Mr. Geragos with a civil restraining order.

March 30

He never seeked that restraining order. He wrote to

Disney 3-27 to see if Arvizo's gave consent to anyone involved in Bashir Video. 3-31-03 From his memo, Mr. Geragos told him he thought there were passports and Janet Arvizo had told him his harassment had stopped. He says Mr. Geragos turned hostile and was unresponsive and adversarial. 4-3-03 communicated with Grenada TV Limited Company. He says any footage they did not give their consent. He wanted things returned **to him. He never called the police on behalf of Arvizo's.** Fee arrangement with Feldman in May 2003. Contacted Sheriff about this case in June or October 2003. He can't remember. 4-11-03 Letter to ABC Mr. Zucker. 4-11-03 Letter to Mr. Geragos no footage of Arvizo's be used by anybody associated with Mj because there's no consent. 4-15-03 Letter from Geragos where to deliver items in storage. 4-16-03 Grenada media letter complaints about use of Arvizo footage. Wrote to Globe newspaper, couldn't find a letter about improper photos of Janet Arvizo. Feldman to plaintiff, civil litigator in California.

March 30

Subpoenaed notes about JC Penney Case. He says he knows nothing about the case. Last letter to Geragos 5-29-03. Letters to Mj lawyer LeGrand continued through July 2003 regarding Arvizo's. He never heard of Mj people paying Arvizo rent while he was representing them. He talked to Feldman yesterday.

Re-Direct

Letter to Michael Kajani. Person at Globe. Never asked for money, just wanted Arvizo's, them, out of that newspaper.

42nd Witness Lt. Klepakis

Investigator fills out a form for a forensic examination. Examination of biological fluids are sent out, not latent fingerprinting that can be done at the Sheriff's. 2 months to go over material from Neverland by Det Bonner. They, Sheriffs, bought adult magazines to practice on. To see what to do that would be best. Got adult materials sent in Feb to DOJ got back in August. 100 plus magazines. Check every page. Got magazines out of the grand jury in Oct 2004. Had to use some forensic people. In July homicide, in Sep Officer Shooting, in Oct homicide.
March 30

He didn't send to Quantico, VA FBI because he wanted to keep control of evidence.

Cross-Examination

90% of searchers were sheriffs. He says they did not alert the media before search. There was a press conference planned before search. He does not know if a press release was prepared before search. The searchers were instructed on how to handle the media. He saw a car on the side of the road on the way into Neverland. Doesn't know if it was the media. Nothing covers their shoes 15 to 25 people in the main house search. He says it was 45 people, sheriffs were in and out of the main house. 1st day search 8:00 am – 11:30 pm. 2nd Search Dec 4 9:00 am – Afternoon sometime. He was in charge of both searches. The people who entered the residence were logged in and logged out. Never asked for Mj DNA till Dec 2004. Asked the FBI with help on computers and backgrounds of people involved in this case. April 1st – George Levine DOJ Latent Fingerprint Analysis. Didn't ask for forensic test on any bottle thought to contain alcoholic beverages from any part of house

April 1st

Fingerprints on bottles and glasses can last many years. He was moving around the estate the entire time. **The fingerprint analysis was only requested on the magazines. They requested no fingerprints on anything else. They never found any DNA, hair or fibers or prints of any Arvizo in anything in Mj bedroom or house.**

Re-Direct

Search had to be done in 1 day on 11-18-03. He says he told the searchers not to talk to the press. He says the wine cellar was locked and (Mj) his bedroom was locked and 1 closet door next to the safe was locked. He says they had certain information and that's what they focused on in search.

Re-Cross

Started investigation Feb 2003. Contacted by Feldman June 2003. Timeline does not include Feb Start.

43rd Witness Jack Green

President Affordable Telephone Systems in Ventura. 20 years. He was trained by AT&T corporate trainers for 10 years. 12-3-04 he worked at Neverland to inspect the phone system and see how it operated. Merlin 2 phone system at Neverland.

April 1st

24 Lines on property. 8 Lines connected to the Merlin system. 15 Lines connected to other things. 1 Line Private not hooked to the system. He had access to everything (all the phones) on the ranch. There were 2 phones on the ranch that you could pick a line or listen in to a phone conversation. The other phones on property were different. The 2 phones, 1 in Mj's bedroom, 1 in the administrative office. The other phones you had to have a code to call out. You could secretly listen in on phone conversations from the phone in Mj bedroom. He says you could hook a recording device to this phone.

Cross-Examination

Standard Business phone system. From the late 80s. Phone systems have progressed quite a bit. He says that system is not unusual at all on a working ranch especially in the 80s. He says it is possible to connect a recording device to any phone. The phones at the ranch were in every room. The main phone for this system was in the administration building. A code to call out is very common to this phone system.

April 1st

No restriction to calling 911 on this system. He just made sure there was a dial tone on the other 15 lines. These other 15 were not in the Merlin System.

Re-Direct

The 15 lines could be for computer alarm systems etc … Private line in the downstairs bathroom area of the Merlin System was taken out of production in the early 90s. He says typically the calls come into the console and then sent out. You can't tell on this system, no audio if someone listens in. He says on a home system there could be a little noise. You couldn't listen in from the other lines around the ranch. The lines had to ring at the console in the administration office. That system was the most widely sold system in the world.

44th Witness Larry Feldman

Attorney since 1969. Kay Scholer in Century City currently. 600 lawyers in the firm. Since Jan 2004 He has represented the Oakland Raiders, Stars etc.. He represented Johnnie Cochran Jr for 10 years. He teaches to Judges, Lawyers and students. Jordan Chandler was 13 years old in 1993. He was represented by Gloria Allred then they

April 1st

wanted to switch lawyers. He alleged 7 causes of action. The sexual molestation of Jordan Chandler. In the Mj case he got a confession of judgement. He had never handled a sexual molestation case before Mj or since. He didn't, Jordan Chandler, appear before Santa Barbara grand jury. Minors right not to testify in molestation case in 1993. He had a person to person meeting with Dickerman in 2003. Dickerman was at a meeting with Feldman and Arvizo's. If Martin Bashir or ABC had consent to put children on television. He decided to let experts spend time with Janet, Starr, Gavin. That was Dr. Katz. In May or June 2003. Got a report in person from Dr. Katz at his office. After this they, Arvizo's, went and saw Dr. Katz after Feldman had called in Arvizo's to his office. The Arvizo's wanted too. HE contacted David Saunders of the LA Family Services. After the 2nd conversation with Katz, he went down to family services with Dr. Katz and one of his colleagues. They didn't take Family Services reports or guide them anywhere. After that he called DA Sneddon.

April 1st

There would be no lawsuit; he (Feldman) was told by Sneddon and that the police would make a decision. He terminated his relationship in Oct 2003 with Arvizo's. He has done a little legal work for Arvizo's in 2004. Janet or Davellin cannot file lawsuits against the County of LA. The minors still can. He's never been asked by anybody to file a lawsuit against Mj in this case.

Cross-Examination

Gavin has till his 20th birthday, Starr also filed a lawsuit for sexual molestation. They would win a civil suit if Mj were convicted in this case. Civil Statute of Limitation 3 years. There was a cross allegation by Mj in the Chandler case of extortion. Confession of judgement does not mean you admit guilt. They had a settlement judgement in 1993 that both sides admit no wrongdoing to each other. His law firm is doing work for Arvizo's in this case. He filed notice of claim for Arvizo's with La County just in case they sue. So they, Arvizo boys, can file against LA County and Mj separately. Dickerman wanted to be involved if Feldman brought the case.

April 1st

He says he's sure that Dickerman wanted money. Both parents in Chandler's case signed his fee agreement. The parents accepted money in the Jordan Chandler case. But he says that was the defense's idea. The mother's new husband David Schwartz also filed a suit in that case. He was referred by criminal defense lawyers Bob Shapiro and Richard Hearst who represented somebody. Barry Rothman represented the father and they both were accused of extortion by Mj camp. Met Stanley Katz 1987. They defended two adults about false claims of abuse by the government. He was called by Lt Klepakis in June 2003. He talked to Mr. Sneddon yesterday for 2 hrs. He was sent his grand jury transcript and he reviewed it 2 weeks ago. He talked to Dr.Katz before and after he testified. He talked to Dickerman before he testified. Dr. Katz told him he was secretly recorded by the Sheriff's office. He has given Jay Jackson advice as a lawyer after they got married. He has represented Janet's parents in this case. When there bank records were subpoenaed

April 1st

From Dec 2004 to Jan 2005 he represented her parents. He says his representation ended after that. He says he's had a total of maybe 10 total conversations in person and on phone. He's met with Mr. Zonen a couple of times. He had a few phone conversations with him. He was interviewed on Today Show by Matt Lauer 1-16-04. He said he had no comment in that interview if he was going to join prosecution. He wrote a letter to Judge Nash to keep Gavin's child welfare records confidential. He objected to any media or lawyers getting those records. He did not let Jamie Masada into the meeting because of losing the lawyer/client privilege. May 2004 stopped NBC from obtaining West Covina police records of Janet Arvizo. He says he never had a meeting with Michael Viner and Larry King at the grill where he said Janet's and the Arvizo allegations are false.

Re-Direct

The baby case in dependency court was physical abuse. He says Jordan Chandler never appeared before the grand jury. He met with the producer of the Larry King Show.

April 1st

Her name was Nancy Baker. **The parents got the money in the Chandler case so the parents would be bound by agreement to be quiet because Mj and his people didn't want anything out. He says he would never want to do a criminal trial then a civil trial.**

Re-Cross

-

Re-Direct (2)

Punitive damages are to punish somebody on top of compensatory damages.

Re-Cross (2)

He says it's good if the defendant is a convicted felon to get punitive damages.

45th Witness Jesus Salas

He stopped working at Neverland June 2003. He worked there 20 years even before Mj bought it. He had 15 people working under him. Middle of 2002 house manager for Mj. He had 8 people working under him. He reported directly to Mj, sometimes the ranch manager. He had an office in the house. Daily contact with Mj when Mj was there. He says Mj expected the best service. His hours are 7:00 am to 3:00 am sometimes. Nobody was fired while he was house manager. Not allowed to talk about

April 1st

what happens at Neverland. The bedroom shutters were closed most of the time, his room was dark. He says Frank Tyson, he thinks, was 18 years old when he met him. He says in 1990 he was Mj right hand man he thinks. Mj spent time with Frank in 2003 on occasion at a ranch in different rooms. He says at 1 point Mj and Frank were close friends but not in 2003. Frank was staying in the Video Library in Jan, Feb, March 2003. His office was in the Video Library. Vinnie was living in the same area, he says. He was a friend of Frank's. The Video Library is outside the main house but is still connected to the main house. He says MJ's control over the house was pretty high. He says he was told by Mj whatever the guests needed to give it to them. When Mj was there everything was kept open all night long. He says the combo to Mj bedroom changed 2 times when he was house manager. He says the main house combo changed every 2 months. All guests of the house had a main house combo. Mj was not happy about Frank bringing guests to Neverland without his permission.

His (Mj) frustration with Frank was after the Arvizo's had left in 2003. He met Dieter early 2002 at Neverland. He says Dieter stayed for 2 weeks and Mj was there. He met Ronald at same time, he came with Dieter. He says Ronald and Dieter tried to have a meeting with Mj once a day. He says their relationship with Mj was mostly business. He says Ronald and Dieter were there for 2 weeks when Arvizo's were there. He says Frank was always there. "Mr. Malnik" was there. "Zia" is a lawyer he met at the ranch. He saw him there at Neverland a couple of times and he was there when the Arvizo's were there. He picked the Arvizo's and Mj up at Santa Barbara airport. He says the Arvizo's stayed a week or 2. Then they left for 2 weeks, came back for about 3 weeks left and then came back and stayed a week. He says Mj was there pretty much all the time the Arvizo's were there. He says the Arvizo boys most of the time tried to sleep in Mj room. He says Mj would play with the kids on a daily basis. He says he would see kids in the house and eating with Mj.

April 4th

He says most of the children were mostly boys and 10-11 years of age. He says Mj drank wine and vodka. He says he never saw Mj drinking but saw the effects of him drinking on a regular basis. He says he saw Mj drunk in front of his children quite a few times when he was house manager. He says Mj didn't try and hide the fact he was drunk from his children. He says there was whiskey and tequila in wine cellar while Arvizo's were there. He says he did see kids go in wine cellar but not the Arvizo's. He has served Mj alcohol in front of children a couple of times. **He says the 1st time was Jan 2003 about 9pm to Mj Bedroom. He brought glasses and white wine. He brought 4 glasses. He also said he ordered soda drinks also.** He says the Arvizo boys were there. The 2nd time was 11pm, Mj ordered wine and 1 glass not sure what kids were there. He never mentioned soda to sheriffs. When he came back the 1st time the bottle of wine was empty. The complaints about wine cellar were from Los Olivos kids. He saw those boys coming out of wine cellar early in the morning.

April 4th
October 2002 **He says Mj was with the boys. He**

says the boys were drunk. He says they weren't acting normal. He says the 2nd time was 2 or 3 weeks after the 1st time inside the house Mj was there. He says the boys arrived at 12:00 noon and left at 1:00 am. He doesn't know where they got their alcohol. He says he doesn't recall any other time Mj was in wine cellar with boys. He has seen adult magazines in Mj 1st floor bathroom. He says the magazines were there when Arvizo's where there.

#777 Picture of statues from Mj office
#778 Picture of items from Office
#779 Same thing

He says the statues were there for a long time. **They are little statues of half-naked women in leather.** He says the Arvizo's were not allowed to leave Neverland. He was told that by Janet. He says Janet was crying when she asked him to take them to LA, it was nighttime. He says there was a safe put in the maids room to keep the keys of the wine cellar and other things when the Los Olivos boys were found to be drinking.

April 4th

He says it was his choice to take the Arvizo's in the Rolls Royce. He told Mj's bodyguard, Chris Carter, he was taken the Arvizo's off Neverland. He says Dieter, Frank were there at that time. He says Janet was concerned about Dieter and Ronald. He got into trouble for taking Arvizo's off

Neverland. Frank told him he was in trouble. He says Frank told him not to do it again. Dieter told him the same thing. When the Arvizo's came back to ranch she asked him a week later to take them off the property again.

Cross Examination

Spoke to investigators for defense Jan 9, 2005 at Holiday Inn in Santa Maria for 30 minutes. He says that the Arvizo boys slept downstairs in the room. He says he never saw Gavin drinking. He says Janet was getting first class service. He says the unit Janet stayed in was the nicest room of them all. He says that Mj was never in charge of watching kids from the tours. He says nobody kept her forcibly at Neverland. He says she didn't claim she was mistreated or abused at Neverland. She just

April 4th

Complained about media attention and Dieter. He says she never complained about Mj. He arranged a limousine the last time Arvizo's left. He says it was his idea and ranch manager to get safe and put keys in. Before that they were hung in the open. He says he saw a lot of Frank's family visit the ranch. He says he saw Frank and Marie Nicole in Mj bedroom. He says sometimes people were allowed in Mj bedroom when he wasn't there if he gave the Ok. He says he was able to buy as many toys as he needed to. He says that kids were caught a lot doing things they weren't supposed to do. He says you can go into the main house 24 hrs a day and get whatever you want. The wine cellar was already there when Mj bought property. She complained Dieter and Ronald were separating her from Mj. He's met with DA and Sheriffs a couple of times. They never asked if he brought non-alcoholic beverages for Arvizo's. Frank has brought a lot of girls on property without Mj knowing. He says he, Mj, would bring kids and adults into his recording studio.

April 4th

He says he knew in advance if he (Mj) was leaving the property. He says when Mj there sometimes you hardly see him. He says Mj does not want weapons on his property. He says that Mj was sometimes gone when Arvizo's were there in 2003. He says the adults will run to Mj and want to touch him just like the kids. He never saw Mj drinking. He knew Mj had a prescription drug problem. He knew Mj was being treated for all kinds of problems in 2002. He says Mj took prescription drugs in 2003. He says Mj stored things in other areas of the wine cellar. He says Mj policy was no kids in wine cellar. He says pretty much nobody watched the Los Olivos kids, maybe security sometimes. He says those kids came on a regular basis. He says they were 15 to 16 years old. Nobody ever called their parents nor were they asked to leave. He says the Arvizo kids roamed freely at Neverland. He says the mother never watched them, nor was she ever with them except at dinner table in main house. He called limousine service 3 times he thinks for the Arvizo's.

April 4th

He thinks Janet left 1 time to get a body wax at the salon she was taken by a maid.

Re-Direct

Those beds in the theater can be used by anybody not just handicapped. He says Frank was at the table when he thought Gavin was drinking, also Vinnie and a couple of Frank's guests. At 9pm Mj was on property but not at the table. He says it was pretty much all boys that slept in Mj room. He said ranch employees had to go through Frank with problems with the Arvizo's. Then he reported to Mj. His daughter has visited Neverland in the early 90s. He says Janet spent most of her time in her room. When Mj bought the ranch the security carried guns. He says Mj had alcohol on a regular basis in 2003.

Re-Cross

He says Mj would give people tours of his home. Janet never asked him to call the police.

46th Witness Jason Francia

24 Years old. Auto Parts Salesman. Mentoring

Program through Church for 6 months but for 6 years. He's lived here pretty much since 1988.

April 4th

His mother was a maid for Mj. He met Mj when he was 6 or 7. He went to Mj house in Encino 6-7 times. Mj's parents lived there and (Mj, Janet, his sister) he thinks. He says the condo had very little furniture. He spent the night here with his mother. He says when he moved here with his mother he was MJ's personal maid. He says he went to Neverland 4-5 times. He was in Mj's bedroom twice, he thinks. He says he was eleven when his mother quit. 1st he felt uncomfortable at the hideout condo. He was 7, he was sitting on Mj lap watching TV, Mj was tickling him and he was tickling Mj and then Mj moved to his crotch area. He said it went on 3-10 minutes. He says he was wearing shorts he thinks. 2nd time he was **8 ½** watching cartoons on a sleeping bag, Mj was behind him tickling him (midday he thinks) in his genital area on top of clothes, he was in shorts he thinks, he says his hand was there maybe 5 minutes. He says Mj gave him money at every tickle thing he says. And it was $100.

April 4

dollar bill and he says it was a don't tell your mom about money. 3rd time 10 ½ at Neverland. In an arcade in the loft area, at night time he says he was playing a video game Mj started to tickle him, they ended up on the couch laying down, Mj behind him tickling him this time. He says he touched his testicles under his clothes this time for 2 or 3 minutes. He says he first told 2 detectives in 1993. They wanted to talk to him. Interview at the Sheriff's Department 1-1 ½ hour was recorded. He told them these stories. His lawyers were Terry Cannon and Chris Coleman. He had them after this interview. He did get a settlement from Mj but he says he never asked for any money.

Cross Examination

His mother went on the Hard Copy TV Show. She took $20,000 dollars. He learned of her going on TV after he saw it. **He's very non responsive.** He told 2 lawyers he was molested. He says he was 7 ½ the first incident with Mj. He first said he didn't tell his mother now he says he told her in counseling.

April 4th

He doesn't know if his mother went on Hard copy in 1993. **He says he never told anybody about molestations before sheriffs came to see him?** Vince Neglia and Russel Burchum were the Sheriffs at an interview in 1993, the 1st time he was ever interviewed by police about Mj. He says he doesn't remember anything about Encino. **Early in his interviews he denied being touched in his genital area he says he was scared. In a 1993 interview he says they just tickled each other and**

then he left. (Drinking A lot of Water) **He says Mj never kissed him. Now he says Mj put the money down his pants and not just gave it to him.** He has received money from the settlement. **He says in the beginning of the 1993 interview he was lying.** He says it was a year from the 1st time to 2nd time and 2 years from 2nd to 3rd. He says 1st incident 87-88? The first 2 events he says he doesn't know where mother is in this big 1 room condo? He says on tape nothing happened at the ranch because there were too many people around.

April 4th

He told the police officers they were pushy.

April 5th

Mj used to tell him he would give him money if he got A's in school and read books. He said in a 2nd tape interview in 1994 that they kept pushing him and he wanted to hit them in the head. **October 2004 Interview with Mr. Zonen, Terry Cannon, his former lawyer was there. He says he isn't represented by him anymore. Now he says he may have asked Terry Coleman to be there.** He says he doesn't know if Mj was ever charged with a crime. He doesn't remember saying he and Mj had a tickling contest before each alleged incident. 11-19-04 Auchincloss and Zonen and his mother. It says in a report that they requested it not be tape recorded the same request he made in Dec

Interview. 10-18-04 1st Interview, not December, he told prosecutors that Mj tickled his testicles for about 10 seconds. Terry Cannon was at both interviews. Now he says he learned last Sunday that his mother was paid $20,000 for a Hard Copy Interview.

April 5

Sheriff says on tape **that he's (Mj) a molester.** He says he's a great guy and he makes great music and he (Sheriff) says (Bullshit). The sheriff complained about how much money Mj has. He never slept in Mj's bed with him. He talked to Attorney Terry Cannon yesterday, the attorney called him. **He says he usually cries when he talks about alleged molestations?** He says sleeping bag near the window on the right side of the TV. He doesn't remember telling Mj he got A's in school and read a book to get money. He received settlement money from Mj when he turned 18 and his mother got money before that. **He says he spoke to a media guy in 92 or 93 who had a British Accent but didn't say anything about Mj.** He says he doesn't remember saying he was aware of another boy suing Mj for money in 1993. He says he was 16 when he learned of anybody suing Mj for money because that's when money was an issue for him.

Re-Direct

He says he was teased more at Church than at

school.

47th Witness Kris Kallman

Attorney Civil Trial Lawyer 29 years. He lives in Santa Barbara.

April 5th

Known Terry Cannon 20 yrs. He associated with him in certain cases. He is again associated with him again. He and Mr. Cannon prepared a complaint beginning a lawsuit against Mj. Late 94 early 95 contact with Cochran and other lawyers. Mid 95 contact with (Mj) his new lawyers. He signed a confidentiality agreement when he turned 18. If interviewed he had to notify the defense team within 5 days. Case settled in 95 or 96.

Cross Examine

They had 2 different settlement agreements 1 for mother, 1 for son. April 96 - mothers. June 98 - for Jason. The time difference he says is because the mother was an adult and Jason didn't turn 18 till June 98. Terry Cannon did not work with him in Oct, Nov, Dec 1994.

48th Witness Blanca Francia

Caregiver for elderly 15 years. Came to the US in

1975 from El Salvador. She was 21 years old. She began with Mj in 1986 in Encino. Janet, Latoya and his parents lived in that house. After a year he (Mj) got another condo. She says she had 3 rooms. She cleaned that condo for a year. No bed at condo.

April 5th

They Mj people paid her to move to Santa Maria. She worked at Neverland. She cleaned his bedroom and took care of all of his clothes and personal stuff. She says Mj asked her to bring Jason with her to Encino house. She continued cleaning the condo after Mj moved to Neverland. She used a key to access Mj Bedroom. He slept downstairs in his bedroom and she said he had a bed upstairs also. Wade Robson was 7 or 8 when she met him. She says Wade was there with his mother and sister. Wade stayed in Mj room. She also washed Wade Robson's clothes. She says Wade first came in 1989. She says Wade would stay at least a week each time he came. She says she usually only made 1 bed when Wade was there. She says only Wade stayed in Mj room at that time. No other kids that visited stayed in Mj room. Big Jacuzzi in the lady's bathroom. **She says she saw Mj and Wade in the shower together.** She says the shower had a glass door. She says it was steamy, she just saw figures that she said was Mj and Wade Robeson. She left the room without saying anything.

April 5th

She says the 1st time she was concerned about Mj

and her son was in 1986 he was 7 or 8. She says she saw things before that with other things. She says she didn't go look for her son when Mj took him upstairs when she told her son to stay downstairs. She says Mj slept on or in a sleeping bag at Condo. She says she saw Mj and Jason in a sleeping bag one time. She tried to get him up to go and eat, not necessarily to get away from Mj. The TV was on 1 or 2 in the afternoon, and the room was dark. Jason was born 5-30-80. Mj gave Jason 2, $100 dollar bills at the condo she says. She first saw money at the bus stop. Jason said it was a secret and Mj said it was for him. **She said it was in his pocket.** She saw Macaulay Culkin at Neverland. She says he was 8 or 9. He was after Wade Robson. He stayed with Mj. He brought his family and parents. She saw Macaulay Culkin in Mj bedroom. She says he didn't always come with his family. She says 2 times he came alone. She says Jason is 1 or 2 years older than Macaulay Culkin. She says the family would stay in Mj room also.

April 5
She says she left Neverland in May of 91 on her own. Law Enforcement contacted her 2 ½ years after she left. **Larry Feldman** subpoenaed her to give deposition. Johnnie Cochran was there and she says Howard Weitzman, deposition went 2 days. 94 or 95 after she had an interview with Law Enforcement. She had no lawyer, she says at the time. **She says in deposition Wade wasn't in shower because she was tired.** Then she says he

was. Diane Dimond from Hard Copy. She went with her friend Evangeline who also worked at Neverland. Her friend was the one that arranged the interview and payment. She didn't think she was going to talk about Mj. She gave her friend money, not Hard copy. He, Mj, called her son, Wade and Macaulay "Rubba". She says she received a lot of gifts from Mj. She took a cheap watch from Mj's room, she says. He was 12 when he gave his deposition.

#781 Picture of her son Jason at about 10
#782 Photo of Jason and his mother date 3-1994, he was 13

Cross Examine
She began in 1986, left in 1991.

April 5th

Sept 87 Jan 89 Mj on tour. Japan, Australia, other numerous cities, Italy, Austria, England. She says she stopped cleaning Encino house in 1987. She still cleaned his bedroom at that house though. **She doesn't remember if Mj gave her money totaling $5,000 all together.** She says Mj was always generous with her money. Dec 1993, Jan 1994 Days of Deposition. She says she never saw him touch anyone, or in a sexual way. Only Mj used jacuzzi on Hayvenhurst in Encino. Jacuzzi in the bathroom in his bedroom. She never saw who used the bed upstairs or downstairs; she just saw them messed up. Sometimes just 1 bed was messed up. She met with prosecutors on Saturday for a couple of hours. She met with Larry Feldman before her deposition. She met with him again and doesn't remember if he gave her advice. She hired Terry Cannon when her son was subpoenaed. She says she never saw Mj molest anybody. In her deposition she said the people from Hard Copy are dishonest.

April 5th

She didn't tell Larry Feldman about the Hard Copy interview. She says she doesn't remember her co-workers' names. Her Hard Copy was a month before her deposition. She doesn't remember if she told Evangeline she would talk to the Enquirer. Just 1 meeting with Diane Dimond she says for 3 hours. She signed a contract with Hard Copy. She remembers Ms. Dimond wanted pictures of Mj, that was part of a contract she signed. She also gave Ms. Dimond a picture of her son and Mj. She said she didn't think anyone would recognize her son from the Hard Copy show. Ms. Dimond stopped returning her calls. She thinks it was twice Mr. Robson was in Mj bed. She couldn't tell if Mj and Wade Robson were touching each other or not. She says she's never seen her Hard Copy interview, just little previews of it. She used to see Mj with kids in the dance room at Neverland. She says she asked 1 time what was going on and he (Jason) said he didn't want to talk about it. She met with Sneddon in 93.

Juror Notebook 3

Chapter 3

April 5th

Jan 11, 1994 Deposition. She was asked to bring the contract from Hard Copy but she had gotten rid of it. She had 3 meetings with attorney Larry Feldman. She doesn't remember if she went on Hard Copy after her son spoke to the police. She says she didn't know her son was going to talk to the police. Norma Staykos that's a secretary for Mj that she reported to. 2 times she had her wages garnished and she phony 55 numbers. Gail Goforth head housekeeper worked with her for year to year and a half. She went into her purse to see how much money she made.

48th Witness Blanca Francia

Mj gave her an oak coffee table. She says she didn't try to sell it; she still has it in the garage. She told Gail she quit. No notice she just left. She got in trouble for being late and time card errors. He often used nicknames for kids. **She says she heard only Michael laughing in the shower in her deposition. She also said she only saw Mj silhouette. Now she says she heard 2 people laughing. She has seen Mj playing with kids not tickling them.** She says children usually stayed in the main house. She does not know Frank Tyson.

April 5th

Re-Direct

She says no kids stayed there at Neverland when Mj wasn't there. Now she says she saw Mj in shower , not just a shadow. She says she wants to say yes there were 2 people in shower, but she can't. She just heard 2 voices laughing. (She says she told Diane Dimond about the bathtub and jacuzzi and showed she cleaned up the toys and stuff afterward.) She says on 1 occasion MJ and Wade had no shirts under the blankets on Mj's bed.

#783 – Picture of Bed downstairs
#784 – Picture of bedroom downstairs
#785 – Same
#786 – Picture of bathroom
#787 – Picture of shower
#788 – Same
#789 – Picture of room upstairs

Re-Cross

People often hung out on Mj bed during all hours of the day.

49th Witness Ralph Chacon

Worked at Neverland 1991-1994 Security. Used to repo vehicles. Worked graveyard 10-6 in the morning. Subpoenaed in May '94 for Grand Jury.

April 7th

Kasim Abdul heard of security he carpooled with him. 1st meeting with Mj attorneys outside Mj office

2nd at Mr. Sangers office. Contracted Mr. Burchem Sheriff's Office. Interviewed in Santa Barbara with Mr. Sneddon and Mr. Burchem. Late 92 early 93 in late evening he was with Jordan Chandler. He couldn't see them but could hear them laughing and playing in the water Mj yelled for security. Mj and Jordan went to the restroom outside the rec room, he approached after 30 minutes. He heard Mj and Jordan in the shower there's only 1 shower he says.

He left and then went back to the same area he looked in the window and saw Mj and Jordan standing nude facing each other. He says Mj was caressing him, kissing him and Mj put Jordan's penis in his mouth he saw this and then he left. He saw them come out of the restroom 30 min after this. Jordan was riding on Mj back with towels headed to the main house. Mj double locked the back door which he says Mj never did.

#790 Picture of pool area
#791 Picture of bathroom area
#792 Picture of BBQ area
#793 Picture of Jordan Chandler
#794 Picture of Jordan Chandler
#795 Picture of Jordan Chandler

April 7th

Brett Barnes another child friend of Mj at rancho many times. He says Jordan and Brett looked the same to him. That's the same story he told the grand jury in 94. They made a report about French doors being open. 2nd Incident with Jordan

10:00pm He was in the BBQ area he saw Brett, Jordan, and another little girl in the rec room. HE saw Mj come out his back door, went to the rec room inside through the back door, he went to Jordan, kissed him and then they took off in Mj golf cart. **Came back went into the breezeway, they were standing, Mj kissed him and then put his hands on Jordan's crotch and then they ran inside the house.** (Mj's mother and father are not in court today. His brother was here but left during this testimony.)

#796 – Picture of behind house office and breezeway.

He never told anybody what he saw ever until his testimony to the grand jury. Guards were armed when they knew Mj under investigation, they were not regular guards. He was pressured to quit by those guards. They filed a lawsuit against MJ the guards did.

April 7th

Cross – Examination

Lawsuit went on for 6 months. **Jury found they were not wrongfully terminated and that he had stolen from Mj. $1,473,116 dollars levied against him and his co-workers owed Mj that money. He filed bankruptcy. Judgement of fraud and malice against Mj.** After he left Mj he said he filed for unemployment not disability. He says in deposition he knew his lawyer asked for $16 million he said that wasn't enough. He said he never had deposition before in deposition he says he had. **Mj's mother**

and brother back in court. Kasim Abdul was part of the lawsuit. Adrian McManus is also part of the lawsuit. **His wages at the time were being garnished for child support.** He doesn't recall if he asked Sheriff Burchum for money. Judgement of $2,600.00 against him by Judy Bird he doesn't recall? He told Kasim about alleged molestations right before they testified to the grand jury. He says he probably asked for money so his wife could relocate. Kasim, Adrian and him went to the tabloid The Star. After they met with their lawyer they requested money from The Star.

April 7th

They did sell their story to Star. It was printed. He says he never told anyone at the ranch that Mj was innocent of molestation. Sandy Dones secretary at Neverland. Book author named Gutierrez went to her before going to the Star. He last worked at Neverland in mid-1994. He didn't like OSS security guards and said they should interfere with his job. Accused of stealing candy bars. Linda Allen his landlady in Lompoc. Gary Morgan represented Tabloid. They were all interviewed by Splash Tabloid. The money $17,000.00 went to the lawyer. They were taking money from tabloids to fund a lawsuit against Mj. He says he told nobody Mj was innocent of everything. **He told Mr. Sneddon new facts about the story from 94.** He says he was the first to go to tabloids about Mj in 94. **He says in the deposition part of his damage claim was for Mj staring at him.** He was upset that the new hires got $12 per hour and he was only getting $9 per hour.

They together approached Mr. Ring to get money from Mj. When he left Neverland he just stopped showing up and that was after he met with Mr. Ring.

April 7th

He hadn't heard about security selling stories to tabloids for $100,000 from Encino house. He says they were listening to his phone calls and he was upset. He was upset the OSS looked at his personnel file at work. He says on deposition Mj should compensate him **for the rest of his life.**

Re-Direct

He says he didn't want to testify to the grand jury or here but he was subpoenaed. He and Mr. Abdul was offered raises before they went to testify at a grand jury. He says he got death threats over the phone. He asked for a gun permit and carried a weapon for 2 years. He says OSS broke security beams and basically tortured the regular security guards. He was not allowed to testify about these incidents in their civil suit.

50th Witness Adrian McManus

She sells diamonds at department stores. Merchandise Assistant Cosmetics. She worked for Mj Aug 29, 90 – July 31 94. She was a maid beginning 9 months later and she cleaned his bedroom. She knew Wade Robeson 10-11 years old. Her son was 10 years old. She says he started, Wade to go to ranch in 92. She says he stayed in Mj room.

April 7th

She says Wade slept in the bed with Mj. She only discovered the bed upstairs used once. She saw Wade in Mj's house. Macaulay Culkin 90-93 at ranch would spend weeks or longer. He was 10 or 11. He stayed in Mj's room in his bed. She says that because she only had to make 1 bed. Jordan Chandler 93. Brett Barnes 11 years old 92-93. He stayed in Mj's room in his bed. Jordan stayed in Mj room in his bed. They all brought family but no fathers. She says she saw Brett and Jordan together there at the ranch at least 2 times. She says those 4 boys never stayed in the guest house, always in Mj room. Macaulay, Brett and Jordan. What she saw with Macaulay was Mj was kissing him on cheek and had his hand on his butt and leg. What she saw with Brett was Mj was walking with Brett to his room and Mj put his hand on his butt and kissed him on the cheek. What she saw with Jordan was that she was upstairs in Mj's bedroom and heard the alarm go off. She heard talking, she thought it was Mj and Jordan. She saw Mj and Jordan changing clothes, Mj kissed him on the cheek and mouth and grabbed Jordan's crotch.

April 7th

She stayed quiet upstairs. She waited till she heard chimes go off and knew they left and then she left. She quit July 31, 94. She found Mj underwear and little boy underwear in the jacuzzi water or on the floor next to the jacuzzi. She says Macaulay Culkin was very wild and destructive. She says Mj didn't discipline him. She says Jordan Chandler was rude and demanding. She says Brett Barnes was not rude and well behaved. She says Wade was wild but not as bad as McCauley. She never heard anybody tell them their behavior was inappropriate. She told lawyers about the 3 incidents. She was sick on the day of the search over Jordan Chandler. She gave deposition in that case. She lied in deposition she was threatened by Mj when she took over cleaning his bedroom. OSS were all armed, she says, they were terrible to her. She says she knew it was a Merlin phone system. She quit because she was sexually harassed and abused by BOSS that's why she quit. She was accused of stealing from Mj.

April 7th

She found a drawing in the trash. She owes Mj $1.6 million dollars from their lawsuit that they lost. Gary Morgan from Splash, Michael King determined the amount of money. Michael Ring got $32,000 or more she says. They had judgement against her and her husband for 17,000 each. They didn't lose their home, they sold it. Gary Morgan sold the drawing she found in trash, she thought Mj had drawn the picture.

#797 – A note Mj gave her
#798 – Xerox of 300 dollars Mj gave her.

Mj asked to see her copy of the transcript from the Jordan Chandler case. Mj gave her a note after he read the transcript saying thanks for everything and gave her the $300 dollars. She says the 3 $100 dollar bills had serial numbers that went in order. She says photos are Brett Barnes not Jordan

Chandler as earlier identified by Mr. Chacon. She says the wine cellar was always locked. Key was in the maid's room.

#786 – Picture of Jacuzzi in Mj room
#799 – Picture of theater.

Cross – Examination

Sued by Rosalie Hill over McManus' children.

April 7th

The judge found that they dissipated the trust for those children. $30,584.89 also awarded the plaintiffs $5,085.27 in attorney fees. Willfully and maliciously stole the money from those children. This was before Mj lawsuit. She sold sketches of Elvis by Mj to Gary Morgan. Mj waived punitive part of the lawsuit for $1 dollar. Dec 7, 1993 her deposition in Jordan Chandler Case. Last night, a 3-hr meeting with Prosecutor Zonen. Russ Burchum was present. Her deposition in her lawsuit against Mj took 8 days. She says in 93 Chandler deposition that she trusts Mj and would leave her son alone with him. She says she never saw Jordan Chandler in Mj's bedroom. She never saw Brett Barnes sleep in Mj room. She says she doesn't know when she first met Wade Robeson. She says she doesn't know how many times Bret visited the ranch or where he slept. She saw Jordan's mom bring his clothes into Mj room in a suitcase. **She says she lied in the entire Chandler deposition.** She says the beeper alarm protects Mj. She said she wasn't lying about that.

April 7th

She says she saw Jordan's mom bring his suitcase into Mj room twice and she would sit down and fold them. She says she was never there when Jordan was there at night. She says she never saw Mj in bed. She says she couldn't ever tell if Jordan Chandler ever took a shower with Mj. She never saw Jordan ready for bed or never saw him wake up in the morning. She says she never saw a chimpanzee in Mj's bedroom. She worked at Neverland during Blanca Francia time for 9 months. She can't recall if she went into Mj room before she became his personal room maid. She heard Blanca sold the story to Hard Copy. The money from the sketch funded her lawsuit against Mj.

April 8th

She says she wanted justice, not money? Why the lawsuit? Lesley Gomez manager of Macfrugals. She says she's never told her anything about Mj. Ludy Trajillo worked at Gottschalks with her. She says she didn't tell her anything either. Jamie Vail says she doesn't know her. Gail Goforth says she never told her anything. She says she didn't know about Ralph Chacon selling stories, nor did they.

April 8th

Secret meetings with Ralph or Kasim. Charlie Michaels never discussed with her about making money selling stories. Francine Orosco was a witness against her in her Mj lawsuit. She says she never discussed anything with her. She says she never took one of Mj's hats. She says she never took toys; she says it was Janelle Wall who stole toys. Sued Bill Bray, topman OSS, sued Betty Bailey, Jimmy Van Norman, Tony Colecam, JJ Johnson switched to her side in lawsuit. Sandy Doms secretary Neverland she says did not go to Hard Copy. She says she got $1,000 of the $32,000. Mr. Ring, her lawyer, collected. She did tell stories to Mr. Gutierrez, an author about Mj. She says she never saw Wade Robeson at the ranch without 1 of his parents. She says Bret Barnes mother would give his clothes to her to wash. She says she never saw the Culkin boys clothes in Mj room. She says she saw June Chandler in Mj room. She says she never saw Mj hold hands with anybody at the ranch. Was on Inside Edition during the lawsuit , she says. She was trying to sell personal information about Mj and Lisa Marie Pressley.

April 8th

She says Gary Morgan was her and Ralph Chacon a media broker. She had a contract with Star Magazine, as did Ralph Chacon. She signed with Splash News and picture agency. She gave information to Splash during their trial. She hasn't talked to Chacon for awhile. She hasn't talked to Kasim since trial. She sees Melanie Badnall every once in a while. She says she got a call from someone in London who wanted an interview, she said no, because she was under a gag order.

<u>Re-Direct</u>

She says she never gave sex secrets about Mj and Lisa Marie Pressley. She says she did see him hold hands with children. She never saw evidence that somebody slept on the floor. She says in her initial conversation with the Sheriffs she still did work at Neverland. She had seen Jordan and Mj in his bedroom. She saw Brett sleeping in MJ's bedroom. She saw them in the bed undercovers once when she brought breakfast. She never saw Jordan and Mj in Jacuzzi. She says Mj would run his fingers through her son's hair.

April 8th

51st Witness – Phillip Lemarque

Worked at Neverland for 10 months in 1991. Lived at a ranch house by the zoo while he worked there. Problem with Norma, Mj secretary. Wanted his wife to sign something about Blanca Francia looking into purses. His wife didn't believe it. 4 or 5 days after that they agreed to leave Neverland. He says Mj showed preference to little boys who were 10 or 11 years old. He went and bought toys for 10 and 11 years old, he says they were mainly toys for boys. He says it was common for Mj to stay up all night with the boys. He never saw Mj sleep with anybody but children.

#721 – Picture of Macaulay Culkin
#800 – Picture of Arcade
#801 – Picture of Arcade

He says he saw Mj and Macaulay Culkin in the arcade at 3:00 or 4:00 am Mj wanted French fries MJ codename was "Silver Fox" Mj was playing a thriller game with Macaulay Culkin he says Mj left hand was inside the "pants – shorts" from the bottom in his crotch area. He says the arcade was very noisy. He never reported it to anybody because he says no one would have believed him.

April 8th

Arnold Kessler was their lawyer. They **never sold their story.**

Cross-Examine

9-10-93 handwritten statement saying he couldn't determine what Mj was doing with his hands. Filed lawsuit against Mj for overtime and not giving references. Paul Beressi met with him several times, he was the guy who taped their conversation with their lawyer and sold it. He had a meeting with Beressi that they wanted $500,000 not $100,000. Never knew Quindoys Never knew they were selling a story he says. Lawyer was Arnold Kessler. Met with him and Beressi about selling their story. Left Neverland in 92. In 93 Beressi and Kessler were trying to sell his story, he says he didn't know about it. Last talked to Kessler 2 days ago. Last talked to Beressi a couple months ago, told him to go to hell. Never knew he was quoted in Globe Newspaper. Last talked to Norma Staikos when they left the last day. He says you couldn't be friends with anybody because everybody was spying on everybody. **Don't recall the month and year of the incident with Culkin but remember it was 3:00am.** He says Mrs. Staikos knew about it?

April 8th

He says he was not **in bankruptcy in the 90s**.

Re-Direct

They didn't litigate their OT; it was settled right away by Mj Production.

#802 – His handwritten note (copy) of what he saw in an arcade with Mj and Culkin.

Re-Cross

He added a p.s. on to his handwritten statement. **He added his left hand under his shorts all the way on his crotch.**

Re-Direct # 2

This statement was prepared for police and they asked him for more detail.

Re-Cross

He wrote this after he talked to Beressi. He made a statement a 1 year after he left Neverland.

Prosecution Rests

April 11th

Prosecution Re-Opens

52nd Witness – Bob Jones – Vice President Comm Relations

In charge of Public Relations 16 ½ years for Mj received a letter saying his services were no longer needed. Terminated in late 2004. Filed a complaint with State over his vacation pay. He is preparing a book. He has been on 3 Tours with Mj and World

Music Awards in 92. He, Mj, brought Jordan Chandler, Jane Chandler and Jordan's sister.

April 11th

He saw Mj and Jordan in Monte Carlo 4 times together. He saw physical contact 1 time on flight from Paris to L.A.. During awards Jordan sat on Mj lap. He never saw Mj lick Jordan Chandler's head. He said in his interview a week ago with prosecutors that he wasn't sure if they were head licking or not. His book is titled The Man Behind the Mask, The Rise and Fall of the King of Pop. He has looked at the manuscript of his book but has not approved it. He says his co-writer has added things that he has not approved of.

#803 – A typed page of manuscript says he didn't write the 1st paragraph but did (write the 2nd paragraph.) He says there was cooing and romantic embrace and a lick or licking of Jordan's head.
#804 – E-mail to his co-writer
#805 – E-mail to his co-writer

1st email he says the licking is important. 2nd email says the stuff with Jordan will **bite him big.**

Cross-Examination

Now he says he doesn't recall any head licking.
Co-writer never worked for Mj but knows the family. Pressure to sensationalize things in books.

April 11th

He says the paragraph he wrote is not completely true. He says the email about Chandlers is true. His office was in his home. He was not a regular visitor at Neverland. Had an office on Sunset Blvd for 10 years. He says Mj insisted the **children** sit with him, Mj, at awards. The mother sat behind them. Mj sat in the front row next to the Prince of Monaco and Linda Evans. He says all of Mj guests were invited to all events. He started writing a book after he was let go by Mj. He says he's changed millions of things that were inaccurate in the book. He says it's 6-8 weeks away from completion. He says in a police interview that he's not sure of any licking and he would be lying if he said he did. They flew on a public jet 1st Class and everybody **could see Mj and Jordan.**

Re-Direct

He says those are his emails. **He says he guesses yes, there was licking of Jordan?**

Re-Cross

He says if it was in his email it **must be his words.**

Redirect – 2

He says he would be lying if he said he remembered the licking.

April 11th

53rd Witness Stacy Brown

Analyst for MSNBC and Author. Co-Authored book about Stevie Wonder. Co-Authored book with sisters Rebe and Jermaine never published. He says everyone had to talk to Bob concerning Mj. He was approached by Bob to write a book. Has worked with 5 agents, currently employing 2 agents. **He says Bob Jones did tell him about an incident of Mj licking Jordan Chandler's head. He says everything had to be approved by Bob before it went to the publisher. Publisher** Select Books. He says he hadn't heard of the licking in this case? He does read papers and the internet and other media sources. Bob talked with him about head licking more than a couple of times. He stopped his recollection **abruptly, he says.**

Cross – Examination

Bob told him he is broke and he needs to make money. He talked to him, Bob, about the book before he was fired. Feldman comes up in the book but not by name just by inference. Randy Jackson delivered a message that Bob was fired. It says Bob never saw Mj act inappropriately with children.

April 11th

Re-Direct

He says Bob stopped complaining about his finances the same time he couldn't recollect any licking.

Re-Cross

He forgot licking when he didn't need money?

54th Witness – June Chandler

Jordan Born 1-11-80 Father Evan Chandler.

#793 – Are not picture of Jordan
#794 - Are not picture of Jordan
#795 – Are not picture of Jordan
#776 – Is Picture of Jordan

She met Mj at her ex-husband's business David Schwartz. Her and Jordan went. She gave Mj there phone #. Mj called a month or 2 after meeting to Neverland Feb 93. She says Mj called 8 to 10 times. Some calls lasted up to 10 minutes to 1 ½ hours. Jordan and Lilly visited Neverland. They spent 2 nights there. She stayed in a guest cottage with Jordan and Lilly. Mj took all of them shopping at Toys R Us. They went back to Neverland 1 or 2 weeks later. They were put in a limousine with Mj and Bret Barnes. They stayed the weekend. She says her family stayed in guest cottages.

April 11th

She says she never saw Brett Barnes in guest cottages. She says it could have been that 2nd weekend visit they went to Disneyland, 3rd visit all slept in guests cottages. Jordan asked to sleep in Mj room. She said no. She says Jordan would get back to the guest cottage around 11:00pm. Frankie & Eddie from New Jersey, Cascio about the same age as other kids. Went with Mj to Vegas March 93 Jordan Lilly and Mj. Stayed at Mirage 2 or 3 nights. They all stayed in the same room until the 2nd night. Jordan and Mj were supposed to go to perform at 11:00 pm and never showed up at the show, they showed up at the hotel at 11:30. Mj was crying upset because she wouldn't let Jordan sleep in the bedroom with him. She did allow Jordan that night to sleep with Mj in his bed. She received a gold Cartier bracelet after she let Jordan sleep in bed with Mj. After Vegas they Mj and Jordan continued to sleep together. She says Jordan went to Neverland 2 or 3 times without her or Lilly. When they went, Jordan slept in Mj room and they stayed in a guest cottage.

April 11th

Mj spent the night at their house more than 30 times and stayed in Jordan's room in his bed. Mj would leave when Jordan went for school and come back when Jordan got out of school. They all went to Disney World in Florida, Jordan slept with Mj. Lilly stayed with Mom. She says gradually Jordan didn't want to be with her or Lilly anymore. He started acting differently dressed like Mj and withdrew. She met Joe and Wade Robeson at Neverland. She only met Joy once. Brett and Wade were usually at Neverland with no parents. She had a conversation with Joy Robeson and then became uncomfortable. They were invited to go on tour with Mj. They were in Monaco for 4 days, Jordan slept with Mj. She did go in the room and she did see them in bed together. Her and Lilly shopped in Monaco with Mj credit card. Mj and Jordan both got the flu. Stayed in the room together. They went to Euro Disney for 2 days. Mj and Jordan slept together. Mj went to NY after his brother got married. Her brother wasn't happy about Jordan spending all of his time with Mj. Jordan slept with Mj at the hotel.

April 11th

There were 2 lamps broken in her room in New York. She says Mj was upset she wanted Jordan back. Mj also gave her jewelry. Gift certificate to Fred Siegel. Mj and Jordan were at her ex husband's house before. 2nd trip to Florida Jordan stayed in Mj room. Father's day 1993, in NY Jordan eventually called his father. Message from ex husband Evan in Mj car Mj not present on her answering machine. Anthony Pellicano P.I. Introduced to her by Burt Fields and Mj. Burt Fields is an attorney who worked for Mj. Jordan was interviewed by Pellicano in the Century City apartment of Mj. She was given papers by Pellicano. 9 -3-93 statement to Lauren Wese LA District Attorney she says Mj was frantic and told her to sign so there would be no lawsuits. She signed paper and gave up custody of children. Her brother and sister-in-law visited Neverland. She left before 8 pm, she saw Jordan and Mj in his Mj's bedroom. Her brother and sister-in-law went into Mj room also. She received money from a lawsuit but she says she didn't ask for money.

April 11th

Mj's gift certificate given to her was for $7,000 dollars.

<u>Cross – Examine</u>

She says the reason she signed the declaration is because her ex husband said he wouldn't bring

Jordan back and she thought she only gave up custody for a week. Freeman attorney who represented her for a short time. She doesn't recall asking Mj for $4 million for David Schwartz or if David was $5 million dollars in debt. Her and Evan divorced 1985. She married David in 1985. They divorced in 1994**. She last spoke to Jordan her son 11 years ago.** She doesn't recall if Mj sued them for extortion. Barry Rothman, Evan Chandler's attorney. She knew of Mj Pepsi deal and of his Beatles catalogue. Spoke to Larry Feldman a few days ago, and 2 months before that. They did talk about this case. She says she doesn't know Feldman represents the Arvizo's. Met with an attorney and Sneddon for 1 ½ hours in LA. She does recall Mj making a trip to see Roy Disney's Widow. She says Mj stayed at her house approximately 30 nights beginning April to May.

April 11th

She says Mj went to an apartment in Century City when he left her house during the day. She did have dinner with Joy Robeson and associated with Wade. She was separated from David when Mj spent those nights at her house. She never suspected on the trip to Florida that anything was going on with Jordan and Mj. She says Mj told her in Vegas that he wanted a family he would be normal with. She told the LA District attorney that Jordan's relationship with Mj was good because Jordan would be taken care of for the rest of his life. She does recall her ex-husband wanting Mj to finance a wing on to his house, Mj didn't do it. She was happy with Mj being around because Evan, Jordan's father, didn't spend time with him and she was separated from David. She was told Jordan and Mj watched the Exorcist movie. She wanted Jordan to go to his room, not Mj when in Vegas. She told LA DA Mj helped Jordan with his homework. She says she went into Mj's bedroom approximately 10 times. She would see the Cascio's, Brett, Wade, McCauley.

April 11th

She did watch Tv in Mj's room sometimes. **After the Monaco trip she allowed Mj to stay at her house even though she said things were starting to get weird in Monaco and going downhill.** She never saw Jordan or Mj shower or bathe together. She got upset over a squirt gun fight at her house with Mj Jordan, Evan and Evan's other son. Mj did spend 2 nights at Evan's house with Jordan. She spent 4 nights at a hotel in NY. She told Mj he's like Peter Pan, everyone wants to stay 24 hours with him. She said Lilly would but she is too young. **She says Mj broke lamps practicing karate just messing around. She doesn't mention Mj, Burtfields or Anthony Pellicano in her declaration.** She did use a gift certificate for Fred Siegel from Mj. She got settlement money in October 93 late August early September, David meeting at Mj apartment. She's never met Norma Staykos and just talked to her on the phone. They initially were represented by Gloria Allred, before Feldman. Met with Pellicano 3 or 4 times in his office.

April 11th

1st saw Pellicano in August. Declaration signed August 10, 93 on Freeman office paper. Met with Robert Shapiro in Feldman's Office**. She says she contacted children services before a lawyer.** She never contacted the police department. Over anything involving Mj. Contacted children services sometime in August.

Re-Direct

Children services do have sworn peace officers. Interviewed 8-7-93 she says Jordan made a report. She spoke to Feldman to make sure it was ok to talk to Sneddon. Cascio own's Aldo Restaurant in New Jersey. She learned the story of a hotel room with lamps and karate was not true. **After she signed the paper she never got custody again.** Mj was present for Jordan's interview with Pellicano. She says she regrets every trusting Mj.

Re-Cross

Evan and her were in custody in August of 93.

55th Witness – Dwayne Swingler

Stand in for Stars. Worked for Mj in June 2003. Met Mj at a music studio.

April 11th

In April, he was hired to be security first but then became House Supervisor of Neverland. He says Mj is the only one who could terminate him. Terminated early August 2003. He was terminated by Joe Marcus without reason. Interacted with Mj more than once a day at Neverland if Mj was there. He says Mj was in total control of the ranch. Grace and Chris Carter he says were closest to Mj. He met 2 German businessmen they met with Mj 3 or 4 times.

Cross Examine

He worked 6 or 7 day a week. He's not sure if there were 3 or 4 meetings. He says he could identify those 2 Germans if he saw a picture of them. He spoke to a lady from the News of the World. He wanted to cash in on Mj. He says he has jotted down things that came up missing from his house. He says David from News of the World had written things and titled it using his name. This David wanted him to speak on Mj behalf.

April 11th

He met Dominic Cascio at Neverland and spoke to him often.

Re-Direct

David Schmidt is Pro Michael Jackson

56th Witness – Jay Jackson

April 12th

Married almost a year to Janet. Went to Neverland Summer 02, left late evening. Left for Miami early Feb, Janet lived at his house 3 or 4 days a week. He asked reporters how they were going to compensate the Arvizo family. He says he didn't tell Janet about his conversations with reporters. David Gardner and Alex Burns. They offered $15,000 dollars and he turned them down. He has not accepted any money for any stories. He says they don't plan to in the future. He received several calls from Janet from Neverland when they got back from Miami. He says she was distressed. Started receiving phone calls from Frank Tyson (Cascio) Frank asked what kind of car he drove. He told him and after that he has seen several surveillance tapes of him. He says Janet would sit in the closet when on the phone with Frank. He called every 30 minutes.

April 12th

She was upset over Dieter and Ronald's treatment of her. He believed Brad Miller worked for Mj. Interview was about 2 hours. She didn't specifically tell him what was happening and he didn't ask? When she came back from ranch without kids, she was frantic but didn't want to talk about it? He says Frank was calling every 15 minutes. Janet said she didn't want to do a rebuttal video. He asked for a copy of the contract Frank wanted Janet to sign but never got it. Frank said he would offer a house and college education. He asked about monetary payment for Arvizo's and Frank said are you trying to blackmail us? Never had discussion with Janet about video. Nobody else was calling other than Frank. He believed the children were at Neverland. He doesn't remember her mood the night after the DCFS Interview. They were gone 3 weeks after that interview. Talking on the phone he said she was distressed. She was concerned not being able to see kids and she was being followed or had a chaperone away from Neverland.

April 12th

He met her at a Salon. He saw Vinnie and Gavin come in the back door of the salon. Vinnie told him he had to check if Jay could take Janet. He sys Gavin followed Vinnie outside. He says Gavin was cocky and obnoxious, not normal. Gavin was surprised. Jay was there. Janet left with Jay. Gavin left with Vinnie. Janet was distressed. He tried to help get children from Neverland. Janet called Frank or Vinnie. He saw the children next night at Janet's parent's house. He says Gavin didn't want to see him. Davellin was crying in the back room. Gavin said he couldn't see him because then he couldn't return to Neverland. He says Gavin was cursing and mean. He says Gavin became his old self after a couple of months. The children went to JEI Tutoring.

<u>Cross – Examine</u>

He didn't know about Gavin's school disciplinary file. Nov 25, 2003 first Sheriff interview. Janet believed Mj was innocent before the trip to Miami. He saw both videos. He thought Bashir was slandering Mj. Met Chris Tucker on the bus to Neverland. He said Janet and the kids had a great relationship with Chris Tucker.

April 12th

He had about 5 discussions with David Gardner. Roger Freeman, People Magazine, etc have contacted him. He says he's never asked if Janet or kids signed any documents.

#5000 – Audio or Brad miller Interview with Arvizo's

Miller interview with Arvizo's. Janet remembers David's her ex husbands, #55 License #, kind of odd? Janet says what she has is to not sell. End of tape 10:25pm Sunday February 16, 2003. She is a guardian and has full rights; her ex has no control over anything. **He says here that he was there but in and out during the interview. Told the grand jury he was there on the couch during the interview. He says there was no enticement by Brad Miller of any of their answers.** Rebuttal video on Feb 20, 2003. He moved into St. Andrews 11/02 Both boys were pulled from school because gangs were pressuring them to join. Oct 01 Aug 04, Worked at Wilshire St. and Federal St. Salon 5 or 6 blocks away. FBI Building close by 405 Fay Close Salon in Brentwood Area. Janet had family court the next day he thinks Vinnie went with her.

April 12th

He spoke to Frank Tyson 2 times. He's never met Frank. He says in a police interview he read on the internet about somebody making $5 million on a documentary. He doesn't know what Janet talked to Mj about? He says he hasn't discussed the case with any Arvizo. To his knowledge Janet hasn't seen Bashir Video or Maury Povich video. Moved to WLA Nov 03 to July 04. Kept Janet's Soto address till March of 03. He's been present for 1 attorney meeting with Janet and Bill Dickerman. Met Jamie Masada 4 or 5 times.

April 13th

Janet was settling welfare assistance. He deposited and endorsed her welfare checks, deposited in his bank. She got numerous checks from the county of LA, some addressed to Soto, some addressed to Raymer. Didn't know of any bank account Janet had. He made about $5,500.00 per month in the months of 03. He never knew about JC Penney Settlement. Never knew of any deposits in her mother's bank account.

April 13th

March 03 deals with domestic problems. He can't say if her rent was paid just from her welfare money. Knew nothing of any account at Washington Mutual. She did receive food stamps. Met Janet July 02. He never wondered why someone on welfare wanted 2 residences. He never asked her why she didn't have a bank account.

Re-Direct

Her rent was $425, her welfare was approximately $780 per month. He says she never had her own car. The child support checks always varied. The welfare checks were the same. Feb 15 and 16 were a Saturday & Sunday. Never believed Frank would give house or college education. He says Janet didn't talk much and wouldn't tell him anything that was going on at the time.

Re-Cross

He called police Feb 11, Tuesday 2003. He denies saying that Janet wasn't in any danger? He calls the police, she leaves Neverland, goes to her mother's house, she goes back to Neverland, she leaves Neverland, she goes back to Neverland??? Every time she left Neverland she was driven Mjs people.

April 13th

Re-Direct (2)

Family was scared of somebody named Johnny. He told the counselor at school that Johnny was stalking Starr & Gavin.

#26 – Picture of Johnny

Re-Cross (2)

He never called the police on Johnny?

57th Witness – Janet Arvizo

Met Mj August 2000. Gavin was 10. She's never been in Mj's bedroom. They had to be separated because they could have brought home a virus (makes sense). 1998-2003 lived on Soto St. May 2001 Gavin in remission. Sept 2002 next time (she) went to Neverland. The boys went back right away after 1st visit with their father. David and Gavin went to Universal Hilton to meet Mj. She says Gavin and Mj phone conversations were hours long. Chris Tucker took them to Neverland in 2002. Mj invited the kids back right after that. Separated from

David since May 2001. Met Jay in July 2002. She says the vehicle Mj gave her looked like OJ Simpson's car.

April 13th

She, Jay and the kids went to Neverland for Chris Tucker's son's birthday party. Sept 2002 kids went to Neverland. This is when Bashir filmed Evvy Tavasci, Mj's personal secretary. She didn't learn of filming Bashir till February. Mj phone call to Gavin early February, Janet got on the phone Mj told her Gavin was in danger because of the Bashir documentary. Her conversation with Mj lasted long enough to convince her. Mj told her he needed Gavin to do a press conference and he could protect him. (She was very animated and won't let the question he asked of her can't wait to tell her story.) Her mother was contacted by the press before Mj talked to her. David Gardner reporter from England. NO other reporters tried to get a hold of her before she went to Miami. Arrived at dawn, saw Mj that day at Turnberry Hotel. Conversation lasted 45 minutes. She met Dieter and Ronald that day. She says the "Germans." She says Evvy told her to look at Mj as "family" for someone so protective she gave Dieter and Ronald a lot of personal info.

April 13th

They spent the next day in Mj room with Mj and her kids. She was concerned about her kids being killed but she let them go with Chris Tucker to spa?

#807 – Paper with her signature on there twice from Feb 7,03 Theodore Goddard authorization to file complaint for Gavin.

She says she never signed the same document twice. She says Mj told her now all of her kids were in danger. Mj told her he didn't want her to see Bashir Documentary. She says Dieter and Ronald and Mj kept pulling Gavin into bedrooms alone to talk to him. She says Dieter and Ronald were the damage control team. She says Dieter and Ronald threatened her when they got back from Miami. She met Frank August 2000 at Neverland, saw him in Miami but he didn't talk to her. She says Aldo and Marie Nicole were not friends of her kids and didn't really hang out till they got back from Miami to Neverland. She says on flight Aldo, Marie Nicole, and Mj kids were running all over the plane and the stewardess was very busy?

#808 – Diagram of inside of plane

April 13th

She says Grace the nanny would throw the stewardess out to back if she wasn't working. She says she saw Mj licking Gavin's head over and over when she got up when everybody was sleeping. She told nobody about that. She says they had to walk a little ways when they got to Neverland. She says her white bag was missing. She never went into the house to see kids in Mj house. She saw Dieter the next day and Ronald a couple days later at Neverland.

#405 – Document Press release from Belliard. Sunday Feb 9, 2003.

She doesn't know how long she was there before Jesus helped her. She told Ronald and Dieter she wanted to leave Neverland. She says the first person to mention the word "killers" was Mj. She says Dieter showed her the script for the rebuttal video. She spoke to Jesus in English and Spanish. She went to a beautify salon to get her legs waxed. She said it was Ronald and Dieter's idea. She says she paid for it because it came out of her stolen stuff.

April 13th

Earlier she was worried about reporters scaring her mother but she had Jesus drop her and the kids off there? After that she went to Jay's house. She says Mj called her mother's house almost immediately after they got there. She says Frank called all the time. She says her mother's table was full of offers to her and the kids for stories. She says one offer was for $100,000 cash. She says the recorded phone call is a compilation of phone calls, not just one.

#809 – That phone conversation

Frank promises she doesn't have to talk to Germans. Frank wants to get her out of there because he says it's not safe. He wants to put a 24hr watch in front of her house. He wants them to go back to ranch. 201-213-****S. Franks phone #. He tells her that they are all going to go somewhere nice. A lot of cut-outs or interruption on the tape? She now says Frank is the worst one of them all? What about Mj who supposedly molested Gavin?

Never wanted a guard posted outside of her parent's house.

April 13th

She says she wanted friends so bad because David always told her she would never have any. She didn't talk with Mj before she left Neverland with Jesus. She returned to Neverland after she was told the Germans were fired. "Say nice things about Mj that would appease the killers." She says that is burned into her brain. The Arvizo's returned to Neverland the day after Brad Miller interview. She saw Ronald and Dieter almost right away. She told them Ronald and Dieter that she had an emergency they told her she could leave but not the kids. Jesus told her he couldn't help her anymore. She asked Chris Carter to take her. She left her kids at Neverland. She said she called Jay over and over, couldn't get ahold of him. She says their phone calls were being monitored at Neverland. She spoke to 3 ladies from DCFS CPS at 3 different times. They never told her why they wanted to meet with her. They told her her kids had to be at interview. He said if she did a good job she wouldn't have to leave the country.

April 13th

Interview scheduled for February 20, Thursday.

April 14th

They returned to Neverland the next day after the interview. Rebuttal video took place Feb 19-20 at Hamid's house. Vinnie drove her that was the first time she met Vinnie. She says Hamid brought the kids to his house for rebuttal. She says the video was done at Hamid's house because she didn't want to go back to Neverland. Christian the guy asking the scripted questions in the rebuttal video. Frank wanted her to say how wonderful Mj was. **She says she was acting on rebuttal videos.** She says Frank told her to wear make-up for Rebuttal Video, she says she doesn't normally wear make-up. Rebuttal started at 3 am and ended early that morning. She says she got no sleep before the DCFS interview. (Vickie Pobereski) attorney for MJ and Mark Geragos who wanted to be present at the DCFS interview. Vickie told her, her kids were going to be taken away from her. Jay was there when they arrived at his apt. Aja arrived the same time DCFS ladies arrived. Assef was there when Vinnie left.

April 14th

She says Frank wanted Aja there, and she agreed because she trusted her. Assef was Mj security. She says Assef told her to do everything she was supposed to do, per Frank and Vickie instructions. She didn't know there was a tape-recorder in the room. The DCFS people would not allow Assef or Aja in the room during the interview. Karen Walker DCFS supervisor. They were all interviewed together. That's what she asked for per Vickie Mj lawyer. First heard a tape at the grand jury. She never knew why the DCFS was there.

#810- CD of that interview

Lots of laughter and talking beginning playing on DVD. Janet heads down not looking at anything or anybody, when tapes are played from today and yesterday, but very vocal and boisterous during testimony. Janet says it is her fault that Aja and Assef are there. Assef tells her this is a tape recorder and not to mess with it, it's all set to go. She turned off the tape recorder to be sure she put towels on it in the closet. All of DCFS 'interviews were not confidential; they got out to the media.

April 14th

She doesn't know how long the interview went on. She says none of the workers took notes and they just said they didn't want to be sued by Mj. Vinnie showed up after social workers left. Assef escorted Aja and her child to their car. Vinnie told her she and the kids did not do an adequate job on rebuttal and they still had to leave the country. She said God healed Gavin; she was supposed to say Mj did. She wasn't supposed to comment about the DCFS thing.

#811 – Document 4 papers. Releases she had to sign before rebuttal video. Kid signature as well and Vinnie's.
#812 – Document Frank and Vinnie wanted her to sign after the rebuttal video. She never signed it.

She was never paid or asked to be paid for doing video she says. She says she just wanted to go let her and her children go.

#814- Document Vinnie handwriting copy of #812

She went to get birth certificates. She had to write a note saying it was an emergency. She says she agreed to go to Brazil because Frank and Vinnie threatened her parents and Jay's life.

#259 – Applications for birth certificates
Emergency note signed by her.

April 14th

#260 – 11 pages of Documents 4 of the pages applications for passports. They say destination Italy & France not Brazil. She signed but writing is Vinnie's.
#261 – 10 pages of Documents
(B) Visa application. Her picture Vinnie's writing and Vinnie signed it.
(C) Itinerary for flights with an address not hers. Feb 25, 2003 Flight
(D) Starr's Vinnie wrote and signed
(E) Gavin's Vinnie wrote and signed
(F) Gavin's birth certificate
(G) Child custody order and visitation, Vinny and Frank told her to get it
(H) Starr Birth certificate
(I) Visa application Davellin Vinny wrote and signed
(J)Davellin's birth certificate

Feb 20 she stayed at Jay's, her kids were at Neverland. Feb 21 she met Vinnie, went to marc Schaffel's house

#806 – 5 pieces of paper duplicates of Birth certificates. 4 passports.

She first saw passports at Neverland. Vinny had them. She says they were always followed by another car. She stayed at Neverland Feb 21-25. She stayed in a guest cottage, Davellin stayed in a guest cottage. Boys stayed in the house, she doesn't know if Mj was there. She never went to the main house for anything. She says she walked around twice.

April 14th

Feb 25 they all went to Gavin's Dr Appointment at Kaiser. Vinnie went and she says they were followed. March 10 scheduled test. Laugh Factory after hospital visit met Jamie Masada and **Bill Dickerman** she says she didn't know Dickerman was going to be there but then she says he didn't tell Vinny they were going to meet a lawyer. Stayed at a hotel in Calabasas Feb 25-Mar 2. They went shopping for clothes 1 of those days. She called Louise Palanker during this time. She says Frank, Vinnie, and Johnny and other people she didn't know were with her all the time at the hotel. She says her calls were monitored. Vinnie told her that she says she called her mother that didn't help. She called Aja and told her and hoped no one heard it? She called Jay, tried to tell him the same way. Went back to Neverland March 2 – March 10. She says Joe was very scary and very loyal to Mj. She says her boys were with Mj. She says they were running around like crazy. She says her kids were out of control. She says they stayed the night with Mj every night. She thought they stayed with other children.

April 14th

She says her kids weren't in school and getting no schooling. She went to an orthodontist to get braces off. At night after hours why would the orthodontist remove the braces if they weren't ready? Ronald and Dieter wanted her to move out of Soto's apartment. She had letters there from Mj to Gavin hidden from David. Frank & Vinny talked to her about moving out of the apartment.

#276 – 2 sheets
(A) Envelope to her from her old landlord
(B) Letter termination of her lease she didn't sign
(B -Back) Saying she's paid in full on her apartment. She never returned to Soto. She used Jay's address so the boys could go to a different school because of gangs they weren't involved in, she says they got beat up all the time.

#271 -
(A) - ?
(B) Check out sheet from boys school 3-6-2003 Signed by Vinnie for Gavin. Says new and going to be Phoenix, AZ.
(C) – Letter to school saying they were moving to Phoenix, AZ signed by her.
(D) – Janet's Drivers license and Vinnie's License.

#272-
(A) – Check out the sheet Starr says is the same as Gavin's.
(B) – Letter to school same as above signed by her

April 14th

They didn't let her turn in his urine on Feb 25th. She got a container at Kaiser. She was supposed to turn it the right way. 24 hrs later? They didn't turn or try to turn it in till March 10 they started collecting urine on March 2nd. Gavin called her at 4 am and told her he drank wine and had to reschedule so they wouldn't find out alcohol in urine, she says Gavin told her Mj scared. She held a urine bottle in the front seat. She had to stop and use the bathroom at Denny's. She came out and the car was gone. 5 minutes she asked Vinnie where he went, the urine bottle moved and the container was almost empty? Vinnie told her it must have fallen. She says it hadn't spilled in the car. They went to Jay's apt after the doctor visit. She called Jay to meet her at nail salon Vinnie took Gavin across the street, she called Jay again Jay showed up at the salon. Vinnie called Frank to tell him she wasn't going with them from the salon. Vinnie and Gavin went back to Neverland. She told Vinnie she wanted to spend quality time with Jay. She knew kids didn't have to be at family court.

April 14th

Michael Manning family law lawyer. Told Jay everything that night before family court. Vinnie came to take her to family court and had none of her kids with him. Vinnie went with her to court and then she went to Jay's, never returning to Neverland. She contacted Karen Walker but she was no help. Jay called her parents from his work, she called Frank from Jay's and negotiated a visit for her kids and her parents for 2 days. She saw her kids that night. She says Gavin was angry and violent, not normal. She told him he wasn't going back to Neverland, she says it took weeks before he was normal. She says Gavin wasn't allowed to bring anything but Starr and Davellin brought their staff and their mom's stuff. She saw Johnny, Frank, Vinnie and new people following them.

#277 – Note slipped through the door from Johnny, to call Frank or Vinnie. She never called. Rocks thrown at parent's house.

Children had been out of school less than 2 months. She said they had to go where there were no hotels in Brazil.

April 14th

She says Frank and Vinnie told Mj would not come to Brazil. She said there was an apartment in Brazil full of surveillance equipment. She enrolled boys back in John Burrows and Davellin in a different high school. She says everything to do with Mj was what was missing from her stuff from her apartment. She says people were telling her the Bashir Documentary was still being shown. Dickerman was trying to get some of her stuff back and to get Mj people to stop following them. Feb 21st, Friday Vinnie told social worker kids would be put in school the next day. She met Larry Feldman through Bill Dickerman. Feldman referred them to Dr. Katz. She says because her house was a cuckoo house that's why she thought they were seeing Dr. Katz. She didn't learn about alleged molestations till after police got involved. She didn't get her possessions back till after police got involved. She says all letters, pictures and anything that involved Mj was gone. She says Gavin wore a watch everyday that Mj gave him, she says **she took it off of him** because it was ridiculous. She then left it at Jay's house and then she gave it to her lawyers? She says they offered to rent her a house and apartment, if she left the country, she said nothing else was offered. She says she never asked for money, it's not her nature. She says she does not intend to file a lawsuit at any time.

April 15th

She says they were followed everywhere they went.

#809- A Transcripts
#810 – A Transcripts
#815 – Surveillance DVD
#816 – Surveillance DVD
#817 – Surveillance DVD
#818 – Surveillance DVD

Apartment on Soto was very gross and ran down, wondering if it was like that when they moved in.

Cross – Examine

She didn't know her phone conversation with Frank was being tape recorded. She says she never wanted Security from Frank. **Frank sounds like Mj on taped conversation with Janet.** She says 1 trip to Miami and she's calling everybody family. These phone conversations with Frank were after she says

Jesus helped her and the kids escape. A report was made that David molested Davellin.

April 15th

David violated the restraining order by going to Davellin's school and having her get into his car. She was at court with Davellin but not in the judge's chambers. Carol Lemure is David's girlfriend. She says she was too scared of Mj people to get a restraining order. Wasn't she afraid of David also? She and David were being investigated by DCFS in 2001. She was investigated in the 1990s by DCFS over Gavin telling the nurse at school he was accused of her abuse and then changed his story. She says in this conversation was the only time she complained about the media. She says she escaped from Neverland 3 times? She doesn't want to look at the treatment receipt? She didn't pay with her money at the salon? **She says what's wrong with telling the truth.** She says the rebuttal video was all scripted. Where's the script? Gavin asked Brett Ratner to take him to Miami to see Mj. Brett said no, she said he was concerned by Dieter and Mj to do that? Frank tells her Germans aren't there and if they are she doesn't have to talk to them.

April 15th

She says phone conversation it's crazy around here and people are calling like crazy. She says it's not safe. She still considered Mj family. **Frank asked her if she wanted somebody outside her house 24 hours a day security and she said "no." She says she meant no she didn't want that?** She says her kid's school is bombarded and her Soto Street apartment is crazy. She tells him numerous times during tape they are family. She asked for Frank's number. She says she believes everything Frank tells her. She does not like the German people. She never says no to security at her house, and she never says yes? She says that she is just being "polite" when she is complying with Frank. She says she has no idea how Frank got her mother's phone #. She says she loves Frank at the end of conversation. She says she filed for divorce after David was arrested for domestic violence. She told LAPD David physically and mentally abused her for 17 years. Deposition Dec 18, 2000 JCPenney. She says David never struck her or the children? She lied, she says!

April 15th

She says she changes her story to the truth after David is arrested. She says she was told of the deadline in the JC Penney case civil suit by her lawyer. Her family was given $152,000 in the JC Penney Case. She testified she had no black and blue marks before this incident. She lied! Did she lie under oath in the JC Penney Case! Yes. She says she did not consider David an honest person, on deposition she says David is extremely honest he's too honest. She said she thought she was going to die in the parking lot from JC Penney and Tower Records security. She says her breasts were touched and her nipples squeezed 10-25 times. Mary Hulser is a giant Mj fan and works for the lawyers that sued JCPenney. She says Rothstein is the firm! She was a loss prevention person at Vons for 1 year.

Georg Owen Feldman lawyer says she's never been represented by him. She says in the JC Penney Case she wasn't interested in suing she just wanted an apology but she and her family kept the money.

April 15th

George Owen Feldman is an attorney for Rothstein, the firm who saved JC Penney for her. Jan 1, 2000 Dec 18, 2003, she signed a document saying she was investigating Mj, but says she didn't meet him in Aug 2000? She says her laughter was part of the script and everything Gavin is saying is memorized. She says she is acting on rebuttal are they lies or the truth, she says she was acting!! She won't say if anything is true or false. Just acting following the script. Answer the questions!!!! If David was so bad from the beginning of the relationship, why did she have 3 kids and why did she stay for 17 years? She doesn't know if she was being scripted in Miami. She doesn't know how long it took to memorize the script. She says even the outtakes are scripted? She says she didn't tell anybody about what was going on because no one would believe it. Andrew Lasek, an officer LAPD, has been her friend since 2001.

April 15th

He's from Hollenbeck Division. That's a very bad part of town. LAPD Patrick Matoyer, Sgt Milt Hernandez. She says she never asked Officer Lasek for assistance, he has driven her home from the welfare department. Sgt Chu Rampart, Cindy Garcia, Det. Angullo (They don't sound familiar.) She had Officer Lasek's cell phone #. She says out of respect because he just got married, she stopped talking to Office Lasek? David was arrested Sept - Oct 2001. She says Officer Lasek never helped with the fundraiser. Davellin, Gavin, and Starr went to a Christmas party at Hollenbeck Police Station. She can't answer if she talked to Larry Feldman in the last couple weeks she can't remember? Now she says she talked to Feldman every time they got a subpoena. She met Feldman in 2003. She says she knew 2 MTA officers well the rest by face only.

April 18th Jan, Feb, Mar, Apr 2003. Represented by Attorney Michael Manning against David for child support and spousal support. He represented her 2001-2004. She says he represented her for free. She never told him about being held against her will or her family? She wouldn't answer, she said attorney client privilege? Oct 4, 2001 went to Hollenbeck detective division to complain about her husband. She brought photos of Chris Tucker and Azja. Met with Ron Zonen and Detective on Sunday. Meeting was 10 minutes, she says. She says her kids slept with baseball bats. She says she's never told Mj, Kobe Bryant, or Fritz Coleman about her domestic problems with David. Her holding knife in the photo she says was for fun? 17 years of violence and she screwing around with a knife for a picture? She says David's brother never threatened her or the kids. She says she never discussed with Jay who Brad Miller was. She says she didn't pay attention to what Brad Miller was saying even when she answers yes? She says the Brad Miller interview was not scripted, it was how she felt at the time.

April 18th

Her Mj and kids were dancing in the bumper car area in their first meeting in August 2000. She says she never spoke to Mj there or at the dinner table that night either? She says this Miller interview was really her words but, 4 days later the rebuttal was all scripted??? She doesn't recall telling Jamie Masada or George Lopez her kids dove into a fountain or coins. She filed a state disability claim for being depressed because she was sad about being a nobody?? She says she last saw Brad Miller was in a rebuttal video. Now she says Brad Miller came to Jay's after the DCFS interviews. She says Aja never drove her to Neverland nor did she drive her anywhere after the DCFS interview. Aja drove her children to Neverland after the DCFS interview. She says she and Davellin never asked Aja for Chris Tucker's car keys. She says she did not tell Aja she was excited to go to Brazil. She met Carol Lemure at dance school. Davellin stayed at her house but Janet says all Carol wanted her to do was to clean her house.

April 18th

She, Davellin, stayed at Carol's house during the time Gavin had cancer. She did tell Aja she was being held against her will?? She knew her boys were staying with Mj on her first visit because she heard Gavin ask. She never asked her boys where they spent the night inside the house on the first visit? She wrote down the VIN number on the Blazer Mj gave her? Mj gave Gavin a laptop on his first visit. It was returned at some point. She says she wasn't upset about that. Mj would leave phone messages for Gavin at his Grandma's house on his private line. Starr never discussed the video he made at Neverland with her. She never asked where the boys stayed on their second trip to Neverland. She doesn't know what celebrities Chris Tucker introduced David too. Chris Tucker introduced the children to Jackie Chan and Mike Tyson, she says that's all she can remember. They didn't have bank accounts when Louise Palanker gave them the 2 checks for $10,000. They cashed them through her mother's bank. They opened an account for Gavin at Washington Mutual she says people

April 18th

would go and deposit money on their own no money was given to her and then deposited she says. She says none of the $20,000 went for anything. She says she used it how David instructed her to do it?? She says she was a waitress full time at Bonaventure Hotel during Gavin's cancer. She says Jamie Masada is still a friend of hers. She says she never knew anything about any fundraisers for Gavin? And they were never discussed with her? She spoke to the newspaper about Gavin's illness. She says the article in the paper was related to David somehow? She says no one from the newspaper ever brought turkey to her mom's house and she says she never told them the turkey wasn't enough. She says "she" never asked anybody for assistance for Gavin! She was not personally introduced to Brett Ratner. She says "she" saw Jamie Masada at the hospital once. She says last time she saw Fritz Coleman was at hospital. She had spoken to George Lopez about Gavin. She was the only signatory on the

April 18th

Washing Mutual account David was not? Because David owed his brother a lot of money. She withdrew all the money and spent it how David wanted her too. She says her and Ajas friendship grew slowly. She says **she doesn't think** she told Aja that David spent all the money from the fundraises on his drug habit. I thought she didn't know about fundraisers. Now she says she didn't discuss fundraisers with anybody. She didn't know Chris wired money into the Washington Mutual account but she withdrew it and gave it to David? Chris and Aja gave her Janet's, Aja's old car for Christmas. She says she never drove it and she doesn't own it today. She did tell Aja about Germans. She says she made Aja aware that the Germans weren't letting her go? She says she didn't tell Aja she had errands to run and could she take the kids to Neverland. She says Miko Brando had many titles at Neverland. She did tell Aja phone calls were being monitored at Neverland. She told Michael Manning her lawyer also. Neither one called the police?

April 18th

She never saw or discussed the Maury Povich show with anybody. She did allow her children to go back to Neverland after she claims to have seen Mj licking Gavin's head. Her telling Mj people were threatening to kill her and her family wasn't told to the police till after her meeting with Larry Feldman? She never called the police . She said she was dropping hints to **certain people so they would**? **She keeps adding specific words to her testimony. She says she's not very smart and still a nobody? But she adds those words at certain times!** She never saw a document that the Brazil trip was only for 2 weeks. She says she never wanted a house or apartment from Mj. She believed Jay Jackson's phones were tapped. She doesn't think Salons phones were tapped, she says she never scripted her children in the JC Penney case like David said.

April 18th

She never talked to anybody about the George Lopez wallet incident. She says she's sure she mentioned killers on the phone with Frank even though it wasn't on tape? She says a man with so much wealth, money, Mj didn't even hire a tutor for them when they were supposed to be in school. She never saw any plane tickets for the Brazil trip. Any forms that were signed by her were signed at the federal facility. She says they told the Germans, Frank and Vinnie, they could get kids to disappear in a Hot Air Balloon from Neverland. She says she told Jay Jackson everything on March 10th. Summer 2003 she learned she was involved in a lawsuit in England involving Bashir. She had no involvement with David Legrand but knew who he was. She says the Ed Bradley interview was set-up but was never going to happen. Feb 8, 2003 article in British newspaper that quoted her. She says she never said she and her family lived in a stable in Bakersfield. She didn't read the document before she inserted words in it?

April 18th

3-11 she called Karen Walker and told her Gavin had been given alcohol, held against their will. Karen told her she couldn't help her that the case was closed. Met with Dickerman first 2-25. She didn't go to the police until months after meeting with 2 lawyers. Feldman was the first one to bring up child molestation? She didn't answer. She says she made no mention during the DCFS interview about going to Brazil that wasn't mentioned till her phone call with Karen Walker. **She didn't know Davellin was leaving school? She signed a paper to allow Starr & Gavin to leave school? She says she didn't know Jay asked Frank how much the family was going to get for video.** She told Mrs. Lizalde the landlord of her apartment that she was leaving the country. **Katie Bernard worked at Neverland. She says she doesn't know her.** Raphael Camacho worked at Neverland. She doesn't know him, she says. She says she asked Frank and Vinnie to drive her to church on Ash Wednesday and they said no.

April 18th

Francisco Fuentes – No
Tammy Gewher – No
Gail Goforth – No
Maria Gomez – No

Curtis Gordon – No
Patty Hankins – No
Chris Hernandez – No
Ryan Hester – No
Anthony Hadley – No
Charlie Kirchoff – No
Julio Magana – No, She talked on the phone once with him she thinks
Kristy Mann – No
Shane Meredith – No
Samuel Moreno – No
Jonathan Bruce Richards – No
Manuel Rivera – No, She never complicated Mj on her trips to Neverland
Brian Salce – No
James Silva – No
Javier Velasco – No
Angel Vivanco – No
Jason Walcott – No
Christian Robinson – Yes, Did Rebuttal Video He had scripted questions.

First met him at Hamid's House at the time she got there. **She never asked Evvy Tavasci for help with her family. She says she had friends and she didn't ask them for any help.** I thought her husband didn't allow her to have friends or told her she didn't have any friends?

Julio Avila – No
Alex Burn – No
Nancy Catallo – No, she says she never talked to Dr. Farshchian
Romero Rubulcaua Garcia – No

April 18th

Gary Hearn – Yes, He was a driver.
Rio – No (Mj Relatives)
Simone – No (Mjs Relatives)
Arlene Kennedy – Yes, She owns the dance school where her kids went. She says her kids didn't have a scholarship to that school. She never told Arlene Kennedy that MJ was clueless and the people around him kept him in the dark. **She says she only called Arlene 1 time from Neverland. She knew Carol Lemure 3 years before she ever met Mj.** She says she never asked for an automobile. She last saw Carol Lemure at David's court date. She never told anybody including the police that David threatened their lives, hers and her kids.

Richard Ramey – No
Marion Arvizo – Yes, Friend of editor of newspaper
Marie Trigs – No
Bruce Richards – No, she says she made no phone calls at Hamid's House Brad Miller called Vicky Pottereski and put Janet on the phone with her.
Violet Silva – No

David got 5 grand from JC Penney settlement. Feb 21st – Outback Steakhouse she says never happened.

April 18th

Robinsons May 2-21-03 Never happened she says. She says it was 2-26 with her children. Vinnie paid the bill.
Lisa is beauty supply (Never happened she says) 2-21

Pacific Sunwear (Never happened) 2-26-03
Luggage (Yes) 2-26-03
Banana Republic (Never happened she says) 2-26-03
Gap Outlet (Never happened) 2-26-03
Levi Outlet (Yes) 2-26-03
Black Angus (Yes) 2-26-03
Footlocker (Never happened she says) 2-26-03
Abercrombie & Fitch (Never happened she says) 2-26-03
Robinsons May (Yes) 2-26-03
No shopping on 2-27-03
Songs Barbershop (No) 2-28
Adidas (No) 2-27-03
Old Navy (No) 2-27-03
Robinsons May (No) 2-27-03
Anchor Blue (No) 3-1
Robins (No) May 3-6
Nails (Yes) 3-10

April 18th

She never asked Neverland employees to shop for her why she was there. She never got any cosmetics. She says while staying Hotel they were allowed only 1 meal per day. She never bought a car 11-9-01, she rode a bus. Met Stan Katz May 2003 through Larry Feldman. She first learned of any alleged molestation Sept 2003

Re-Direct

Mary Holzer is a huge Mj fan she says. She says Gavin and Starr were 6 and 7 years old during the JCPenney suit. She says to the man and woman beating up her husband in the parking lot of JC Penney. What are you doing, and what's going on here. She says they started beating her up. They were arrested. **<u>She never touched Starr & Gavin's money from JC Penney settlement because she can't.</u>**

#820 – Documents Gavin $25,595.00
#821 – Documents Starr $8,576.00 She received $32,000. David received $5,000
#819 – Photo's of her injuries from JC Penney suit. Gavin's injuries also

April 18th

How can we be sure all of the bruises and marks are from JcPenney. Maybe from abusive David?? She never talked to Chris Tucker again after the Miami trip. She did talk to Aja after that trip. She says she's never bought a car on her own.

April 19th

She says she didn't ask Louise Palanker for any money David did. She says she never asked Jay Leno for money. She says she doesn't know to this day who offered a large amount of help that Jamie Masada told her about. She says she never had a conversation with Mj before phone calls to ask her and kids to come to Miami.

<u>Re-Cross</u>

She says she saw David getting beat up by a man and woman at JCPenney, but she says David didn't get injured? She says it was 2 males, a female and someone else from tower beat her up that day. She says it was late afternoon 6:00-6:30 pm and doesn't know what day it was. **Driving around the parking lot kissing David couldn't find a parking spot.**

April 19th

She says one of the males and the female was the ones that were cursing at her. **She says the woman hit her in the head with her handcuffs but they didn't show any injuries on top of her head in photos. She remembers distinctively where they parked how there were no windows out of public view but she can't remember other things?** She said David is honest and extremely honest when talking about stealing clothes. **She says she had makeup on at the time at the police station that's** why she just showed marks not bruises she says the bruising got worse and worse as time went on. **I thought her husband didn't allow her to wear make-up.** She never knew about anything even though she talked to all these people and lived with her family?

April 19th

She used her credit card for cosmetic surgery. She never had any discussion with the contractor who fixed up Gavin's room at her parents home? She endorsed a $10,000 check with her name on it and never asked or knew it was cashed through her mother's bank account. She doesn't know if David had his own bank account at that time? She says David hit her all over her body during their marriage. **<u>She says David took her immediately to get pictures of her bruises in the JC Penney case, but I thought she said she didn't have bruises right away. She said they got blacker and blacker as time went on?</u>** 2-21 met Bill Dickerman she says. She says she didn't know Gavin was trying to call or call Jay Leno, she wasn't there if he talked to Jay Leno she never talked to Jay Leno.

<u>Re-Direct (2)</u>

She contacted Jamie, Louise and George when Gavin became ill.

58th Witness – Det. Alvarez

#822- Seized an item that had fallen out of a bag. Magazine Wicked Intention

April 19th

#815 – All DVD's, Surveillance of Soto, Ramer, Jay Jackson, Davellin
#816 - All DVD's, Surveillance of Soto, Ramer, Jay Jackson, Davellin
#817 - All DVD's, Surveillance of Soto, Ramer, Jay Jackson, Davellin
#818 - All DVD's, Surveillance of Soto, Ramer, Jay Jackson, Davellin
#823 – VHS Tapes of Surveillance made into DVDs
#824 - VHS Tapes of Surveillance made into DVDs
#825 - VHS Tapes of Surveillance made into DVDs
#826 - VHS Tapes of Surveillance made into DVDs

<u>Cross – Examine</u>

The #822 magazine was not booked right away as #3048 just #304 as a group.

#822 – The art of Dave Nestler Wicked Intentions. Surveillance Tapes were found in Brad Miller's office who worked for Mark Geragos for Mj. Those tapes were consistent with what a P.I. would normally do.

Re-Direct

Magazine was found in Mj bathroom out in the open

59th Witness – Maria Ventura

She's never been to Neverland, didn't know what it was, didn't know who Mj was. She says Channel 52 reporters were the worst. She had to lie that she was ill to get the children to her house. They arrived the following day. Her husband's name is **David**. Janet and Jay arrived later. She says the kids were different and still she says Gavin is different?

April 19th

She could hear messages being left on her phone. She could see Neverland on screen and sometimes it was Frank. She doesn't know how many calls there were. She heard rocks hit her house and they went out and saw a man throw a rock who was standing next to a car.

No Cross Exam

60th Witness – William F. Caldwell

Sgt Sheriff Dept. 27 years. Det Sgt 4 years. He searched Brad Miller's office at 9:30 am Inv Tonnello and Det Forney and an officer from Beverly Hills P.D. Office was closed and they got in by the office manager. They gained access to inner doors with sledgehammers.

#831 – Photo of cabinet video and audio tapes
#832 – blowup of audio tapes
#833 – Blowup of video tapes
#823 – Arvizo 2-19-2-21 video tape
#824 – To Brad Ray Arvizo video tape
#825 – Arvizo move, 3-5-3
#826 – To Brad, Janet, March Johnny Mj Arvizo 2003
#827 – Audio Mj
#828 – Audio Michael Jackson. Arvizo Stmt.
#829 – Video tape Arvizo Move

All seized in cabinet with TV

April 19th

Cross – Examine

Det for 16 or 17 years as detective. Assignment came from Klepakis and Kitzman. They also searched a storage locker related to Brad Miller. He was told Brad Miller worked for Mj later he found out Brad Miller worked for Geragos.

Re-Direct

Had search warrant with him ---"Joe Dispenza"

61st Witness – Rod Forney

Det Santa Barbara County Sheriff. 11 years. Det 5 years. 211 5 Beverly Dr Ste 108 Brad Miller's office address. All Audio and video tapes were seized from conference room in Brad Miller's office

Cross – Examine

Worked in Bakersfield as a cop for 14 years. He says you wouldn't want to find a piece of evidence that fell out of a bag.

62nd Witness – Michael Davy

Retired. LA School District. John Burrow's 2,400 students when he worked there. He worked at John Burrows for 5 years. Total 4 counselors. They star Gavin attended John Burrows sometime during 2002-2003. He was their counselor Starr and Gavin's. Steven Kaurfman wants to make contact with Arvizo's.

April 19th

He says Janet came to the school regularly. His conversation with Janet was about the kids attending school. He told her that the kids had to return to school or be checked out of school. Vinnie came with Janet's note and driver's license and his ID to check the boys out of school. Before Vinnie came he told Janet that if she couldn't come and check them out someone could come with a note and her ID and their ID and check them out. Books were paid for when Vinnie checked the kids out. Mr. Geralt worked at John Burrows during this time. He says Geralt was an aggressive drill Sergeant type. Had problems with students and parents Gavin & Starr came back to John Burrows 3 weeks later. He says Jay Jackson approached him at the school about a week after boys returned. He went down and saw a man videotaping students. Nissan Sports Car. He told him to stop videotaping students and he did.

Cross – Examine

Met Arvizo's fall of 2002. They both were in the 7th grade. He says Gavin was a constant discipline problem.

April 19th

Gavin was generally an all around bad student. He doesn't recall saying to Sgt Robel that Gavin's grades were the same at every school he went to not good! He says he saw no change in Gavin from Feb Prior 03-March 03 return. He doesn't know how many meetings he had with Janet over Gavin's behavior. He says Gavin's disciplinary problems began Nov 02. Gavin had a tardiness problem, Gavin banged on doors. Gavin had problems with teachers, Gavin had problems with students. Gavin had a negative impact on his class. He was interviewed by Sgt Robel. 12-4-03. He counseled Gavin on his disruptive behavior. He had 6 individual meetings with Gavin and sometimes Janet and Jay. **He saw no difference in Gavin's behavior prior to Feb 03 to after return Mar 03.** Mr. Gerralt did ROTC and ran the detention after school. He would also process people who were late to school and give them a detention slip parents had to sign. 20 minute discussion with Sneddon last night on the phone about grand jury testimony.

April 19th

He met Vinnie and said he was businesslike and cooperative.

63rd Witness – Janet Williams

Retired Santa Barbara County Sheriff. 29 years. She was assigned to search the downstairs bedroom of Mj, the sitting area.

#590 – Bag with 4 books in it
#590A – Book- found in box
#590B - Book- found in box
#590C - Book- found in box
#590D - Book- found in box
#590A – Bob and Rob Title Cover two nude men, no genitalia showing
#590B – Before the hand of man
#590C – Room to play
#590D – Dian Hanson naked as a Jaybird
#591 – Binder with 2 magazines in it
#834 – Bags with 4 magazines
#592 – Magazine – The Nudist
#593 – Magazine – Sunbather
#594 – Magazine – The Nudist
#595 – Magazine – The Nudist

These were all found in boxes.

#596 – Book – Man Sexual Study of Man
#597 – Book – Golden Age of Neglect
#599 – Taormina

All found in boxes

#835 – Bag
#598 – The Nudist
#600 through #613 – The Nudist and others

All found in boxes

#836 – Bag
#614 – Binder Magazine
#615 – The Nudist
#616 – The Nudist
#617 – The Nudist
#618 - ?
#619 - ?

All found in boxes. All chemically treated.

April 19th

#837- Bag (All found in boxes)
#620 – Eden (All found in boxes)
#621 – The Nudist (All found in boxes)
848 – Poo Chi Book (Found in Bookcase in Den)

Cross Examine

Retired Feb 2004. Det 2 different times. Once for 10 years and once for 9 years. Her specialty was mostly sex cases. Most of the books in the bookshelf were art and entertainment books. No books unlawful to purchase or possess for adults. She went to the 2nd story pantry room, 2 bedrooms and a room with toys. She did no research to the authors of any of the books seized.

#838 – She described it as a book of female groin area pictures. It was actually a spoof book of armpits and other folded areas.

April 20th

64th Witness – Brian Barron

Police Officer. City of Guadalupe. Security at Neverland over 3 periods of time 5 to 5 ½ years. Quit April or May of 2004. He mostly worked nights 6:00 pm to 6:30 am.

April 20th

Average 1 Security check per hour. He says none of the security had the code to Mj bedroom. He only talked to Mj if he needed to. He says employees were more tense when Mj was there than when he wasn't.

#300 – Notebook fall
#335 of documents Logs of people who came in or out accident reports. Daily logs etc…

Guests were not allowed on the property if the proper forms weren't filled out. He says Frank was or became an employee of Mj around 2000. He says Frank would sometimes stay there for a month. He says he saw Frank and Mj together 75-100 times. He says Frank spent the night 100s of times in his 5 years, Vinnie friend of Franks. Vinnie spent the night sometimes. Mark Schaffel came 3 or 4 times a year. Never met Ronald, knows the name. Dieter he says would stay a couple of days and then leave. 2002-2003 is when Dieter was there on a continuous basis for a couple of months. Boys from Los Olivos visited quite often, he says at a period of time.

April 20th

He says those boys were very destructive. He saw a directive on the grease board concerning Gavin Arvizo saying Gavin is not allowed off the property. It was on there for a week approximately and it was Jan-Feb 2003 he thinks.

Cross – Examine

Started in Guadalupe Sept 28, 1998. He worked at Neverland moonlighting as a security guard. He didn't leave because he saw anything unlawful. **He never saw anything unlawful go on.** If he says anything unlawful occurred, he would at the least have to report it if not do something about it because he was a sworn police officer. **Gate Activity Log. 2-19-03. Says at 17:52 The kids are not to leave per Joe kids meaning like Gavin, Starr, etc… Kids are not allowed to leave the ranch without supervision. He doesn't think their parents were there that day.** He says Franks other family members would stay overnight or longer also. Started seeing Vinnie late 2002. Started seeing Dieter late 2002. The intruders caught some had cameras.

Juror Notebook 4

Chapter 4

April 20th

He did bring people or family to many family days. They have 1 working fire truck on the ranch. He felt the operation was run professionally. There are 2 private schools across from Neverland. He says Mj had personal bodyguards. When he talked to Janet on the phone, which was 2 times, he felt she wanted to be there. April 12th, 2004 was his grand jury testimony. He says Janet had full access to the house. He says the seldom times he saw Gavin and Starr they appeared to him they wanted to be at the ranch. Det Bonner contacted him in Dec 2003. Det. Bonner wanted him to be an informant. He refused to do that. 6-21-02 Gavin wrecked Batman Cart into the theater fountain. Was reported and warned by security. M. Bashir was seen in at 12:05 and left at 2:40.

Chris Tucker, Gavin, Starr, Davellin all arrived at 3:00 pm and did not leave that day.
What Day? **6-21-02**
6-22-02 (Carry still over there)
6-23-02
6-24-02
6-25-02 (Left 7:54 am)

6-29-02 (Arrive 12:46 am)
Starr, Gavin, Davellin

6-30-02 Still There. They were not cleared for quad runners. Jet Skis or horseback riding like before on 6-21-02 with Chris Tucker visit.

7-1-02 Gavin, Starr, Davellin (Left 9:14 pm)
9-15-02 Chris Tucker, Gavin Starr, Davellin, Chris's nephew (All arrived, no time given)
9-16-02 Stayed overnight (All left at 6:54 am on bus)
9-26-02 Martin Bashir arrived (2:00 pm, left 6:13 pm)

Gary Hearn, Driver, Starr, Gavin, Davellin (Arrive at 2:30, stay overnight)
9-27-02
9-28-02 (Left at 4:00 pm)
Gary Hearn picked them up

Medical Report
Log 2003

2-8-03 Starr fell on a scooter. He says they don't routinely stop Mj vehicle on the way into the ranch.

2-6-03 paper says owner and guest?
Not typical wording

3-7-03 Gavin, Starr, Davellin, Janet, Marie Nicole, Aldo, Dr. Farshian (All stayed overnight)
No Date when CBS Ed Bradley etc showed up.

April 20th

2-9-03 Marie Nicole, Gavin, Starr, Davellin (Left at 1:30, Came back 4:15, Spent the night)

2-10-03 Spent night, Janet also

2-11-03 Janet (Left 5:04, Ret 7:57)
Katie Bernard took her in black van, dropped her somewhere?

2-12-03 Janet, Starr, Gavin, Davellin (Left at 1:38 am)
Jesus Salas shown checking Rolls Royce out at 1:38 am and returning at 9:08 am

2-17-03 – 2-20-03 Davellin, Gavin, Starr, Janet (Leave 7:51) (Leaves 9:46)
Stayed in Dance Studio

2-18-03 Doesn't show all stayed but he says they did

2-19-03 Doesn't show them again. Just shows a new guest.

2-20-03 Shows Aja Pryor, Gavin, Starr, Davellin, Dustin Tucker (Shows them coming in at 2:20)

April 21st

2-18-03 Marie Nicole, Davellin, Aldo (3:05 staying upstairs theater)

2-19-03 Hamid and couple others (Arrive at 4:10 approx, Leave 8:10)

2-21-03 Janet Arvizo arrives at 10:55, same time as Vincent Black

2-22-03 Janet in Guest Unit 4. Davellin, Marie Nicole Upstairs in theater. Starr and Gavin in Unit #2.

2-23-03 Same as day above

2-24-03 Stayed in the same places as previous day. No Marie Nicole though

2-25-03 All the Arvizo's leave ranch at 7:25 am. Vinnie left at 7:25 am.

2-27-03 Frank Cascio returns at 5:35 pm

2-28-03 Frank still there

3-1-03 Frank still there

3-2-03 Frank leaves at 4:30. Comes back with Vinnie and Arvizo.

3-3-03 Vinnie leaves 12:10. Frank and Arvizo spend the night.

April 21st

3-4-03 Arvizo still there

3-5-03 Arvizo's still there

3-6-03 Arvizo's still there

3-7-03 Kids still there. Not sure Janet name on there but crossed off

3-8-03 Kids, Frank and Vinnie, still there, No Janet

3-9-03 Kids still there. Frank and Vinnie Leave and come back, No Janet

3-10-03 No guest information log page. Janet does not return with Vinnie and Gavin

3-11-03 Arvizo's leave for a couple of hours and come back, No Janet

3-12-03 Arvizo's kids leave at 12:15 with Vinnie. Vinnie returns later that evening

<u>Re-Direct</u>

He says most intruders were just trying to see Mj at the ranch. He says the Brando family maybe visited as much as Frank. ATVs were not allowed off the property. The guards were discouraged in engaging in conversation with guests. Nobody outranked Joe Marcus on the ranch when he was the ranch manager. He says just because it says assigned area log, that doesn't mean they spent the night there.

April 21st

Chris Carter started to come to Neverland in late 2001 and early 2002. He's never seen a directive to note let a certain child or children off ranch. Dr. Kline a visitor to Neverland? The Bentley with the darker tinted windows was the one most used to transport Mj.

Re-Cross

He says there were 80-100 employees when he worked there. Dr. Kline was a dermatologist for Mj. **No indication on paperwork Arvizo's left ranch if in fact they were in LA on 2-19-03. That is the same day the directive to not let kids leave ranch per Joe. Kids meaning like Gavin and Starr? Appeared on paperwork.**

Re-Direct (2)

That order to not let Gavin off property was on board for a week.

Re-Cross (2)

He has no knowledge of Mj giving those instructions on Gavin. He never saw Mj write anything on anything.

64th Witness Stephen Cleaves

Sgt Santa Barbara County. 25 years. Lead officer to search security offices. To look at or for computer files. They found no records for 2003.

April 21st

Cross- Examine

Special operations is a detective job. He searched the garage and the video library. The warrant was possibly not for every building on the property.

65th Witness Timothy Sutcliffe

Santa Barbara Sheriff. Criminal Forensics Unit. Helped Sgt Cleaves in searching for records of individuals. He found nothing from 2003.

Cross-Examine

He didn't search the administration building either. He didn't search the office at the gate. He just seized records pertaining to the names he was looking for. There were logs from 2003. He just didn't seize them.

Re-Direct

He could only seize items pertaining to people that he was searching for.

66th Witness Tim Rooney

Santa Barbara County DA. Senior Criminal Invest. Searched security area. Seized items from boxes and file cabinets. He took no documents after 2002. Nothing for 2003.

<u>Cross-Examine</u>

He helped search the video library and guarded guest units and back employee area till sheriffs came

April 21st

He didn't search the administration building or front gate office.

67th Witness Steven Moeller

Santa Barbara County Sheriff Deputy. 30 years. He searched the security office. He was also the scribe. All documents were from 2002 except for 1 page.

<u>Cross-Examine</u>

No prior experience as a detective other than 8 months which was within this search warrant time period. He did not search the administration of the front gate office.

68th Witness Jeff Klapakis

Lieutenant Santa Barbara County. Jan 31, 2004 Search warrant served at Marc Schaffel.

April 25th

69th Witness Kassim Abdool

Worked at Neverland Mid 1990-Mid 1994. Security guard. Head of Security. Worked graveyard shift most of the time he worked there. He knew Jordan Chandler. He saw him on the ranch many times. He says Mj and Jordan arrived at the ranch together alone 2 or 3 times. He says Jordan crashed a golf cart. He says Jordan was wild and wouldn't associate with security or talk to them.

April 25th

He says Wade Robson acted with that same behavior. Brett Barnes was there sometimes without parents. He says there were no rules that he knew of on how to discipline children who were out of control. French doors left open. He saw MJ for the first time that night at 10:00-10:30 pm. He saw Mj and Jordan going towards jacuzzi in swim trunks. He says it was dim lighting in the pool and jacuzzi area. He went to the chef and asked for 2 sodas for Mj. He saw Mj and Jordan walking towards the restroom area. He later saw Jordan riding on Mj's back with Mj with no shirt and a towel wrapped around him and Jordan had a bathrobe on. He says Mj and Jordan went into the house and Mj locked the doors which he says was odd because Mj never locked the doors, that was security's job. He says it was ½ hour from when he saw them walking toward the bathroom till he saw them go in the house. **<u>He went to the locked bathroom where MJ and Jordan were and saw their swim trunks on the ground next to each other.</u>** He asked Ralph Chacon to lock the French door a couple of times. He refused and said he wasn't going in the house. He says this Jordan incident was 93.

April 25th

Peter Pan display outside of Mj office, in the back of the house. He saw Mj and Jordan coming from the hill area by the theater. He saw Mj standing behind Jordan both facing the same direction toward Peter Pan display. He saw Mj give Jordan a kiss on the cheek. He didn't want to testify in LA at a grand jury in 94. He was offered advice, transportation and help from Steve Cochran, Mj attorney in 94. He received a $1,000 per month raise before he testified to a grand jury in LA. He had asked for that raise a couple of months before that. He received death threats toward him and his family. He reported it to the police. He asked to be put in a witness protection program. He says the OSS guards who came on during the first investigation of Mj carried guns. He says he saw them drinking on a ranch. He says they were big people. He says Van Norman, one of the OSS, put a gun to the head of someone at the gate. Told him how to beat people up on Mj tour. Told him he knew a hitman in Europe. Used to walk back and forth in front of his office and stare at him.

April 25th

He says money from the interview was supposed to be used to carry on a civil suit against Mj. Mr. Chacon did tell him what he saw the night that he found the swim trunks next to each other.

Cross Examine

He says there were 3 meetings at Mr. Sanger's office with Steve Cochran, Mj's attorney and an investigator before his grand jury testimony in LA in May of 94. He doesn't remember signing a statement in Jan 94. Now he does after he read it. Worked at Neverland since Jan 91. He says in a statement he never saw Mj do anything sexual to children. Never saw Mj unclothed or any child unclothed with Mj. He says he has 2 children, 9 and 13 and would have no problem leaving them alone with Mj. He says no one at Neverland ever complained about Mj doing anything sexual with children. He and other security sued Mj and the OSS security guards and lost. He has never paid Mj the $1.4 million he was ordered to pay. He was counseled for stealing Mj gasoline. He says he was just replacing what he used when using his own car to go to Solvang. He claimed to be emotionally disabled from what happened at Neverland.

April 25th

He says he was so distraught and depressed that he couldn't work. He was seeking millions because of this in their civil suit. Talked to Gary from Splash, told he was going to be quoted in the "Star". Quit July 31, 94. He never complained to Mj about Van Norman carrying a gun, drinking alcohol or anything else. He never complained to Mj about any of the security OSS at Neverland. He had his photograph taken by Gary for the tabloids. They were called the Neverland 5. They didn't make that name up. He was a former police officer in Trinidad. He didn't call the police when he saw MJ's actions with Jordan. He brought his family to Family Day at the ranch after he saw these things happen with Mj. He says as far as he knows all of the money from interviews went into a fund for a lawsuit against Mj. He was head of security the last 3 to 4 months of his job there. He says they didn't walk around the pool or jacuzzi area when Mj was there with guests. He requested that raise to the head of Mj company.

April 25th

He says that was the first time the OSS security came on ranch was in 93 or 94.

Re-Direct

He says Mj was with little boys sometimes at 3 am. After the gas incident he was still promoted to head of security. He says he wouldn't have lied in his interviews.

Re-Cross

He's not allowed to talk to anybody about this case. He's under a gag order.

70th Witness Jeff Klepakis

Jan 31, 04 Served warrant on Mark Schaffel's home.
#400 Document found in Schaffel's master bedroom.
#401 Document found in locked room in file cabinet.
The house was unoccupied.

<u>Cross-Examine</u>

They booked approximately thousands of documents from that search. They seized computers on a different day. Schaffel did not have other people working out of his house.

71st Witness Det. Craig Bonner

#843 Photos of what was found in Black Briefcase
Did photos July 20

April 25th

#404 3 page document. Seized in a locked closet upstairs in a file cabinet. Stuart Backerman File?
#405 1 page document with Belliard at top. Same file drawer.
#406 14 page document. Hale Lane. Same file

drawer.
#407 10 page document. Spain deal. On top of file cabinets. File titled Ronald.
#410 4 page document. On top of the file cabinet. File titled address book.
#411 – 2 page document. From locked file. Enterprise.
#412 – 5 page document. Same file drawer. Artists Releases.
#413 11 page document. Same file drawer. Model Releases.
#415 47 pages. Living with Mj tape 2 at top. In a black binder on the shelf above the file cabinets.
#417 12 page document. Same locked closet. Folder above file cabinets. David LeGrand File.
#420 28 page document. Same file drawer.
#421 10 page document. Law offices Armstrong Hersh. On top of file cabinets.
#422 Letter of intent from Royalty Advance Funding. 19 pages. On top of the file cabinet. Royalty.
#423 7 pages. Same file drawer. Foreign Rights.

April 25th

Cross-Examine

He wore gloves when he took pictures of briefcases. He was aware that other people were working out of Schaffel's house. He says the 400 exhibits were only 5 to 10 percent of the pages seized. He says they seized thousands of pages.

#414 Copies of floppy discs. Janet Expense and Janet Backup Expense. Found in the same file drawer.
#416 Summary of petty cash expenditures. Receipts etc.
He didn't seize them. He was informed where they were seized from.

#421 Have numbers
#422 On top that
#423 Weren't on there when seized. Put on by DA. Numbers not in sequential order.

Re-Direct

Those numbers were not put on original documents.

#420A Pages that correspond with #420 but has some more pages
He only took photographs of pertinent pages.

Re-Cross

He doesn't know why there are paper clips on the documents.

72nd Witness Det. Victor Alvarez

#402 11/01 Balance Sheet 2 pages. Upstairs Office Desk.
#403 13 pages upstairs Office desk. Fires Brewing.

April 25th

#409 1 page document upstairs office desk. Phone Number.
#419 3 pages. Check, check, stub, etc. Upstairs office desk.

He interviewed Cindy Bell. She said she serves white wine in Diet Coke cans on flights with Mj and he says she told him it was either Mj's idea or Dr. Farshian's idea.

April 26th

73rd Witness Cynthia Montgomery

Travel Consultant. Based in Los Vegas. 21 years in business. Served mostly musicians. She arranged for travel to Brazil. Before she knows Mj through Mark Schaffel. She's known Mark Schaffel for 20 years, not friends anymore. Mj became her client in 2000. Met Dieter Wiesner through Schaffel. She was with Dieter and Mj twice. She met Ronald Konitzer in Las Vegas through Schaffel. She's met Frank Cascio once. She has made private and commercial flights for those men. Mj or Evvy Tavasci set up or called her for Mjj Productions. Schaffel contacted her through Neverland Valley Entertainment. Her billing instructions came from Schaffel or Evvy Tavasci.

April 26th

#251 Documents. Flight manifest. Bill from ExtraJet. Pilots Report. Trip Sheet.
#253 Sept 16, 2003. Documents of arranged flight for Mj. Same documents as above.
#254 Documents. Information on 2 individual flights. Boca Raton to CA Feb 26, 03.

She would call in the catering for Mj flights. She says it was Mrs. Wallace who told her that Mj asked or told her that he wanted his wine served in Diet Coke or soda cans.

#252 Passenger profile for Mj.
#848 2 page F/B document. Passenger Name Record.
#849 Document. Same for Schaffel.

He, Schaffel, called her to set up a 1 way flight to Brazil for the Arvizo's. You can't have a 1 way ticket to Brazil. So she set up the return date. Flight to Brazil was for 3-1-2003.

Cross-Examine

She is testifying under immunity. Her attorney is Robert Moore. **She would not testify without immunity.** She is under investigation by the FBI that she and others secretly videotaped the flight with Mj.

April 26th

She last talked to Schaffel 11-20-03. Schaffel is currently suing Mj for millions of dollars. She is currently suing Mj and Mj is currently suing her for invasion of privacy. She made the arrangements for that flight 11-20-03. She did discuss this flight with Schaffel. **A different airplane company was asked to be used but she and Mr. Schaffel said to stick with XtraJet.** She learned of the videotaping of Mj on that flight 11-21-03. She started booking flights in late 2000/early 2001. She first met Mj at his ranch in 2003 and a 2nd time in October 2003 in Las Vegas. Granted of use immunity. She can still be prosecuted for perjury. Mark Geragos was on that flight with Mj that was videotaped. She has booked many flights for Marc Schaffel to Brazil. She assisted Marc Schaffel with fundraising at Neverland. Schaffel was the one she talked to about the Brazil flight involving Arvizo. No tickets were ever bought, no bill was ever sent. Schaffel still went to Brazil at that time, she thinks. She can't recall. She did buy a ticket for him indirectly.

April 26th

She paid for the flight Mj was videotaped on in cash to XtraJet. She is suing Mj for $50,000. She flew from Las Vegas to Santa Barbara on a different XtraJet flight. The same day as Mj flew from Las Vegas to Santa Barbara on XtraJet, he was videotaped. She was told only by Schaffel things about Neverland Valley Entertainment and 1 of the bookkeepers. **She has knowledge that Schaffel sent bills to Mj's accountants about the money he spent on the Arvizo.** She has booked flights for Cascio's. She last booked a flight for Mj 11-19-03. She filed a lawsuit against Mj in 2004. Company called Oneness. She donates travel for charities. She met with prosecution 1 time. She called the Sheriffs to give info about Mj after she saw a 60 Minutes Special with Ed Bradley. She's had several conversations with Sheriffs regarding things to do with Mj. She called "someone" knowing it was going to be secretly recorded by the Sheriffs.

Re-Direct

She says it was her attorney's idea for immunity. She called after Bradley's interview over the statement that he was mishandled at his arrest.

April 26th

She was there when Mj was arrested in 2003 Nov. Schaffel gave her the address on Trent Court in Calabasas for Janet Arvizo.

Re-Cross

She says everything dealing with immunity was generated by her attorney.

74th Witness – Lt Jeff Klepakis

That address for Janet Arvizo in Calabasas does not exist.

Cross – Examine

He met with Mrs. Montgomery and her attorney on Jan 22, 04. She agreed to make a phone call to be recorded.

75th Witness – Hamid Moslehi

Video Production. Still photography since 1990. He does pre-production and post which includes editing. Mjj production has used his services on 40-50 projects from 1996 to 2003. Mj called him personally a few times. Mj would sometimes be involved with the finished product. He was called to supervise a shoot for Martin Bashir. He became the personal Director of Photography in 1997. 3 sessions. 7-30 Neverland, Neverland 7-31, and Florida 1-03 for Bashir's documentary. He helped Bashir with lighting.

April 26th

1-3 Shoot took place in Florida. Shot video of Arvizo's 3 times. 1st 9-200, 2nd 10-2000, 3rd 2-19-03. He was not present for shots of Gavin and Mj in Bashir video. 9-2000 took video of Gavin and Mj walking around Neverland. 10-2000 The pilot with Starr was host of the Neverland channel. Gavin and other kids were in it. Frank Casio was co-producer. He met Frank on Mj 1996 world tour. He says Frank was there on that tour for 30% of it.

#844 Nov Dec 2002 Picture of Frank and Michael
#27 Christian Robinson
#41 Miko Brando
#39 Joe Marcus

#42 Stuart Backerman
#23 Brad Miller
#18 Ronald Konitzer
#17 Dieter Wiesner
#19 Vinnie Amen
#16 Mark Schaffel
#845 Photo of Mj, Schaffel, Rudy and 2 others
#846 Mj, Nick Carter, Frank, Schaffel, Aaron Carter, Rudy and Brad Buxer
#193 Hamid's House
#194 Hamid's House

He met Brad Miller at his house 2-19-03. He met Stuart at Schaffel's house 2-10-03. 2-18-03. 5 or 6 projects took place the remainder of 2003.

April 26th

Interview with Debbie Rowe at Schaffel's house 2-5-03. Mj new managers at that time were Ronald and Dieter. It was to respond to the Bashir video, the video footage of Debbie Rowe. He says Schaffel was the producer. Schaffel took the video of that interview of Debbie Rowe. He had no employees with him in Florida. He met with Dieter and Ronald at their hotel room in Florida. Mjj Productions owed him about 250,000 dollars from unpaid invoices over 1 ½ years. He was never informed why he went to Florida, he was just informed that it wasn't going to happen. He told Dieter and Ronald that he had behind the scenes footage of Bashir video. They told him to call Schaffel and tell him. He met with Schaffel about it and showed him the footage. Rebuttal documentary of Bashir Documentary. Video footage of Mj family and Arvizo family. He was told by Schaffel to interview Arvizo's. The original shoot was supposed to take place at Neverland. He went Feb 19 to Neverland and arrived at about 6:00 pm. Janet was not at Neverland that day.

April 26th

He talked to Schaffel about Janet not being there. Hamid, he talked to Janet on the phone. He says in the beginning, she was not happy to do the rebuttal video, because of all the media and problems from the Bashir documentary. He did try to persuade her to do it so he could get the production done. After the phone conversation, he says she agreed to do the video rebuttal. It was 9:00 or 10:00 pm after the phone call. He was told on the phone by Schaffel that it wouldn't take place at Neverland. **They shot it at Hamid's House because Schaffel didn't want the Arvizo's to remember where he lived.** Hamid informed **Joe Marcus that he was going to take Arvizo kids to his house to shoot the rebuttal video. Joe told him the Arvizo kids are not allowed to leave the property.** He was allowed to leave Neverland with the kids. It was 30 minutes from the 1st conversation with Joe. They arrived at Hamid's house around 11:00 pm. Starr and Gavin played video games Davellin said he doesn't know. Christian Robinson and Paul were first to arrive at Hamid's house, then Brad Miller asked Christian who he was. They said he was a P.I..

April 26th

Vinnie and Janet arrived at midnight. **He says Janet did her own makeup.** He says there was a problem with the contract or release Paul, Vinnie and Christian were asking Janet to sign. 2 hours passed from the time Janet arrived until they started shooting the video. He says Janet wasn't happy about the contract? He said she must have signed it because Mark Schaffel's people were happy? Shot 1 hour of video for this. He says Paul, Schaffel's associate, wanted those tapes that night. Hamid refused. He wanted to make copies and there were apparently still some issues to resolve. He met with Janet after shooting the video . He says he gave her a loan, he says Janet didn't ask for it, he just offered it. He says Janet never asked him for any money or anything. He gave Janet $2,000. He told her it was a personal loan and she could pay it back when she could. Did most of the rough editing at Schaffel's house. He heard Schaffel on the phone saying we had to get them out of the country.

April 26th

He doesn't know who he was referring to or who he was talking to. Feb 21, 2003 he received a letter from David LeGrand saying his services were no longer needed. He was still owed a lot of money. Mj called him Feb 21, 2003 and told him he did a good job on the video. He received that fax letter from LeGrand after that phone conversation with Mj. He was supposed to meet with Mj 2-26-03 about his unpaid invoices. He went to Neverland to meet with Mj. He thinks Mj saw him, but Mj never acknowledged him. He received a call 19 min later from Evvy. After that conversation, he left Neverland. He didn't know about any surveillance of him, nor did he give permission to anyone to tape him. 2-23-03 day of surveillance of him.

Cross – Examine

4-23-05 He had an interview with Sgt. Robel and his lawyer present and Gordon Auchincloss. One of the purposes of that meeting was to explain why he gave him two thousand dollars. He told Janet it was a loan not a gift and he did expect to get paid back but he never has been paid back.

April 26th

I Films Inc. is the name of his company. Brad Lachman Productions Fox TV hired to put a rebuttal documentary together. He was interviewed also for a rebuttal video. He was filming right next to Bashir's people during Bashir's documentary making. He knew there were positive things that Bashir said about Mj that were left out of Bashir's Documentary. He signed an agreement on 2-14-03 for them to use his voice and words and likeness in his interview of the rebuttal video. He doesn't recall any filming of Mj doctor. The footage of Arvizo's never appeared in that rebuttal documentary. 3-2003 represented by law firm Greenberg Toureg Dieter and Ronald promised him a percentage of net profit of the documentary and the $250,000 he was owed from invoices. He says he has the copyright to the footage of that video he says he owns it because he was never paid. He met Dieter in 1996 on Mj world tour. He says Dieter was a merchandiser for Mj and met Ronald late 2002.

April 27th

Janet never told him she was getting support from Jay Jackson. She didn't tell him about the JC Penney suit either. She (Janet) basically told him nothing about any monetary help she got from celebrities, fundraisers, etc. He understood it to be okay for him to drive the Arvizo children to his house from Janet Arvizo. He does not know the area he was at when he was surveilled. The rebuttal he was filming was supposed to air 2-20-03. He says he worked 250 hrs in 11 days to get this rebuttal done. He says since the equipment was already set up, he just finished Arvizo part of the rebuttal even though he already knew they were past the deadline to use it. He says there was 1 payment made of $200,000 wired to him. He has to this day never turned over the Arvizo video, it was seized by Sheriffs. He hasn't spoken to any Arvizo since Feb 20, 2003. Konitzer told him not to speak to Mj or Evvy. Dieter and Ronald told him they were taking over and would smooth out all of Mj's business problems. He asked Bashir for copies of his footage. Bashir told him he would but never did.

April 27th

He says Bashir wasn't happy that he was also filming. Christian Robinson did the questioning during Arvizo's filming. He is not sure if Christian went over the questions with the Arvizo's. He says the person asking questions usually has a sheet of paper with the questions. He never saw the Arvizo kids or Janet memorizing questions or answer before filming started. He never saw Janet sign any document. He never saw anybody coaching Janet or kids before or during the interview. Vinnie asked him to sign a document and he refused. Feb 8, 2003 at Neverland to meet with 60 Minutes. He was Mj's director of photography at the time. He was there a few hours. He's seen Janet Arvizo at Neverland 2 or 3 times. He first saw her between 2000-2002 at Neverland. First met Miko Brando 1997-1998. Last saw him at the end of Feb 2003. Debbie Rowe interview took place before Arvizo interview. Schaffel didn't want Arvizo to know where he lived but didn't care if Debbie Rowe knew. Evvy didn't want to see his footage. She said Mj's lawyers would take care of it.

April 27th

In a phone conversation with Janet on Feb 19, she was not happy with the media. Janet never told him she was going to be murdered, had death threats or anything else. Never asked him to call the police on her behalf. He is suing Mj for unpaid invoices and damages for use of other footage he did. When Mj called to thank him, he couldn't and didn't see Arvizo's.

Re-Direct

He says they tried to get a rebuttal done as soon as possible. When Fox bought this idea, they set the date. 15 minutes delay due to conversation about release between Janet and Vinnie and other parties. He says Janet seemed more energetic when they started filming. He's seen Mj's bodyguards carry cell phones. He says Mj doesn't carry one but he has seen him, Mj, on a cell phone. Any footage that would have been turned in by midnight of 2-19, it would have been part of the airing on TV. He says Christian and Paul should have known about the deadline. He says it wouldn't have made a difference if he had known about the $20,000 from Louise or the JC Penney money because it was 3 years ago. He still would have lent her the money.

April 27th

Mj told him to call David Legrand about invoices not being paid.

#851 Document letter from David Legrand Feb 21. That his services were no longer needed. He received this a few hours after his conversation with Legrand on the phone.

Re-Cross

He says he probably wouldn't have lent her the $2,000 if he knew she was being supported by Jay Jackson who made almost $80,000 per year.

76th Witness Terry Paulsen

Huntel Systems. 27 years. Air to ground telephone calls.

#850 Documents phone calls made from Aircraft. Feb 7 2003 bill sent to XtraJet.

The ground station has a number that shows up on the bill. Last call from Aircraft was at 9:28 pm over Grand Canyon, AZ.

<u>Cross Examination</u>

They can't tell which plane makes the calls, they don't know who makes the calls either. She doesn't know if people actually talked to each other. She just knows it was connected.

April 27th

76th Witness Gabriel Dominguez

Custodian of records for T-Mobile. Worked there for 4 years. Testified 60 to 70 times.

#452 Billing records

Call detail records for Chris Carter, Frank Cascio, Vinnie Amen, Evvy Tavasci and Christian Robinson. From Jan to March of 2003. Chris Carter's work number is the same as Evvy Tavasci's home number.

Cross Examine

You can have similar numbers for large amounts of phones.

77th Witness Anne-Marie Sims

SBC Phone Company. 25 years. Custodian of record 2 years.

#451 Billing Subscriber Records
Evvy Tavasci (#1)
2 Home Phone #
Aja Pryor (#2)
Neverland Valley Ent. 5 different lines (#3)
Miko Brando (#4)
David Ventura 3-14 section. Call to Santa Ynez
Long Distance (#5)

These are completed calls because they don't register if somebody doesn't answer.

Jay Jackson (#6)
Mjj Productions (#7)
Chris Tucker (#9)
Country Inn Calabasas (#10)
Burrows Jr High (#11)
Kaiser Foundation (#12)
Enterprise Rent A Car (#13)

Cross-Examine

Chris Tucker (#9)

818-757-****
Jay Jackson (#6)
213-739-****
Call Chris Tucker twice on Feb 4
David Ventura (#5)
626-575-****
Several calls to a number in Guadalupe 805-343-**** in March

All these phones listed are land lines

78th Witness Joseph Shebroe

Verizon Wireless. 7 years.

#456 Billing and Subscriber Records

Debbie Rowe (#2)
Jesus Salas
Paul Hugo
Frank Cascio

Account Summary for Frank Cascio (#3)
213-07** # (#4)
(#5)
Switch Records (#6)
Apr 2003 (#7)
Acct info for Debbie Rowe (#10)

There is a 3-way calling feature with Verizon Wireless. Letter (0). Call forwarding. Letter (F)

April 27th

Cross-Examine

All Cell Phones

79th Witness Jeanne Mulcahy

Cingular Wireless. AT&T Wireless.

#453 Records AT&T
Paul Hugo (#3)
Mjj Productions Miko Brando (#4)
Rudy Provencio (#5)
Mjj Productions. Paul Hugo, Rudy Provencio (#6)
Mjj Productions Miko Brando (#7)
(Mjj) Miko Brando, 5 telephone # Assoc, 3 Entries for Evvy Tavasci (#9)

#454 Records Cingular
Ann Kite (#1)
Evvy Tavasci (#2)

3 W for 3-way Calling_

Cross-Examine

No

80th Witness Deborah Rowe Jackson

1997-1999 married to Mj. Knew Mj for 20 years. Divorced Oct 1999. They never shared a home or apartment. Mj had custody of the children. She could see the children every 45 days for 8 hours. Lasted 1 ½ years. Voluntarily agreed to give up parental rights in 2001. She last saw her children 2 ½ to 3 years ago

April 27th

Arnold Kline Dermatologist. She was his assistant 1979-2001. After speaking to Dr. Kline, he and she spoke to Marc Schaffel on Feb 7 in the morning. Prior to this, she didn't know Bashir or about the documentary. She talked to Mj 30 minutes later. The last time she had talked to Mj was Oct 1999. Mj told her there was a bad video coming out. He asked her to work with Ronald, Dieter and Marc. Ronald asked for her help in the rebuttal video. She was supposed to work with Schaffel. She told him she needed a confidentiality agreement. She signed a confidentiality agreement when her and Mj got divorced. She couldn't talk about Mj, the kids or her life with Mj. She got an exemption to this so she could talk to Schaffel about helping Mj. Her interview was at Schaffel's house. Hamid, Stuart, Marc, Christian, her lawyer, Iris, Rudy and Ian Drew. She did this interview because she promised to always be there for Mj and the children. She wanted to be re-introduced to her kids and Mj. She didn't know what questions were going to be asked.

April 27th

She didn't want anybody to say it was rehearsed, that's why she didn't want to prepare or see questions. She didn't answer those questions truthfully and honestly. She said it's her personal life, the media would twist it. 9hr interview only 3 hr tape. Mj parenting the children was some of the questions she didn't answer truthfully.

April 28th

Her attorney was at the interview but not with her the entire time. Mr. Drew told her there were 105 questions on interview papers. Schaffel would ask her to rephrase an answer or ask Mr. Drew to rephrase the question. Schaffel told her they were excited and they would be going to Neverland soon. To this day, she has still not seen her children. She has parental rights again after going back to court. Her motivation to do this interview was so she could see her children.

Cross-Examine

She called Schaffel every week for 3 months. She agreed to call people and let sheriffs record the conversations. Schaffel, Ian Drew, Dieter.

April 28th

She met Ian Drew and Schaffel for the 1st time at the interview. Entire interview she was completely positive towards Mj. She says she thought Schaffel was using and trying to take advantage of Mj, manipulating Mj so he, Schaffel, could make lots of money. She thought the same of Dieter and

Ronald. She definitely got the impression that Dieter, Ronald and Marc were working together. She says Mj is removed and he a lot of times is not consulted on a lot of decisions that are made. She still considers Mj her friend. She met Dieter once, and talked to him on the phone twice. She learned from Schaffel that he was making money off her interview. Schaffel told her he was going to sue Mj 6 months ago. Schaffel told her he was involved in business with Dieter and Ronald in Europe. She considers all 3 to be liars. Schaffel told her Drew was a plant at a tabloid. Schaffel bragged to her constantly about the money he was going to make off Mj. Dieter told her he and Ronald were going to take over all of Mj's business dealings. She says it was a mistake whoever hired Mark Geragos.

April 28th

Last talked to Schaffel 2 weeks ago. She last talked to Ian Drew a month ago. Last talked to Dieter a while ago. Last talked to Ronald shortly after the video. She didn't know if any discussion on the phone with her was recorded. She told Sgt. Robel that Schaffel told her he made $7.5 million dollars off her interview. She says Mj is very easily manipulated if he is scared. She thinks Schaffel told her it was FOX and someone in Europe is how he made the $7.5 million. She says Mj is generous to a fault. First met Mj in the 80s at her work office with Dr. Kline, a dermatologist. She worked with Kline for about 20 years. She went on the

Dangerous Tour with Mj. She also went on the History Tour. They were married at that time. She says Schaffel was giving information to the tabloids. She met with Ron Zonen last night. She watched her interview.

Re-Direct

They told her she was helpful in doing the interview. Schaffel told her he was on the outs and he wanted to get back in. She hasn't spoken to Mj.

April 28th

Mj has known Konitzer since the 90s. She may have met Dieter in the 90s, she's not sure. She knew Frank Cascio. She met him when he was a teenager. She says Mj was close with all the Cascio's.

81st Witness Iris Joan Finsilver

Lawyer since 1986. California since 1989. Family Law lawyer. Rowe's attorney since 1996. Schaffel said at least twice Mj would be happy with her answers and she, Debbie, would go to Neverland and see Mj and her kids.

82nd Witness Andrew Dietz

Air Apparent Inc, Los Angeles. Arranges travel reservations etc. Since 1980. Mjj Productions has been a client for 15 years. He pays and then sends out an invoice to the customer for payment.

#223 through #249 Documents dealing with his business with Mjj Productions
#224 Itinerary slash. Invoice #. Agent Coupon. Their copy of the transaction.
#852 3 page document Air Apparent
#853 5 page document Air Apparent

April 28th

Each customer has an account #. Void stamped on the ticket means that ticket wasn't used. Marie Nicole Cascio, Aldo Cascio, M Lerraque (All tickets voided). Only Mj tickets were used. Return tickets to LA.
#854 Documents Transactions 2-1 – 2-11
#855 Documents Transactions from 2-12-03 – End of 3-2003
#853 – 0143505 Invoice #. $6,646.00

Only 1 person traveled on 3-1-03 of the 4, just Mj. He doesn't know if he's seen #854 and #855 before the prosecution showed them to him.

Cross-Examination

He doesn't know for sure if, in fact, it was Mj that used that ticket. Evvy is the one who contacts him for flight arrangements etc. Doesn't mean Evvy called it in but she has to approve everything.

Re-Direct

A person cannot travel on somebody else's ticket.

83rd Witness Jeffery Schwartz

Talk America. Long distance Internet provider and phone.

#458 Subscriber. Paper for Jay Jackson Toll Records Jan, Feb, Mar 2003.

Feb 18-Feb 19 Completed calls to Wyckoff, Nj

Cross-Examine

They, Talk America, doesn't provide cell phone service. (Phone # 213-739-**** Jay Jackson) Records start Jan 1, 2003. His regular carrier was Pac-Bell. He's been in the phone business for 9 years.

#451 Phone Record
(#6) PG-3 – Calls to Reseda Long Distance?

That shows up on the Pac-Bell bill, not on the Talk America bill. 3 calls on 2-11 to Santa Barbara.

84th Witness Crystalee Danko

#455 Sprint call phone record and land line records.

(#1) 702-362-****

D Legrand 702-222-****
Law Firm 702-365-****
Hale Lane

(#2) Geragos and Geragos
213-864-****
213-625-****

(#3) Vincent Amen
201-838-****

(#4) F. Marc Schaffel
818-87*-****

(#5) Maria Farshchian
Jan, Feb, March 2003

April 28th

Feb 7 2003 billing information for Schaffel

85th Witness Jennifer Simmons

#450 Nextel Phone Record

Feb 2003

(#1) 310-901-****
818-402-****

(#2) March Billing for those 2 numbers
(#3) April Billing Evvy Tavasci
(#4) Subscriber History

Numerous phone numbers listed to Evvy Tavasci. All bills going to a P.O. Box. Some say Mjj Productions, some don't.
(#7) 4 additional Phone's registered to Evvy Tavasci. Feb 2003
(#8) Numbers March April
(#9) 2003 Evvy

These are all wireless phone #s

86th Witness Joe Corral Jr.

27 years Verizon

#457 Verizon Telephone Records California
#459 NY Records. Frank Cascio Billing add in New Jersey Landline
#457 Landlines Neverland Ranch Jan-Mar 2003

(#5) Rudy Provencio
310-47*-****

#457 All Calls

Tab 4 #22 PG to

April 29th

87th Witness Det. Craig Bonner

#827 Audio Tape. Rec Janet Arvizo and Frank Tyson, taken to Lab to determine if any breaks in tape.

<u>Cross- Examine</u>

He did not seize this item that he took to the lab. This tape came from Brad Miller's office.

88th Witness Dr. Harry Koons

Scientist at Aerospace Corporation in El Segundo. 37 years. He is responsible for the audio forensics work. "Normally" they can tell if a tape is a compilation of different taped conversations. Started doing forensic work on audio tapes in 1995. He's done about 200. This is his first time testifying in court. His first impression was that it was continuous. 13 seconds into tape a gap in the continuity of tape. He found 34 gaps in tape.

(#1) Pause Button
(#2) Press to talk telephone
(#3) Mute button on telephone
(#4) Voice activated line

Small microphone on handset. Plug-in device or in line sensor. These are the ways to record phone conversations. He says there's evidence this is a 2nd generation tape.

April 29th

<u>He cannot determine if this is a compilation of</u>

tapes or not. He doesn't know for sure if this is a first generation tape or second generation tape.

#858 Record of amplitude from tape beginning.
2:37 into a tape.
#857 Different look at break in the tape at same time on the tape.

He says he thinks all the breaks in this tape were all for the same reason? He says this is not a voice activated recorder used for this tape.

Cross-Examine

He doesn't know how long the tape was stopped for each time. He says it stopped automatic gain control on this recorder. He did not do a physical analysis of the tape. There are Labs that do this. He says it's a possible malfunction of the recorder but not likely he says.

89th Witness Det. Rose Smith

LA Police Dept. 20 years. Investigates stalking and workplace violence. 9 years Sex Crimes Investigator. Aug 93 search at Neverland. She searched the master bedroom.

#841 Boys will be boys. Hardcover book.

She seized that book. Clothed and nude pictures of little boys. Found in the file cabinet. Locked inside. Locked room inside Mj bedroom.

#842 The Boy. A photographic essay.
Some clothed, some nude little boys. She also seized it. Found in a file cabinet in a locked room in Mj bedroom.

#856 A photo of a search warrant and a photo of a file cabinet where books were seized from the 3rd drawer.

Cross-Examine

Warrant issued by LA Judge in 93. Those books are not unlawful to possess by adults in California.

#842 has an inscription to Mj from your (heart xxxooo) Rhonda? 1993 Chicago maybe.

#841 Has inscription also. Look at the true spirit of happiness and joy in these boys' faces. This is the life I want for my children.

May 2

90th Witness Beverly Wagner

Works for US Bank. Worked at Santa Monica Branch in 2003.

#418 PG3. Check from Neverland Valley Entertainment. Amount $1,000,000 dollars. This check was cashed Fred Marc Schaffel

#419 PG3. Check for $500,000. This check was cashed also Fred Marc Schaffel

Cross-Examine
Schaffel had 3 accounts at this bank. Mj on account. She's not sure if Mj ever signed anything on this account other than a signature card.

May 2nd

91st Witness Det. Craig Bonner

He analyzed and put together all phone records.

#859 - #882
#859 Feb 5, 2003 Call regarding parties involved.

Records and spreadsheets for all these phone calls (below)
#859 - #867 Feb 5, 2003 , Feb 16, 2003.
#871 Feb 20, 2003
#875 - #879 March 5, 2003 , March 9 2003

All these exhibits listed were created by Det. Bonner. #200 - #218 Records from Turnberry Inn, which he used to make some of his charts. Phone calls 2 on 2-4-03 from Janet Arvizo's parents. Calls from Frank Cascio to Schaffel or vice versa started at around 1:00 am and ended around 9:00 pm. Frank to Evvy calls 1st 3:42 pm last around 9:00 pm. Schaffel to Brandon Room started 10:40 am and ended around 10:00 pm. Evvy and Jay Jackson lasted 3 minutes. This call was after

Presidential Suite Call 2-5-03 , 2-6-03. 19 calls between Schaffel and Cascio. 38 calls between Cascio and Schaffel on 2-12-03, started 12:24 am. 19 calls between Vinnie and Frank, interspersed throughout the day.

May 2nd

2-13-03
Frank 12 calls with Vinnie and 7 with Schaffel.

2-14-03
Frank 2 calls to Vinnie, 3 with Schaffel and 4 with Janet's parent's phone.

2-15-03
Frank 11 calls with Vinnie, 14 with Jay Jackson's phone. Appears a lot of these calls revolve around Frank's phone.

2-16-03
Frank 3 calls with Jay Jackson's phone. 4 with Vinnie, 1 with Schaffel, 1 with Neverland.

2-20-03
Frank 13 calls with Schaffel, 7 with Neverland and 31? with Vinnie's phone.

3-5-03
Frank 5 with Neverland Miko Brando, Mjj Productions. 14 calls with Evvy Tavasci home phone.

3-6-03
Frank 4 calls with Neverland, 12 calls with Mjj Production Miko Brando with Mjj Production Evvy Tavasci.

3-7-03
Frank 5 with Neverland, Neverland 6? Calls with Mjj Production Evvy Tavasci. Evvy Mjj Production 20 calls with Mjj Production Miko Brando.

3-8-03
No Frank calls. 12 Evvy home calls with Kenneth Morgan room at Beverly Hilton Hotel. This day calls related to Evvy 3 phones, Neverland, Miko Brando.

3-9-03
Frank 3 with Neverland, 2 with Schaffel. Evvy Mjj Production 12 calls with Schaffel. This is incorrect, should be 12 calls with Neverland started at 8:48 am ended 8:19 pm

Cross-Examine

He couldn't determine if Mj was ever on a single one of these phone calls. Some calls under 30 seconds were omitted completely. **1st call involving Rudy Provencio was Feb 8, 2003.** Calls going to the Hotels only show going to Hotel, they don't actually know who was spoken to. **Feb 4, 2003, he didn't do a chart for. There were calls involving people in this case on that day.** 2 calls on Feb 4, 2003 from Jay Jackson phone to phone #

in Reseda 818-75*-**** Chris Tucker. 6:11 pm and 6:14 pm 4 minutes each. He does not know how many rooms the Presidential Suite has or how many phones or how many people went in or out and used those phones. No summary chart for Feb 11th. Jay Jackson phone long distance 3 calls to Santa Barbara. 1 call to the Santa Barbara Police dept. . 2 calls **possibly** to the Santa Barbara Sheriffs Dept.

May 2nd

3-12-03 Summary shows no calls from Janet's parents' house to Buelton or Guadalupe. Guadalupe 343-50** didn't determine whose phone # this was. 1st call 11:25 pm, next call 3-13-03 8:45 pm. 3-14-03 through 3-18-03, 8 calls to the same number in Guadalupe lasting a total of 84 minutes. 3-19 through 3-21, 7 calls to the same number in Guadalupe lasting a total of 83 minutes. Nobody tried to figure out whose number this is in Guadalupe. Could it be Mr. Vivanco? Whoever that is. Evvy was responsible for getting phones for other people or employees.

2-7-03
13 phone calls from Gavin, Franklin Turnberry Room to Jay Jackson's phone and Janet's parents' phone.

2-15-03
Second time Rudy Provencio's phone shows up. 8 of 14 calls between Jay's phone and Frank. 1 of 5

Janet's calls with Frank. Janet's parents called Frank's phone.

12 - Feb 15, 2003 calls from Jay Jackson home phone to a phone # in New Jersey related to Frank Cascio.

May 2nd

92nd Witness Det. Paul Zellis

#868 Phone Record Charts

2-17-03
#869 Phone Record Feb 18
#870 Phone Record Feb 19
#880 Phone Record 3-10-03
#882 Phone Record 3-12-03
#881 Phone Record 3-11-03

2-17-03
12 calls from Carter phone # to Jay Jackson phone #, none longer than a minute. 4 calls from Rudy Provencio # to Schaffel #.

Feb 18-03
Jay calls Carter phone # at 6:00 am. Call to Cascio phone # at 6:06 pm.

2-19-03
Frank 10 calls with Vinnie. 9 calls with Jay and 13 calls with Neverland and 6 with Schaffel.

3-10-03
Frank 13 phone calls with Neverland. Vinnie 1 with Jay. 4 with Neverland. 5 with Schaffel.

3-11-03
Frank's phone calls. 11 with Neverland. Vinnie 1 with Neverland. 2 with Schaffel. 2 with Janet's parents #. 1 with Rudy Provencio. 3 with Jay Jackson.

3-12-03
Frank 13 calls with Neverland. 4 with Vinnie. Jay 6 calls with Neverland. Vinnie 4 with Schaffel. Schaffel 1 with Provencio.

May 2nd

Cross-Examine

2-19-03 was the day of Rebuttal that was originally supposed to be done at Neverland but had to be done in LA because that's where Janet Arvizo was.

May 3rd

93 Witness David Saunders

Chief investigating officer. District Attorney 2 ½ years. Police officer 19 years.

#872 3-2-03 Diagram of phone calls
#873 3-3—03 Diagram of phone calls

#874 3-4-03 Diagram of phone calls

3-2-03
Frank 1 phone call Evvy home, 6 calls, Evvy Mjj Production. 4 calls Vinnie. The calls from Paul Hugo to Schaffel came from Brazil. Last call from Brazil by Paul Hugo was to Neverland?

3-3-03
Frank 4 calls with Neverland. Vinnie 6 calls with Neverland.

3-4-03
Paul Hugo calls Vinnie 5 times from Brazil. Calls Schaffel 3 times from Brazil. Vinnie calls Neverland 3 times. Frank calls Neverland 4 times.

May 3rd

<u>Cross-Examine</u>

He is aware there are multiple phone #s at Neverland and many extensions. Cannot determine from phone records who actually called from Paul Hugo's phone in Brazil? Or who answered the phone at Neverland on that day. He was not aware that Paul Hugo was a production associate of Schaffel, he just knew they were connected somehow.

94th Witness Lt. Jeff Klepakis

310-49*-**** called that number yesterday

morning. Talked to Brad Miller.

Cross-Examine

They knew of Brad Miller before the search on 11-18-03, but they just called his number yesterday to determine that was his number?

95th Witness Sgt. Craig Bonner

None of the information from Phone Company records related to Brad Miller.

#884 4 page document compilation of phone records of Miller's number and other numbers of people involved in this case.

#885 22 page document. Diagrams of information contained in #884.

May 3rd

These are all cell phones. Frank, Vinnie's and Evvy involved with Brad Miller's phone #.

2-15-03
Frank calls Brad Miller 7 times. Brad Miller called Frank 4 times.

Video of Mj having a conversation with Bashir was found at Schaffel's house. Mj saying "during flying you don't have a little bit of Jesus Juice, a little bit of wine."

Cross-Examine

They don't have any toll records for the Brad Miller phone. They have one page that shows subscriber info Hamid Mosefarian? Tape Mj/Bashir summer 2002. Louise Palanker's interview lasted 45 minutes with Sgt. Bonner and Det. Zellis.

96th Witness Det. Steve Robel

Debbie Rowe Interview March 3, 2004 with him and Klepakis was taped with her knowledge. She refers to Mj as a sociopath and his children as possessions. She told him that her statements were false and it was all part of her, Debbie Rowe and Mj's plan after their divorce and during any interview. No loss seized from Ranch are after Dec 31, 2002.

#335 Log entries
#334 from 2003

These have been in the defense possession over a year.

Cross-Examine

Debbie Rowe said things in open court that he did not ask her in their interview! He did not know she was in a custody thing with Mj over their children.

97th Witness John Duross O'Bryan

CPA Alex Partners. Managing Director. He has participated in Financial Accounting Investigations. Forensic Accounting Investigations is much more invasive than just an audit. He was asked to look at the financial state of Mj up to Feb 2003. Financial condition assets compared with liabilities. Assets minus liability gives you a net worth.

6-30-02
Balance sheet only
Total Assets $130 million
Total Liabilities $415 million
Net Worth (-$285 million)

Assets could have higher or lower value. Same for liabilities. They did see financial advisor statements. They didn't get everything they wanted to look at in case.

May 3rd

Expenditures have exceeded income. Liabilities have increased. Ongoing Cash Crisis as of Feb 2003. Spent $20-30 million. Spent more than he made per year. Reduced his net worth. Debt rose approximately $70 million from 1999 to Feb 2003. Mj 3 main assets. His catalog Mi-Jack, Sony Catalogue, Neverland.

Holthouse CPA from Mj CPA
10-13-99 memo
Short $780,000 to meet outstanding

liabilities. $11.5 million received on catalogues. Expenditures of over $20 million in 1999. $11 million (1999) of interest with 2 loans from Bank of America. So total expenditure is 99, $31 million. $11.5 million in earnings.

1 Line of credit. 1 set loan started at $140 million and has grown to $200 million. Additional $26 million owed to Sony. As of 2000, $3.5 million of obligation. There would be a substantial tax on selling those catalogs.

May 3rd

$20 million line of credit. June 14th, 2000, letter concerned about Mj's rate of spending. Debt $200 million. Line of credit $35 million. Unable to pay vendors. Threatening action. Catalogues are now at risk. Ming Ho Lee, Oct 01. Mj financial advisor. 16 month period. $31 million spent. Looked at his debt increase from 2001 to 2004.

Feb 13, 2003
IBM Financial Consultants for Mj at the time concerned about his excessive spending habits. Loan Balances $70 million Mi Jack. Bank of America Loan (Sony) $200 million. $10.5 million of unpaid vendor invoices. $38,000 in the bank.

Cross-Examine

1999 – 2000 - 2001 – 2002 – 2003
1999 They liked to see financial statements, bank statements and ledgers. Were not made available by the **prosecution.** He hasn't talked to anybody from the defense. Sony Catalogue estimated value at $1 Billion dollars. He never hired an appraiser to appraise Sony Catalogue's worth. Not aware of anybody wanting to purchase Mj interest in Sony Catalogue.

May 3rd

He never saw that specific document from David LeGrand regarding Mj selling his part of Sony Catalogue. He would be able to pay off his debt and still have $200 million before royalties. Mj has never gone bankrupt. He didn't see current appraisals of Mj assets. He never advised anybody in the entertainment industry. 1999 value of Mi Jack catalogue $128 million dollars. Less debt and taxes if sold. Debt as of Feb 2003. $200 million Bank of America Loan. $24 Mi Jack Loan. $10.5 million to vendors. He says $7 million from a rebuttal video wouldn't make much difference. 2000 value on Neverland about $50 million dollars.

Re-Direct

He says the Mi Jack catalogue had decreased in value from 99 to 03. Has put an option on

December 05 on Sony Catalogue for $200 million. His tax liability would be $40 million. His loan is due on Dec 20, 05, from Bank of America $200 million. Neverland is cross-collateralized with the Mi Jack loan that has reached $70 million. Mj was accruing $20-$30 million per year in debt.

May 3rd

Re-Cross

He considered the values of catalogues but did have them appraised for his evaluation. Mj shares Sony Catalogue in Feb 2003, he believes was worth $200 million. He is not aware of someone offering Mj $400 million for his part of the catalogue in 2003. He, the witness, has done this kind of analysis for David Bowie.

98th Witness Rudy R Provencio

Independent Contractor. Music for film or television. Entertainment business 20 years. First met Schaffel in high school in 1983-1984. Benefit single "What More Can I Give" Charity single to benefit people of the charities Mj picks. Would have been different versions of the same song called CD-5. He was invited into enterprise with Schaffel and Mj in June 2001. He was hired on salary for this. June 2001-Feb 25, 2003, was his tenure. Aug 2003 was when he stopped going into office. He was GM of Neverland Valley Entertainment.

May 3rd

Neverland Valley Entertainment he says is Marc Schaffel and Mj Company. Mj, Schaffel, himself, Dieter and Ronald were on the fringes. He says Mj told him this had to make more money and be bigger than "We Are The World." His salary was $225,000 and a point on the record which is a 1 percent of gross sales. Mj and Schaffel signed documents giving him this 1 percent. Schaffel was president of Neverland Valley Entertainment. He says Mj came to the studio in the beginning 3 to 4 times a month. He says Mj would call him at home late at night. Neverland Valley Entertainment offices were at Schaffel's house in Calabasas. He frequently overheard Schaffel's phone conversations with a lot of people including Mj. He says Mj would call 10 times a week and be on the phone for hours. He says Mj was financing this project from a loan Mj and Schaffel got for $10 million dollars from Parvise. Deposited into Schaffel's bank "US Bank" in Santa Monica.

May 4th

The artists on "What More Can I Give" were not going to be paid. He says Mj has 2 different voices, 1 normal, 1 angry. He says Schaffel would call Mj "Arnold". Mj would say French Fries to Schaffel and that would mean Mj wanted money. He heard Mj a couple of times get cash from Schaffel. Schaffel got fired in Nov 2001 by fax, by one of Mj's lawyers. It was about his past in Adult

Entertainment. He, Schaffel, still continued getting paid and still had that bank account at US Bank. He gave 1 percent in this venture back to
Mj. Rebuttals, RMA Awards and the Bambi's in Germany. These were other things Neverland Valley Entertainment was involved in. June 2003 was the last time he, Rudy, talked to Mj in Gary, Indiana. Katherine Milofski, press person from Great Britain. She sent him a transcript from Bashir Documentary. Phones were very busy at NVE before this aired on television. The press was asking, "Who is this boy Mj is sleeping with", that was there #1 question. He says Stuart Backerman and Vinnie were brought in.

May 4th

Schaffel contacted Ronald and Dieter about the content of the transcript of the Documentary or after it was seen on TV. Feb 1st conference call between Schaffel, Dieter and Mj, he listened to it in his office. Mj was asked to call Debbie Rowe so she could do a rebuttal. Schaffel and Dieter told Mj that the Arvizo's could Black Mail him and ruin his career. Discussion of rebuttal so he could put some money in his pocket and save Mj career. Schaffel told Mj that the network could make the money or he, Mj, could make the money. Mj brought up the point of the Arvizo's needed to be in rebuttal. Feb 2 or 3, 2nd Conference call, he listened as
well. Dieter, Mj and Schaffel. He says Mj and Dieter were not at Neverland. Dieter, **Ronald?,** Mj involved in the video. Schaffel told Mj about taking

Arvizo's to Florida. Dieter told Mj they needed to do a press conference. There was no concern about Arvizo's he says. Debbie Rowe was not talked about in 2nd conversation. Debbie Rowe's interview took place a couple of days after the second phone call.

Juror Notebook 5

Chapter 5

May 4th

Debbie, her lawyer, Schaffel, Ian Drew, Hamid Moslehi, Stuart Backerman, Christian Robinson and himself were at the Debbie Rowe Interview.

#888 – Picture of Interview (Debbie) in Schaffel's house. Schaffel's working on the questions and answers in the picture.

Ian Drew sent over 100 approximate questions. At the time there were no answers, later there were answers. He says Schaffel was telling Debbie Rowe a lot how to answer questions to make them better. (1) About Mj's parents skills, she said Mj was a good parent. Schaffel told her she was going to see her kids soon. She was doing good. Schaffel thought Debbie Rowe could cry better and she did. Mark Geragos called a couple of times during the interview. Before that if Vinnie was at the house, Geragos called all the time.

#887- Mj cd "Invincible" Credit to Schaffel. Thank you for all your help Love Michael. Credit to Frank Casio. Pretty much the same thing. Other Casio family Bob Jones? Love Mj.

May 4th

#400 Work agreement for Schaffel with Neverland Valley Entertainment

#401 4 pages agreement over song and gives him his point.
#402 Reports of money spent.
#405 Document from Belliard Feb 2003
#409 Compilation of phone # Gavin Arvizo's is on there
#410 Same as 409
#413 Paper Vinnie's handwriting
#423 Parvise documents for the loan that Mj and Schaffel signed.

He says Mj was a main decision maker for Neverland Valley Entertainment. Mark Schaffel and Vinnie talked about "killers." Gavin had 2 visits to Schaffel's home. The "Killers" that were after the Arvizo's. Rudy was alarmed by those comments. He asked Vinnie about this on the phone, Vinnie told him there were no killers and they were calling him a faggot at school. Mark told him he can't talk right now he says they just escaped. He was in Michigan during this time 3-6 or 3-7 taking care of his dying father. He called Vinnie and Vinnie told him the same thing. He left Neverland Valley Entertainment at the beginning of March.

May 4th

<u>Cross – Examine</u>

He says he's been taking notes and keeping journals since he was a teenager. He first talked to Sheriff's in 2004. Middle of Feb 2003 was the first time he "met" Arvizo's at Schaffel's house. Gavin was with Vinnie. Mid February was the talk of "killers" that happened. He says Schaffel called the Arvizo's "stupid Mexicans." He says he took notes only to keep track of what was going on. He wrote "killers" Feb 1 2003 in his notes this was before Bashir Documentary was on tv. He's recorded phone calls with Mrs. Milofsky 20 times, Vinnie 10 times, Schaffel 10 times. 4 people. Quite a few times. He says he never recorded anybody's phone calls before he went to law enforcement. **He never called police when he thought something was going on or was concerned about the Arvizo family?** In February? He waited until after the Raid on Neverland to cooperate with Sheriffs. He stayed in contact with Schaffel after the Arvizo's had escaped quite often.

May 4th

5 months after the "escape" he goes to Gary. Indiana with Schaffel and Mj? 1st week of March, March 6th is when he says he heard the Arvizo's had escaped. Debbie Rowe Interview in his notes 2-2-03. Either a lot of his dates are wrong or he didn't write down a lot of dates. Formed LLC with Vinnie, Mark and possibly Frank in early 2003. "Steal the stage LLC" registered in New Jersey. Mj was not part of this. He, Rudy, had no meetings with Schaffel and Vinnie about this company. He started cooperating with Sheriffs in 2004. Maury Povich Interview took place on the 3rd week of February. He inquired about a month ago who helped the Arvizo's "escape" Neverland. He says Janet Arvizo was weird and she was flipping out on 2-1-03, but he's never met her. He's just listening to other people and writing it down. He says everything

started going crazy on Jan 24th after they got the script of Bashir Documentary. He says Mark told him the Arvizo's were poor and ghetto in late Jan but Mark hadn't met them yet.

May 4th

He told Milofsky Mj had no idea what was going on. He knows Mark and Vinnie gave Arvizo's money to go shopping. He says everybody was making money with and off of Mj, but he says Mj has no idea how much money people made off of him. He never had a business relationship with Dieter or Ronald. He says he spoke with Mj on the phone twice and met him in person 10 or 12 times. He helped Schaffel pick up stones for his house in summer 2003. He talked to Vinnie about another benefit, not Schaffel, after he left Neverland Valley Entertainment. He kept in touch with all the people he says were part of Train Wreck going on in 2003. Jan 31 2004 interview with Sgt Robel. He, Rudy, told him Mj probably didn't know what was going on with the Arvizo family. Mark Schaffel directed everything. He found his notes in his storage unit about a month ago. Schaffel rejoined the team of Wiesner and Konitzer in the beginning of February 2003? He didn't tell police about answers, just questions regarding the Debbie Rowe Interview.

May 4th

He never mentions the word "Killers" to Sgt Robel in the January 31, 2004 interview. He didn't want this interview tape recorded and he would tell them everything he knows. Mj usually tells people he's giving credit to that he loves them. He first met Christian Robinson in 2001. He says he heard that Christian had made $10,000 selling a picture of Mj to ABC. He last saw Christian in Gary, Indiana. He says Chris Tucker and his girlfriend were witnesses to Arvizo's ability to come and go at Neverland. He doesn't remember saying this. He says Mark was the mastermind and let everybody know what was going on. He learned Schaffel had stolen money from a woman in Japan and still kept working with him. Cyndi Montgomery he met her around the time of the supposed "Brazil trip." He says Schaffel was a prolific liar. He ran into Schaffel after 9 years when he was working for Warner Music in 1993. He told her Cyndi he wasn't giving his detailed notes because that's a book money even though he says he has no intention of writing book?

Ian Barkley worked with Christian. He, Rudy, never saw Ian with Mj. He talked to Schaffel last month. He last saw him in person in Ohio. He says he was tempted to go to the tabloid but he didn't. He told Vinnie that Mj gave a million dollars to Marlon Brando. He told Vinnie, Schaffel stole a million dollars from the woman in Japan. He has discussed this case with Ian Drew, most recently a couple of days ago. He says Schaffel wrote the note about Larry Schiller in his (Rudy) notes. Larry Schiller writes books about trials? Never re-written his notes. Never added to his notes he says. He says Backerman came on to work on fallout from Bashir Documentary. He says he probably talked to Cyndi Montgomery about her secretly videotaping Mj on a flight. He says he was uncertain if she had done it or not. He says it was an accident that he recorded Cyndi. **Once or twice**. September 13 of 2003 he Rudy worked with Cyndi at a party at Neverland for charity. He wasn't certain all money was going to charity.

May 4th

He says Schaffel went to Brazil that he knew of 5 times over a couple of years. Cyndi booked all those flights, he says. He says he saw only questions and no **answers** to Arvizo's rebuttal. He says Ian Drew and Schaffel don't like each other. He says he never listened to any conversations between Schaffel and Geragos. He heard conversations between Vinnie and Geragos but only Vinnie's half. He's taking notes right up to this point in present time. He made corrections for a police report of a past interview he had. DA Gordon gave him a report. 2 months ago. This interview was very old. Report he added Mj to this report? Of Schaffel and Dieter and Ronald were doing illegal or wrong things.

Re-Direct

He says Mj did know what's going on and he would ask questions frequently. He says his notebooks random entries not like a diary dates weren't made in order in notebooks. Different styles of writing for different paragraphs.

May 4th

He says Schaffel spoke derogatory terms to everybody. At some stage, Vinnie, Frank, and Marc started talking favorably about the Arvizo's. He says Marc said the Arvizo's are deeply religious. Vinnie, Frank, and Marc called Janet Arvizo "crack whore." Marc told him "mom" flipping out. Never heard threats. Mark would use Mj's name to make money. "They" always said Mj new of all projects going on. Now he says he doesn't believe Debbie Rowe was honest in her answers in the rebuttal interview. He thought they were all giving their points back. He says he was offered a million dollars for that point from some guy from Korea. He was told not to talk on the phone at Neverland because calls were monitored. The million given to Marlon Brando came from the Parvise Loan.

Re-Cross

He said he'd give his lawyer the bullet points but not my notes. That's a book baby, he told Cyndi that in a taped phone conversation. Now he says the handwriting is similar but still different.

May 4th

He says he gave notes to Sgt. Robel during the January 31, 2004 interview. Mid April 2005 was when he found his notes in storage.

Re-Direct (2)

Follow up interview in Calabasas 2 weeks after search warrant.

Prosecution Rests 5-4-05

May 5th

Defense

1st Witness Wade J Robson

He met Mj after one of Mj's concerts in Australia. Met him, Mj, again in 1989 at a record studio. First he went to Neverland that night and stayed a week with his entire family. Would come back twice a year and stay with Mj at his ranch or an apartment. September 1991 moved to the USA permanently. Stayed at Neverland 25 times. He considering Mj a close friend. **He says Mj never absolutely not has ever done anything sexual to him. First time he was at Neverland, he spent the night in Mj's bedroom, his sister, also.** He says he has stayed in Mj's bedroom 15 to 20 times. Never showered with Mj. He has gone into the jacuzzi with Mj and (Wade's) his sister. Mrs. Chandler at Neverland, he says she acted like Neverland was hers.

Cross -Examine

Home- study high school, no college. Sister slept with him and Mj the whole first week. **He asked Mj if he could stay in Mj's room with him.** His mother has seen Mj's bedroom. He says Mj never grabbed his crotch when both were doing dance routines.

May 5th

He would stay alone overnight sometimes with Mj. 3 or 4 times over the years he didn't sleep with Mj. **His mother was never upset that she felt like she was losing her son to Mj.** Wade says that Mj took him to Las Vegas. He stayed with Mj in his room and his mothers stayed in a separate room. Met Jordan Chandler 1 time. He, Jordan, Macaulay Culkin, and his brother Kieran all stayed the night in Mj room. He and Mj threw pebbles at the lion. Never spent a night with Brett Barnes. Mj told him he was family and told his mother also. He, Mj, told him he could trust him and he would take care of him. He spent 1 night at Century City apartment with Macaulay Culkin. Last time he slept in Mj's bed was at a Sheraton Hotel when he was 14. Mj would kiss him on the head and cheek and run his fingers through his hair.

Re-Direct

Mj never encouraged him to dress like him. Mj would kiss him on the cheek in front of his mother and sister. His mother and sister would hug and kiss Mj. He never saw Mj do anything sexual with any children.

May 5th

He's never seen Mj do anything inappropriate with any children or adults. He says his mother was with him every time except 1 time at Neverland. His mother would hang with Mj and all the kids and play with them.

Re-Cross

Mj slept with him on the couch at Wade's apartment.

Re-Direct #2

Mj reading Playboy Hustler Penthouse would not have concerned him.

Re-Cross #2

Looks at a book with nude children and says it's not pornographic, just a book. Shows him more graphic books of men engaged in sexual acts and says he probably would have a problem. He says because "Rhonda" is in quotation marks, it means that's not the real name. All books he's looked at are of nude men or boys, some bondage and some sex acts. Wade considers some bothersome, some art. Looking at magazines with women engaged in sex acts or inserting things into themselves and oral sex. If he knew the person, he wouldn't have a problem letting his kid sleep with this person because of these magazines.

May 5th

Re-Direct #3

No books with children having sex or adults having sex with children.

Re-Cross #3

He never knew or saw any of this with Mj or at Mj's house.

Witness # 2 – Brett Barnes

23 Years old. Lives in Melbourne. Had to quit his job to come here and testify. Dec 91 first visit to Neverland, his whole family went. He says Mj never touched him in a sexual way, he would not

have put up with it. He considers Mj a part of his family. He never took a shower with Mj. He says he's very upset about these allegations that Mj inappropriately touched him.

Cross – Examine

He flew to Neverland alone from Australia. He last slept in Mj's bed with him 4 years ago when he was 19. Mj never showed him any sexually explicit material. He traveled with Mj through North America without his mother. He says Mj always wore pajama bottoms and a t-shirt.

May 5th

When he slept with him and he wore the same. **He can't remember a lot of things?** He doesn't recall Mj traveling with a friend or girlfriend. He knows Wade Robson, but they're not friends, he says. He and Wade are staying at Neverland right now. Mj told him to trust him and he would take care of him. Frank, Macaulay, and Eddie Casio, he says they shared Mj's bed with him.

May 6th

3rd Witness – Joy Robson

She's known Mj for 18 years. Been to Neverland at least 50 times. 1st time in January 1990. She has seen Mj's bedroom. Wade and his sister asked to stay in Mj's room with him. She's never seen anything inappropriate with Mj. She says they all played together. She's been in the jacuzzi at Neverland 6 or 8 times.

<u>Cross – Examine</u>

First met Mj in 1987 in Australia. The first night she says her kids told her they slept on the mezzanine level, not in Mj's bed with him. Mj took her kids to Toys R Us. They could get whatever they wanted.

May 6th

She says she probably would not have let Wade go to Japan with Mj. She says Mj had a business trip to Japan he canceled because Wade wanted to stay at Neverland. Came back to the USA when Mj set up for Wade to be in a LA Gear Commercial. She says LA Gear paid for their trip, not Mj. She would walk him, Wade, across the street to Mj's condo from their hotel room late at night during this LA Gear Commercial. She knew Wade was sleeping with Mj. Charli Michaels security at the ranch was told by her Joy that she was upset about not seeing her son on Mother's day. She says Wade would rather be with Mj than her. September '91, came to the USA for good with her son and daughter separated from her husband. She says they have only been at Neverland 4 times with Mj there. She told Jordan, Chandler's mother, that Jordan would be replaced soon by one of Mj's other special friends.

(90 – Wade Robson)
(91- Macaulay Culkin)
(92 – Brett Barnes)
(93 – Jordan Chandler)

Met Brett Barnes in Chicago when he went to shoot a video. She says Brett's mother and sister were there.

May 6th

Mj referred to some kids as his cousins so that some kids wouldn't get jealous of each other. They originally came in September '91 to work on the Black or White video. Mj told them he would help Wade with his career. She said in the grand jury that Mj had 3 deals set up and she considered that a personal commitment from Mj, but now she says she doesn't remember saying that. Mj paid their rent the first month in September '91. She says that it was part of the video shoot deal. June of '93 deal for a record contract completed Dec '93. Wade's share was $30,000 ; they got $15,000 in advance. She was aware of Jordan Chandler going to CPS and authorities to report molestation. Anthony Pellicano, Mj's private investigator loaned her $10,000. She says she paid him back? Loan from Mj in '92 for $10,000 was never paid back. Mj paid the balance on a car for her. She says Wade has been to school in the valley. She says she doesn't know Kenneth Clark.

Re-Direct

She says Mj is very special and she trusts him with her children. She says Wade spent a lot of time at a recording studio with Mj.

May 6th

She says Wade was learning from MJ all aspects of the entertainment industry. She says Mj never did anything that made her suspicious of anything. Mj was always very supportive of Wade. Wade told her about him and Mj throwing pebbles at the lion cage and not at the lion. She says Mj called various kids' cousins. Not good friends with Brett Barnes or his family. Wade did 3 music videos and a Pepsi commercial and the LA Gear shoot. Last worked with Mj in 2000 to choreograph his Mj's dance routine with N'Sync. She freely walked in and out of Mj's room if she wanted to, but she always knocked. She was paid for 3 years through Mjj Productions when she worked for a cosmetics company. She did not like June Chandler, she thought she was a gold digger and was trying to use Mj.

<u>Re-Cross</u>

She saw Mj trying to elude June Chandler for the entire weekend when they were there when Chandler's were there.

<u>Re-Direct #2</u>

She says there were no contracts, but Mj would help if he could.

May 6th

4th Witness – Chantal Robson

Friend of Mj since she was 10. Last spoke to Mj 2 nights ago at the ranch. 1st visited Neverland in

1989. She has slept in Mj's room 4 times. She has never seen or been suspicious of Mj doing anything to her brother or her. She says her parents and grandparents knew her and her brother were sleeping with Mj. She never felt that she was being kept out of Mj's room. She's a dancer. Mj never helped her with her career.

Cross-Examine

She had Mj's albums. She says Mj's friendship with her brother was very important to Wade. The 1st night she slept upstairs. She says that Wade and Mj slept downstairs together. The next night they all slept in the same bed together. She says this wasn't an idea, they just fell asleep. Never heard of Apple head or doo doo head "club." Just the sayings of no club.

Re-Direct

She believed Wade had a good friendship with Mj. She says Mj is her friend and she loves him.

May 6th

She says Mj has never done anything to make her suspicious. She says she has no reason to feel guilty about her friendship with Mj. She says Wade and her are very upset about allegations of Mj and her brother.

Re-Cross

She would have to re-evaluate her trust if she believes these allegations. She does not believe these allegations.

5th Witness – Marie Lizzete Barnes

Lives in Melbourne, Australia. Has 9 sons and a daughter. She says she's stayed at Neverland 10-15 times. December 1991 their first visit to Neverland. They stayed in guest units the first night. Being in Mj's room several times, she says she had free reign. Mj told her she could come in his room and borrow whatever she wanted whenever she wanted. She says Mj has never done anything to make her suspicious or uncomfortable, and she still trusts Mj to this day.

May 6th

Cross-Examine

Brett was 9 when he first met Mj. First time they went, they were there for 3 weeks and traveled to Disneyland and Las Vegas. Her daughter was 12. Spent 4 or 5 nights at the Disneyland Hotel. Brett slept with Mj on occasion. She was present on several occasions when Mj and Brett traveled. She was in Chicago for the Jam Video. Spent 2 months traveling through South American with Mj on tour. She says Brett was 12 at this time. She had conversations with her husband about Brett sleeping with Mj. Whether or not it inconvenienced Mj if he slept in Mj's room.

#897 – 2 page letter. Letter she wrote. She says she loved Mj as much as her family. September 9, 1992.

Bill Bray was head of security for Mj. She says she remembers causing him some grief. She was upset over not having a VIP Pass to his show and couldn't go. She felt like killing herself, she says in the letter. She was being overly dramatic, she says. She had no discussion with anybody about her testimony.

May 6th

Re-Direct

She has been his friend since 1987, she says. She loves Mj very much and she's proud of it. She's never been asked to leave Neverland.

Re-Cross

Met with Mesereau and Scott Ross from the defense team for 25 minutes

6th Witness – Karlee Barnes

She says MJ is a very good friend of hers. She spoke to Mj on the phone for the first time. She spoke to him a lot on the phone. She says she has been in Mj's bedroom. She recalls sleeping in Mj's room twice. She says they would do things kids do when they were with Mj. She has been in the jacuzzi and swimming pool. She's never seen Mj do anything inappropriate with her or her brother and she's never been suspicious of Mj.

Cross-Examine

She says her and her brother stayed up all night on the first night. Out of 100 visits, she can recall 2 times sleeping in Mj's room. Brett slept in there all the time.

May 6th

Re-Direct

She says the whole family is a special friend of Mj. She never thought she or her brother were victims of molestation. She thinks the allegations that Mj had molested her brother are lies.

May 9th

7th Witness – Francine Contreras

Worked at Neverland for 2 years. 1991-1993. Worked with Adrian McManus, good friends at times, not now. She says that McManus always talked well about Mj. Never mentioned any molestations. She stopped talking to her after McManus filed a lawsuit. She says McManus had a lot of Mj's items in her house. She used to steal his stuff in a laundry basket. She says McManus kept toys that she was supposed to wrap.

Cross-Examine

She was fired from Meruyns, she says for trespassing.

8th Witness – Gayle Goforth

Worked at Neverland. Started in 1989. Housekeeper. Supervisor of housekeeping in 1990. She knew Kasim, Ralph, and Adrian.

May 9th

They had facilities at the ranch to do laundry, and ironing could be done there. She says it was not necessarily one of McManus's duties to take Mj's clothes home to iron. McManus stopped showing up for work in 1994. She says McManus thought she was better than everybody else when she started cleaning Mj's room. First time Arvizo's whole family came, she said 4 or 5 more times, just the father and kids. She says Janet told her she would move to the Valley to be closer to the ranch if she gave her a job. She saw Mj drink alcohol a few times during meals. She wouldn't see alcohol just lying around Mj's room. She says Mj was very private.

Cross – Examine

She, Janet, told her she would sleep in her car outside of the ranch. Janet told her she just needed to work and needed money. She wanted to be a maid for $8.00 an hour. She was suspended for selling items she wasn't supposed to. She quit because she didn't like the way she was treated.

Re-Direct

She never sold anything for her benefit.

May 9th

She was directed by someone else to sell furniture, but the money was going to the ranch. Apparently, MJ didn't want furniture sold.

9th Witness – Violet Silva

Safety Coordinator at Neverland ranch. Her office is in the administration building. She shares her office with the fire chief. Started July 1st, 1991. Ranch manager is Joe Marcus. She retained her current position in November 2004. Terry Cooney was chief of security at that time. She says she knows Mj well. Their contact is limited to Mj making requests pretty much everything else is funneled through the ranch manager. If Mj had a suggestion about security, he would let her know. Mj never asked her to do anything that she thought was inappropriate. She never saw anything inappropriate or illegal at Neverland. They have had ambulances and even a medical helicopter at the ranch. They don't have to ask M j before they pull any privileges from anybody.

May 9th

They try to have 4 security officers 24 hours a day. Security is also a fireman and EMT. She does know Brian Barron, and that he is a police officer. Enter the security office from outside. Confidentiality agreements are not used to hide anything illegal, just to keep people from profiting from selling anything. They have cattle on a ranch from someone that's leasing property. Front gate automatically opens if you're driving a car or gold cart of a quad runner. There's always somebody located at the main house. Most of the staff carry radios. Security would go inside the house sometimes. She says the intruder who got into the main house train room was possibly there for 10 hours and recently caught a person with a 9mm gun, but it didn't work. Most guests who stayed overnight have a code to get into the main house, not Mj bedroom. The security does carry pepper spray. She arrived after the search on 11-18-03. She says the search ended about 10:30 -11:00 pm. She says nothing was hidden or tried to be kept from searchers.

May 9th

Gate logs for 2003 were in a file cabinet insecurity office. They never seized them? She gave them to Mark Geragos eventually. Gate logs contain directives for all security officers for an extended amount of time. Some guests were cleared for certain things and some weren't. She knew the Robson family. Never saw anything inappropriate with this family. She knew the Culkin's and the Barnes families also. She knew the Chandler family also. It could be appropriate for staff to override a decision of a parent if it reflected on the child's safety. She says the wine cellar was normally locked. Children were not allowed down there. 2 keys to it, one in the staff break room, and one in the security office. Boys and girls had the same run of the ranch. Gavin 1st came in August 2000 with Dad and brother. She has no knowledge of any underage drinking. She says kids became more rambunctious when father David was not there. She remembers Arvizo's February 2003, they were there for quite a while off and on. She says they were pretty destructive and would drive vehicles they weren't supposed to.

May 9th

She says Arvizo kids would litter a lot and would wear the same clothes for a few days at a time. She says Davellin was taking care of the boys February, March 2003. Mother is very seldom seen. Arvizo kids would visit the security office and never complain about anything, when she saw Janet, she never complained either. She knows Ronald and Dieter and they were there February -March 2003. She didn't see the interaction between Arvizo's and Ronald and Dieter. Kat Bernard took Janet for a salon visit. Violet didn't see any film crew follow them. Nothing prevents you from calling 911. She says the Arvizo kids were not allowed to leave without adult supervision. Arvizo's children never said they wanted to leave the ranch or were kept from leaving. Janet would have been allowed to leave if she wanted too. She never told her directly that she wanted to leave the ranch.

Cross-Examine

She says Barnes' father was there 2 or 3 times after the initial visit. She never met a father Robson, or a father Chandler. She says Culkin was with his parents mostly.

May 9th

She says the whole Casio family is close to Mj. She was aware of Frank Casio working on a project on the ranch for Mj from 2000-2003. Frank changed or started using a different last name during February, March 2003, same time Arvizo's were there. She never saw meetings with Frank, Ronald, or Dieter with Mj, but she wouldn't have known if they met in the house. Shane Brando 13 or 14. 2003 Miko's kid. 4 drawer cabinet. 2nd drawer from the top is where she retrieved logs that weren't seized. Day of the search she had to get a key from a housekeeper to open an arcade and wine cellar. Groundskeepers and maintenance and zoo and maid staff were all day shifts only. She has been in Mj's bedroom and has heard the chime. There is a deadbolt on Mj's bedroom door and his door has to be opened from inside. Ace Protective Group, security used at Neverland from an outside agency. She says all the young boys had to be reminded of the rules. She says Mj put security in situations where they were the "bad guys." Chris Carter security for Mj. Never seen Mj carry or use a cell phone.

May 9th

Doesn't recall Mj being with Gavin Arvizo other than 1 time at teepee for dinner 2003. It would be against the rules for anybody under the driving age to take quads or golf carts or any vehicle off ranch property. Left keys in vehicles on the ranch? "Don't let kids leave ranch like Gavin, Starr, etc." she never seen that before for any other child. Coultree brothers on the property after Arvizo's. Very rude and destructive. She had adult materials left in her office from Japan. She is very graphic.

Re-Direct

Father and Chris Tucker supervised Arvizo kids (boys) but the mother never did when she was there. She has not reviewed gate logs from 1991-1993. **That entry about Arvizo kids on February 19 was only for that day.** She says Wade and Brett did not have behavior problems. The **entire** Cascio family asked to be called Tyson, not just Frank. She says Mj and Frank didn't always get along, especially after Frank threw a big party.

May 9th

Security only had a keypad combo for the back door. You can open Mj's room with the key she thinks. She wasn't complaining about having to be the "bad guy" per say. She did not have set hours during these times. They never checked to see if Arvizo's boys stayed in their assigned guest unit.

Re-Cross

She would have not let her children act like or take part in the way the kids acted at Neverland. February 28 says the Cascio family will be called Tyson from now on. Vinny Amen to Vinny Black?

Re-Direct #2

That Casio directive as per Joe Marcus. She has brought her kids to family day at Ranch.

Witness #10 – Ramon Velasco

He does understand or speak some English. Prefers Spanish. Started in 1989. Stopped in 1999. Not Consecutive. Had back operation. 1991 off 8 months. Gardner several years of assisted cook washing dishes. Worked full time in the kitchen as the cook when he left in 1999. Nephew Carlos also worked at the ranch. Ramon knew Blanca and Jason Francia.

May 9th

When he first met Blanca, he got along with her. He has heard Blanca talk with other employees. Blanca worked there before him and left long before he did. He says Wine Cellar was kept locked at all times. He saw MJ in several water balloon fights with guests. He never saw Mj do anything inappropriate with any children. Mj would complain sometimes about the food his guests were served but not his food he was served. He was contacted by telephone last night by 2 Sheriffs.

Cross-Examine

He was not permitted to go into Mj's room anytime he wanted.

11th Witness – Joe Marcus

Property Manager. Neverland Valley Ranch. Known Mj for 18 years. William Bone owned the Ranch before Mj bought it, it was called Sycamore Valley Ranch. He became security when Mj bought a ranch. Golden Gate ¼ to ½ mile from the main gate. He says there are 5 or 6 exterior clocks. February, March 2003, clocks were working. Clocks visible all throughout the inside of the house.

May 9th

Security officer for 5 years. Became ranch manager in 2002. 1993 search by LAPD he was aware of. He was a security guard at that time. He didn't observe anything in the early 90's as illegal or inappropriate with adults or children. He says he would have reported it, He knew Brian Barron and knew he was a police officer. He doesn't recall any interaction with Arvizo's on his 1st visit. He recalls Janet being there before and after Chris Tucker's visits. February, March 2003, he saw Arvizo's on the property having fun. He didn't see any sign that the Arvizo kids wanted to leave Neverland. February, March 2003. He did see Janet outside she would talk with people, Cooks, Dieter, etc.. He would knock before he went into Mj bedroom. Even though he had a combo to get in. Janet never complained to him about anything, nor did she seem like she wanted to leave the ranch and couldn't. He took Janet and the boys shopping in Solvang, in February, March 2003. He stayed in the car while they went shopping. Less than 1 hour, he says they were done shopping.

May 9th No film crew followed them. He met them at a local orthodontist in Solvang. 511 5th street Dr. Seamont. He went inside. Vinnie dropped them off there. He was not there to guard them or restrict them in any way. He says they were there for 1 hour to 1 ½ hour. Nobody asked for help.

May 10th

Those instructions to not let kids leave per Joe on February 19, 2003, was to let guards know that not to let Arvizo kids out driving Mj's vehicles. Never told anybody to hold Arvizo's against their will. He says Jesus contacted him about Jesus taking Arvizo's off property early morning February 12,

2003. He says there's been 5 to 10 peace officers working or retired worked as security at Neverland and at least 20 firemen. He was advised the media was trying to contact the Arvizo's. He says Janet or the children did not complain about the Brazil trip. They keep nicer fan mail memorabilia, collectibles, etc. at Neverland Ranch.

May 10th

Cross-Examine

He says there are multiple people who have worked there as long as he has. He was an armed security guard. He only answers to Mj. He says it's up to Mj who comes on the property and who doesn't. He thinks the guest cottages are direct dial phones, but he doesn't recall for sure. He never saw Mj throw stones at lions. He's never seen any of the animals abused. He's seen other children be destructive at Neverland. He says Mj does have special bonds with children, not just boys. He says Frank was at Neverland in 2003 for about a month. He says Vinnie would come and go a lot. He saw Frank and Vinnie with the Arvizo's at different times. He says Mj has had a lot of special relationships with boys. Only his phone and Mj phone are the only phones that can be used to monitor other people's phone calls. He doesn't recall just guarding Mj's hallway to his bedroom in 93. He doesn't recall refusing to turn his gun over to the head of security, his father Zimmerman at some time.

May 10th

He's been interviewed 1 time by Mj investigators. **He believes his interview with Eric Mason, Mj investigator was not on the record? He's never seen Mj drink alcohol? He says honestly, he's only met Janet when asked if he met the Arvizo family? He states in the interview the kids never stayed there without their mother?** He says it's possible Neverland was on a skeleton crew in February 2003. **He lied about knowing kids slept in Mj room in his interview**. He says Jesus told him Gavin drove the van from the theater. He has access to all of Neverland with permission.

Re-Direct

Nude women figurines on Mj's desk in his office where children can go. He says he was concerned for the employees and guests on the ranch during the November 18th search. The employees were calling him on the radio during this search and he said it was chaotic. He says he never saw Arvizo's sleeping in Mj room he just knows from somebody? Guests are instructed on how to use the phones to get outside lines. He says adult guests enjoy areas just like children. He says Mj had special bonds with girls also, not just boys.

May 10th

He says he had adult women that he had a special friendship with. Frank went and bought his own desk that he used in the video library. Living area in the West end of the video library. February, March 2003, he said Frank was there and Vinnie wasn't.

He had a guard card when he carried a weapon as a security guard. Events have a specific meaning when talking about alcohol being served. Ranch was bought by Mj with a collection of wine Wasn't the first time they went somewhere after hours with a guest of the ranch. He doesn't know Inter. Nation Business Management. He says they don't need as much staff if MJ is not there and there are no guests. He says the adult material was no on "display" and he's never seen Mj with this stuff personally.

Re-Cross

He doesn't think it's appropriate for children to see those nude figurines in his office.

May 11th

He asked the interviewer during the search to turn the tape recorder off during the question of children sleeping in Mj's room.

Re-Direct #2

He was trying to cooperate during the search so he didn't have to talk to them.

May 11th

Interview continued 5 or 10 minutes after he asked tape to be turned off.

12th Witness – Macaulay Culkin

Friend of Mj since he was 9 or 10. Mj called him first. Visited Neverland more than a dozen times. He was very impressed with Neverland. He says they just have hung out in LA, NY, Neverland and

London. He says Mj has never touched him in an inappropriate way sexually or made him feel uncomfortable. He's never been asked by anybody, police or media, about the allegations he was molested by Mj. He never felt his family was excluded from him or Neverland, he says real open door policy with Mj and the ranch. He's never seen Mj do anything he felt was inappropriate on any trip they went on together.

Cross-Examine

He's not aware of law enforcement trying to interview him in 93 or 2003. He and his lawyer said they would not give an interview to either side. Mj gave him a Rolex watch when they went to Bermuda. He says he doesn't remember if Mrs. Goldstein told him he couldn't go off with Mj alone.

May 11th

He says he still has Rolex but it doesn't fit anymore. He says it possibly he shared a bed alone with Mj prior to going to Bermuda. He says most every time he was at Neverland, his siblings were with him and were almost always with him while he was there. He says he would probably know if someone was doing something to him while he was sleeping. He says since he's older, he enjoys his privacy that's why he is sleeping in the guest unit now. Mj would call him a lot and they would have long phone conversations. He says sometimes there would be other boys who would fall asleep with him and Mj in Mj's bedroom. At age 20, he spent 10-14 days at

Neverland, Mj was not there. He says Mj and him would go shopping late at night when stores were closed. He says his father would sometimes wake him up in Mj bedroom. He says his parents had an issue with it., He says Mj had the alarm back then when walking to Mj bedroom. He says Mj's bedroom door was never locked at these times.

May 11th

Re-Direct

He says Mj could be related to him as being a child star. "People out to get you type of thing." He says Mj was very child-like. He says no doors were ever locked at Neverland. He never thought anything Mj bought or gave had any ulterior motives. Mj never pressured him to do anything he said.

Re-Cross

It was okay for people to go through his closet on the tour of Neverland. He says it's not surprising to him of the magazines Mj had or has.

13th Witness – James Van Norman

First met Mj in 1990 or 1991. Personal security for Madonna. He eventually started working for Mj. The A Team was with him all the time. The B Team was mostly at venues. 1991-1994 part of A Team. Billy Bray was head of security at this time, OSS. Bray had been with MJ 25 or 30 years. Wayne Nagan second in command. Better Bailey, Bray's assistant. Bray's background was law enforcement LAPD. 6 on A team. 6 and 8 on the B Team.

May 11th

He usually stayed right next door to Mj in the hotels. He says it wasn't easy for Mj to go out in Europe or the USA. Mj would wear a disguise if he went out without security. In 1994 Mj asked him to look after the ranch he lived in until 1998. He carried a firearm at the ranch in 93-94. He says he never displayed his firearm or pointed it at anybody. He says there would be 500 to 6,000 people hanging out at the front gate. There were keys then no keypads. He says celebrity stalkers are very dangerous. He knew the Barnes Family. He would travel with family. He knows Macaulay Culkin, and he knows Robson's family. He says he never saw Mj do anything inappropriate with any of them. If he had seen anything unlawful or inappropriate, he would have reported it to Bill Bray. He says Ralph, Adrian and Kasim all stopped coming to work pretty much on the same day or time. He says they all sold stories to the media along with Blanca Francia, who he didn't know. He would make policy decisions when he was ranch manager and he didn't have to ask Mj.

May 11th

Cross-Examine

He never carried a weapon on tour or video shoots. Mj went to England from Mexico he didn't have any security with him he was there for 6 weeks. He had no guard card while working for Mj. He carried a gun and a stun gun. He says Brett Barnes stayed with Mj on all his travels with Mj. He did buy security equipment to upgrade security at Neverland. He says there are 3 phones that could eavesdrop. He doesn't not recall if foreign trespassers were arrested and prosecuted. He says Chacon's, Abdul's, and McManus time cards were all correct. He also never saw those 3 take anything from the ranch.

Re-Direct

He never carried his weapon off of the ranch. He says Mj didn't like to have guns around him. He says they would patrol woods usually in a truck and sometimes on horseback. He says Mj was like one of the kids that he hung out with. He says Mj related better with kids he was more shy around adults.

May 11th

He did find some people were cheating on their time cards. He did find out things were being stolen from the ranch. At the time of his deposition, before he was sued, he had no knowledge of theft by McManus Chacon or Abdul.

#5009
(A) Videos seized by
(B) Sheriff's out-takes
(C) of Bashir Documentary

He's never been betrayed or deceived by a child, as he has with adults. He says he's prejudiced against ignorance. He says he goes to as many hospitals as concerts. Bashir says people are scum and no one understands. Mj says the bigger the star, the bigger the target. He says he's a tenor never taken female hormones. He says mannequins are like friends he never had. He says he would walk the streets looking for people to talk to just because he wanted to have normal friends. He says he was forced to do it for his career, but he loved it. He, Mj, says he doesn't drink? If he doesn't, why not be honest. Little bit of Jesus juice, a little bit of wine, Mj asked Bashir if he had any when he flew.

May 11th

He says he can be very lonely and then he can be fine. He says he usually feels lonely in hotel rooms. He says he tried to do things normally but he can't. It just doesn't work. Why is Mj coming to our house? Mj says you want to be somewhere. He says he does worry about his own future. At age 11, under contract with Motown, sometimes he didn't want to go to a recording studio. He wanted to go to the ballpark and play with the other kids. He wanted to know what it was like to have a slumber party, birthday party, and that's why he does them now. He says his mother, a very strong Jehovah's Witness, taught him these were all pagan holidays. He says there is always someone there to bring you down. His vision was to have a National Holiday for children. He says he would feel different about his father today if his father had played a game with him. (Who is the lady putting makeup on Mj and hugging him and rubbing him, Mj? Karen is his makeup lady.) Mj rips a picture of little boys and girls out of a magazine in a hotel in Bashir's room. He, Mj, says if he would have had one day with his father, he would feel different about him.

May 11th

Mj says he would slit his wrists before he would hurt a child. He says he hangs with kids now because he grew up with adults. Mj says he is too isolated. He doesn't watch the news because of all the bad news about the world and children. He says he showed his baby over the balcony to German fans because that's what they were chanting. Once again, he says he doesn't drink alcohol? He says he has to give great credit to Dieter for Germany. He can't keep his children locked in a room like a prison. TRUE. He says he's only had 2 surgeries on his nose? Nothing else? He tells Elizabeth Taylor all the time that he's crazy about her. He says she can't Debbie Rowe handle being with her children. He knew she didn't like children or didn't want to have children when they got married. He says she told him they're yours just take them. Bashir tells Mj he's great with his children. End of DVD's outtakes.

May 12th

14th Witness – Carlos Velasco

His father works for Mj. He has gone to family day 20 times, and he's worked there twice in 97-98. He met Jason Francia. He's seen him at family days. He went to high school with Jason Francia. He never saw Mj do anything inappropriate with Jason Francia.

Cross-Examine

He never wanted to sleep with Mj. He said he has no idea if there was molestation for sure, but he was never told nor given any sign that he was.

15th Witness – David LeGrand

Attorney in Las Vegas. Late January 2002. Started with Mj on March 28, 2003. Terminated September of 2004. Worked on 1 case for Mj. He has been a prosecutor doing security frauds for 1 ½ years. Entered private practice in 1982. Worked for a firm he represented Mj. Introduced to Mj by Ronald Konitzer. He considered himself Mj's primary transactional attorney. January 2003 started to bring in a new team of lawyers, accountants, etc. for Mj.

May 12th

January 2003, when the trouble in the UK started over Bashir Documentary. His concern was Mj "camp" never saw the finished product before it aired on tv in the UK. Grenada is a big TV station in the UK. The right documents were not prepared for Mj with Grenada over this Bashir documentary. The 2 that were done were horrible contracts he says that were (or oral) signed by Mj. He says that Mj was misled by Bashir and Grenada. **Mj did not seek compensation from Bashir, just a large donation to a charity.** Mj never asked to be paid even though Bashir and Grenada were going to make millions of dollars. He says the lawsuit against Grenada and Bashir is still going on today, but he is not part of it. Bashir had made numerous misrepresentations to Mj that was the basis of the lawsuit. He says it was a media event for sure regarding this lawsuit involving Mj, Arvizo, and others with Bashir and Grenada. The new management team, cash management, lawyers, etc.. He says Wiesner and Konitzer were trying to take over Mj management. End of January, mid-March. Just a few days he didn't talk to Ronald.

May 12th

Konitzer wanted to be the day to day manager of Mj affairs. He became suspicious of Konitzer and Wiesner. They were in a position to divert funds, proper tax paperwork, etc. and Konitzer was making bad decisions. Close to a million dollars diverted to Konitzer and Wiesner. Some of those funds came from the Fox Take 2 show? He ultimately got the contract for this show. He never found out what happened to the $965,000. He did have the background investigation of Wiesner, Konitzer and Schaffel. He was doing all this to protect Mj. Mj did give power of attorney to Konitzer and Wiesner. He had Mj revoke the power of attorney. Investigative firm was based in New York. He met Janet Arvizo at Neverland when the 60 Minutes crew was there. He says Janet wasn't upset and expressed support for Mj. Janet was around the crew of 60 Minutes throughout the day. There was a desire to get the Arvizo's in the rebuttal Take 2 show. He says he was only getting 4 or 5 hours of sleep a day during this time.

May 12th

He says there was no secret to this Take 2 Production going on. He says Fox wanted this production done for sweeps week. Dealt with other countries other than the UK over this production. He says there was interest by a number of people companies for this Take 2 show. He has no knowledge of the Arvizo's to be held or being held against their will. He says Mj didn't have a lot of liquidity in his assets. He suggested Mj sell his part of the Sony Catalogue. He said Mj could pay his debt and still have 200 million dollars. He did have some discussions with people about projects that involved Mj to make money. There was also the payment to a company for Mj to acquire back his name for marketing for making money. He says he had many proposals during this time in 2003 that Mj could have made money. Mj had about 10 or 11 law firms involved in his affairs at this time. He says Mj has never gone bankrupt. Konitzer and Wiesner told him they wanted to take over management of Mj business and financial affairs. They wanted to control everything involving Mj.

May 12th

It took weeks for him to become suspicious of Konitzer and Wiesner. He says everybody wanted to benefit from Mj, so he was suspicious of everybody. He was constantly trying to get Schaffel out of Mj affairs. He says Debbie Rowe's lawyer didn't express any concern over his interview for the Take 2 video. He's not aware of any secret that the Arvizo's were going to be involved in the Take

2 video. He says Arvizo's are not part of a lawsuit any more in the U.K. Dickerman contacted him in Spring 2004. He's never had contact with Feldman.

#5037 – Outline of Business structure for Mj. Faxed on March 14, 2003, to Malnik, Konitzer put this document together. He found this document to be somewhat disturbing.

Cross – Examine

Met Konitzer through his business Hi-Tech America. Met Mj in Florida at Turnberry Resort at the end of January. He says Konitzer and Wiesner were there. He stayed in Florida for 4 or 5 days. 3 or 4 meetings with Mj. Conference call involved him, Konitzer, and Mj with the U.K..

May 12th

He says Mj wasn't too concerned about PR fallout from Bashir video. Mj was more concerned about his kids not being shown and to see the final edition after editing. Mj never said he did interviews to reignite his career. He says Mj just wanted an accurate and sincere depiction of his regular life. Mj saying he liked to sleep with boys and him hanging his child over the balcony were 2 major issues that Bashir did not misrepresent, also the amount of plastic surgery and his trip to the zoo with the kids were also other concerns that weren't misrepresented by Bashir. He says Mj had a good relationship with Dieter. He says Mj told him he wanted to put Ronald and Dieter in charge. He considered Mj to be a smart businessman. He says this was a public relations crisis and Mj knew that.

Mj decided his mind in doing the 60 Minute interview maybe because of the Jordan Chandler thing coming out on the internet "Smoking Gun." He was trying to get knowledge of Mj's finances.

May 12th

He says Mj was on the verge of bankruptcy if something didn't change. He did not consider all the possible factors of the value of Mj's part of the Song Catalogue. Fire Mountain LLC, owned by Mjj Productions, formed in Nevada. Ann Gabriel wanted the Take 2 video not to be a money maker she thought that would be bad, but they didn't listen to her. Mjj Productions eventually had the power to sign for fire mountain. All the money made on Take 2 went to Fire Mountain in a trust 3 million dollars from Fox came in February.

$898 – Trust listings from Hale Lane sent to Mj 4-1-03.

He doesn't recall getting an ok from Mj for any specific expenditure. Royalty Advance Funding an advance on royalties, the Parvese Loan First met Schaffel at his residence in Calabasas. He doesn't remember discussing anything about a script for the Arvizo interview. Discussed Arvizo's with Schaffel quite a few times. He says it was obvious the world was going to want to know about Gavin Arvizo from Bashir video.

May 12th

He had talked to Mj about the Take 2 video. He gave his files to Mj's former lawyer. He had two meetings with Steve Cochran. He turned over 5 boxes of documents. He doesn't know where his notes are pertaining to Mj. He perceived Arvizo's as a potential liability to Mj. No release was ever gotten for Gavin for Bashir video. Mj never made a statement to the effect of blanking out Gavin's face. He thinks that may have come up in a conference call. Janet was never paid for her appearance in her video. He offered Janet $25,000 to stay on with the complaint against Grenada with the Broadcasting Stands Board. His offer was turned down. After he informed Mj of the $965,000 Dieter and Ronald took or got? He was fired?

May 13th

He discussed Fire Mountain LLC with Bank of America and he says he wasn't aware of any problem. Marcel Avrum, a promoter who entered into business with Mj. Who sued Mj. He called Al Malnik about his wife having a baby last night. He has taken directive from Malnik per Mj.

May 13th

He has attended maybe 2 meetings with Al Malnik and Mj. Malnik was one of the people he had investigated, He had pretty much everybody investigated that could do damage to Mj. He doesn't know what the $965,000 was for. He believes Konitzer was upset that Finkelstein gave him David Legrand that account. The "plan" was made before they knew Mj's financial status. The hope was to make hundreds of millions of dollars. He, in having these people investigated, was just trying to gain knowledge of these people, not necessarily to get rid of them. He's met with Messereau 3 or 4 times. Started dealing with Fox about Mj Home Movie, this was going to run through Fire Mountain also. His concern with Schaffel was his background in Adult Entertainment. He was concerned about being paid for his services. Konitzer told him to calm down he would be first in line. He says he doesn't remember removing any documents from the files he turned over for this case. Geragos came into picture February 2003. It was the lawyers idea to bring in Geragos in case of criminal legal action over the Bashir video.

May 13th

He has not met with Geragos 4 or 5 times. He knows Brad Miller was hired by Geragos to do something with the Arvizo family. The consent forms were prepared having in mind they wanted to use video or make a video of Arvizo's for Take 2.

#263 – 9 pages of consent and release forms for Arvizo's sent to Neverland. At the top of some of them is the Mjj Production logo not all of them have this logo.
#899 – Letter prepared by him to Barry Siegel. Turning over management to Legrand's Co.
#406 – Final agreement for Take 2
#412 – Consent and Appearance forms to Hamid Moslehi and Mjj Productions. With Ann Gabriel Productions on the top page but sent by Legrand.
#413 – Pg 7 – Fax to Vincent at Mjj Production. Releases for Arvizo's to sign for Take 2.

#413 – Pg 8 – Consent form 12:57 am, 2-21-03
#807 – Document authorizing Theodore Goddard to file complaints on behalf of Gavin Arvizo. Janet claims this document was forged. He says Konitzer might have delivered it to him
#811 – Signed releases for Arvizo's

May 13th

Arvizo's did not sign consent forms the 1st time. Vincent Amen told him the Arvizo's didn't want to sign. Vinnie was the one who called him early in the morning 2-21-03 to revise releases that were eventually signed by Arvizo's. He doesn't know where his personal notes for Mj are at this time. He said he would walk away as soon as he plugged a few document holes.

Re-Direct

DA never subpoenaed documents from him, and (DA or Sheriff's), they never called him to see his files. The firm that represented Mj also represented Sony. Mr. Branca Ziffrin Law Firm. The same time he had Inter 4 investigate Branca he was having them also investigate Konitzer Wiesner and Schaffel. Investigating an off-shore account maybe involving Branca maybe in the Caribbean. Investigators report indicated Branca was involved, (Tommy Mottola), and Sony had transferred money to that account. Internet search of Malnik Show ties to organized crime related to Meyer Lansky. He was concerned that Branca and Mottola could get Mj half of the Sony Catalogue.

May 13th

He says Mj did not throughout history surround himself with good people, he had or was being taken advantage of, according to LeGrand. He was once of the lawyers that hired Geragos, He never felt he was Janet's lawyer or gave her advice, Janet wanted the release more understandable to her simpler, but he says they would sign them if this happened.

Re-Cross

He doesn't know if Finkelstein was directly representing Mj. He was hired for Fire Mountain LLC. He thought the 2 million dollars that went to Finkelstein was to pay bills, litigation fees, etc.. He had no credible evidence that Mottola and Branca ever tried to defraud Mj. His view on the Inter 4 reports was incomplete.

Re-Direct #2

Mj has waived his attorney-client privilege with LeGrand. Prosecutors never asked for anything since December.

May 13th

16th Witness – Mark Geragos

Mj lawyer for 16 months. February 2003 started. Retained regarding allegations about his children's parental rights, welfare, etc.. Mj was usually not involved in conference calls. He heard Janet's name before he heard Gavin's. He pulled the plug on the 60 Minutes interview in February 2003. He saw

Janet talking to the producer of 60 Minutes and Gavin talking to Ed Bradley. Dieter, Jack Sussman, Simon Woman, another lawyer from his office, and 30-40 production crew. He has never spoken to Janet on the phone. He heard bad things about Arvizo's. He had somebody tell him that Gavin was told to call Mj daddy, and Mj was uncomfortable with that. He researched databases on Arvizo's and found the JC Penney lawsuit. He says this finding concerned him greatly. He had Brad Miller document (follow) the Arvizo's and see what they were doing. He also told Brad to get a statement from Arvizo's tape recorded. He says Schaffel seemed to be running things concerning rebuttal. He had Brad Miller go to the filming of that rebuttal.

May 13th

He knew of Asaf and knows now that Johnny was working with Brad Miller. He had way more contact with Konitzer than Schaffel. He told Brad Miller to store Janet's things and to film it so he couldn't be accused of stealing anything. Brad told him Janet wanted Brad to move her stuff. He directed Janet's stuff to be dumped at Dickerman's office. He has met Frank Tyson. He felt Mj being involved with Arvizo's was a pending disaster. He knew of a trip to Brazil planned for Arvizo's he had nothing to with it. He learned of the planned trip after Mj was arrested. He had their (Arvizo's) passports filed with as an exhibit. Konitzer told him he was running Mj business affairs. His retainer was signed by Konitzer and Wiesner on power of attorney signed by Mj. He thinks power of attorney was revoked right when Legrand was fired. He thought Arvizo's were going to shake down Mj.

<u>Cross-Examine</u>

His client was Mj, no one else. He was concerned about Mj being on 60 Minutes.

May 13th

He **<u>did not</u>** question Mj about sleeping with boys when he was at Neverland on February 7th. He knew nothing of any press conference in Florida on February 7th when at Neverland. He never told Mj the Arvizo's should be taken home immediately. He gave Mj no advice on February 7th. NO discussion revolved around Mj sleeping with boys. Mj told him he, Gavin, might have spent the night with him, Mj, in his room but that nothing sexual or anything else happened. He told Konitzer in March that Arvizo's needed to be gone away from Mj. He does agree the Brad Miller tape was turned off 3 times during the Arvizo interview, He did not ask Mj about the Chandler incident on February 7th. He made no notes of conversations that he can remember. He has a file on his computer pertaining to Mj. He has no information of any other trip with Mj and Arvizo's. He doesn't think Mj was at Neverland when he said that Arvizo's should be out of the picture. He was aware of 1 tape recorded phone call Brad Miller had. He, Mark, didn't tell him to do it.

May 13th

He was told that the Arvizo's wanted to be compensated for their rebuttal interview. He never thought about the commercial value of Arvizo's to Mj. He never asked Mj if Gavin was a cancer survivor in February. Arvizo's could sell their story to any tabloid they wanted to without a problem if it were true? Brad told him that Janet wanted a lawyer. He referred to Mike Nasatier. He would have asked him what was said with Janet if he talked to Mike Nasatier. He says Janet kept asking Brad to be at the interview. Brad never told him he was present during the DCFS interview.

May 16th

17th Witness – Jean Seamount

Telephone's behind the front counter. Doors in the examining room lead to her office and a back patio. Doors cannot be locked from inside, are they always unlocked during business hours? She never met Mj. Appointment with Arvizo's was a Monday evening. 6:00 pm, called by Joe Marcus, to have braces removed requested by Janet. She says Janet was angry at another orthodontist who put braces on. She advised her not to remove braces.

May 16th

Braces were installed properly. Janet refused to fill out paperwork that is normally filled out. February 24th is the night they went. Nobody asked for help, left out the back door, and used the telephone for nothing. She saw no bodyguards, no film crew, nobody guarding Arvizo's. She says Gavin was undisciplined and was going through her office drawers. Starr's behavior is a little better.

Cross-Examine

They were told they were high profile patients. Told that by Joe Marcus. It was her who decided the time of appointment.

18th Witness – Tiffany Hayness

Worked for Dr. Seamount 4 ½ years. She's on maternity leave. She's never met Mj. She says Neverland paid the bill. She never saw Joe in the examination area, only in the lobby. Arvizo's got there 6:45 that day and they were open until 7:00. She says "older boy" was rude. He told her he was from LA. She says boys were not scared of anything. She did put a proposal together for a set replacement braces. Nobody asked for help to use the phone, nothing.

May 16th

She saw no tension between Joe Marcus and Arvizo's.

Cross-Examine

She says Joe didn't say they were high profile.

19th Witness – Carol McCoy

Licensed Esthetician. Manges Café Angelica. Got my license 8 years ago. Bare Skin AromaTherapy Day Spa. February 11th call for Waxing last appointment of day 5:00 pm.

#5087 – Bill of work done.

She had a full body wax. She believes Janet never asked to use the phone. She says Janet was dropped off and no one stayed with her. She never asked for help. She says a woman dropped her off. She saw no one with a camera or no film crew.

20th Witness – Kathryne Bernard

She lived in Santa Maria for many years. She worked at Neverland for 3 ½ years. 2001-2004. She had an office in the Administration Building. It was just her and Joe Marcus. She coordinated events, etc.. She always got overtime. She would transport people sometimes. She has met Janet Arvizo. She's talked to her on the telephone requesting different things.

May 16th

She says every phone has a phone list. She took Janet to the day spa. She, Janet, called her on the phone to make that request. For waxing and to get her hair done. Janet wanted it done right away. No one else went with them in the van. There was no discussion about who was going to pay. She says Janet was talking about her ex-husband and how Mj was so great and a father figure to her kids. Set up hair appointments for the next morning. **Janet never complained to her about anything**. She says there were no cameras or film crews. She says Janet has asked her to be taken shopping for clothes for her and her kids. She told her she lost her suitcases and didn't have clothes. This wasn't the first time she asked for this. She told her she was being hassled by the orthodontist who put braces on for payment. She told her she couldn't afford to pay, and she wanted them removed and wanted to send braces back. Saw Janet alone in the main house at the kitchen bar. Always needed okay from Joe Marcus.

May 16th

21st Witness – Maria Gomez

Worked for 10 ½ years. Housekeeping. Cleans guests' units usually mid-day when guests go to lunch in the main house. She cleans the wine cellar area. She has met Janet Arvizo. She does recall seeing the Arvizo's all the time at Neverland. She saw the Arvizo's many times playing games in the kitchen area. Spent a lot of hours in the sitting room next to the kitchen watching tv. She did see Janet's children in the guest units. She says those children would make a big mess in their rooms quite often, so they clearly were using those rooms. She says Janet spent a lot of time in her room. She says the wine cellar was always locked and didn't have a lot of people going there so it did not have to be cleaned a lot. Food stored close to wine in the wine cellar. The wine cellar itself is refrigerated. She doesn't recall any key hanging in that area for the wine cellar during this time. She says she and the cooks had to ask for a key to go to the wine cellar. The key used to hang in the maids' room a long time ago.

May 16th

Never saw Gavin appear to be intoxicated, or Starr or Davellin. Never saw them drink either. Never saw Mj drink alcohol with Arvizo children. She says Janet told her or she heard it that Mj was like a father and that she wanted her kids to call him dad. Janet told her Mj was a blessing to them. A week later she, Janet, began saying she was being held against her will. 3 people, including Dieter, were also interfering with her relationship with Mj. Frank Casio, Vinnie Amen and Dieter were the one's interfering with her relationship with Mj. She saw adult magazines on 1 occasion. **She saw them in unit 2 in a backpack where Starr and Davellin were staying.** The backpack was open. Also, 2 magazines under the sink in Mj's office area. No adult magazines were ever seen by her just laying around.

Cross-Examine

She's only been in Mj bedroom 3 times in 9 years. She had an idea that her phone calls could be monitored. She said she was intimidated on search warrant day when she said the Arvizo children were nice and polite.

May 16th

Cross-Examine

She never heard Arvizo children call Mj daddy. She doesn't know why or if the Arvizo children were taken out of school the month they stayed there February – March 2003.

22nd Witness – Shane Merideth

Lived in Santa Maria for 5 years. Worked for Mj 2002-2003. Security officer. Trained by Julio Magana and Curtis Gordon. His shift was 6:00 pm – 6:00 am usually. He has met Janet Arvizo. Saw Janet 5 times at Neverland, mostly just hanging around the front of the house. Has met Arvizo children. Never saw Mj with Janet. He has seen Mj with the Arvizo children. He never saw Mj do anything inappropriate with Arvizo children. Saw Mj nephews sleeping in sleeping bags on the floor in Mj bedroom. He did bring popcorn and soda to Mj's room with Arvizo children there. He says that night, the Arvizo children slept in their guest quarters. They would check the wine cellar sometimes. He did find Gavin and Starr in a wine cellar without anybody else with them, they were drinking.

May 16th

He says half the bottle of alcohol was drunken. He says he helped them pack up the luggage in the limo the last time they left. 1:00-2:00 am Arvizo's told him on his next visit. He says Arvizo's never complained about anything. Janet would call to talk directly to Mj through him. He says the wine cellar door was not always locked. He says there were periods of time where the wine cellar would be left open. He says they would sometimes destroy things and throw trash everywhere, but he says they weren't too bad.

Cross-Examine

The security wore uniforms. He says it wasn't uncommon that kids became rambunctious. He says security would have locked the cellar door if they found it unlocked. He doesn't know for sure if the Arvizo kids drank the ½ bottle wine.

23rd Witness – Brian Salce

Worked at Neverland on and off for 6 years. Trained firefighter. 7 to 15 firefighters. Firefighters at Neverland 24 hours a day. He has met the Arvizo family in the theater. She invited him to LA to their house for Mexican food.

May 16th

As firefights, they patrol Neverland. He had to get the Arvizo kids by the front gate because Davellin needed asthma medicine.

24th Witness – Russel Birchum

Commander Santa Barbara County Sheriff Department. Detective in 1993. Worked with Det Monk. Contacted Kasim Abdul and Ralph Chacon in 1994 for grand jury testimony for LA County.

4-29-94
Neither gave information of any illegal activity at Neverland

5-4-94
Kasim called him for a meeting in a secluded area away from Santa Maria and Lompoc with Ralph

Chacon and Det. Monk. Met them at a rest shop in Gaulota.

5-5-94
Kasim did most of the talking. They wanted to have a meeting with Sneddon.

5-6-94
They did not state they had eyewitnesses of illegal activity. They said they might have information. Hypothetical questions. They asked about witness protection. Ralph said he owed child support.

<u>Cross-Examine</u>

Kasim told him he was afraid to talk because he didn't want to lose his job and he would fear for his life. Chacon said the same thing.

May 16th

He didn't go to interview them just to serve them a subpoena. He was a lead detective in 93 cases. They wanted a meeting in an isolated place for fear of someone Mj people or others seeing them meet with law enforcement. They told him they would be in danger by Mj people, and they wanted to go to the DA to see what kind of protection they could get. They were told no assurances could be given to this kind of protection even if they testified. They indicated they may have knowledge of Mj fondling, kissing and sucking the penis of a boy.

<u>Re-Direct</u>

They did in fact go to tabloids like they said they wouldn't do. They said they might know someone who has information. Everything was a hypothetical type.

25th Witness – Angel Vivanco

He worked for 3 years. Chef Assistant. 1999-2003. Lived in Guadalupe. Phone calls on David Ventura's phone bill to his phone number in Guadalupe. He saw Arvizo's with their mother.

May 16th

Never saw father had interaction with Starr during a birthday party Mj was not there. He says Starr asked him for a milkshake and wanted him to put Mexican liquor in it. He put it in the milkshake. Starr threatened if he didn't do it he would tell Mj and would be fired. He said Gavin also told him one time to give him the fucking Cheeto's. Starr put a knife an inch from his neck. Starr showed him magazines Mj was not there after the Bashir documentary. Starr and Gavin would take food to guest units. He recalls Janet and Dieter talking at a breakfast bar and they asked for champagne, he said Janet was flirtatious. They went to the family room on the couch , drank champagne, talked and she was still flirtatious. They left together. The same thing the next day but Janet wasn't as flirtatious and wasn't as happy she was more serious. He talked with Davellin, made her food. He would deliver food and take her to the theater. Worked 7am – 10pm.

May 17th

He would meet with Davellin after work at the parking area around 10:00-10:30 pm. Spent 5 or 6 evenings with Davellin on a personal basis. Continued to have personal phone calls after the family left. She never complained to him about anything or anybody at Neverland.

Cross-Examine

She did see the Bashir Documentary. He did not report the knife incident with Starr to anybody. Didn't report the obscene word Gavin used towards him. Didn't report the alcohol incident either.

Re-Direct

He didn't report to Mj directly. If he felt he could deal with it he would report it.

Re-Cross

He reported knife and alcohol and swearing to Rudy Lazano, his supervisor and Jesus Salas.

26th Witness – Irene Peters

Social worker DCFS in LA for 30 years. Works out of Wilshire and Vermont offices. She does not have a license. She was in the unit in 2003 that deals with high profile cases. She has met Janet Arvizo. She received on 2-14-03 Gloria Allred's name was mentioned. She read a referral of general neglect.

May 17th

She went to Jay Jackson's home with 2 LAPD officers. She went to the school the children were at and Janet happened to call while she was there. Her supervisor and another coworker went with her to the interview. Jackie Bowen, and Karen Walker. Janet told her they lived there periodically. She told her they were hiding out from the media because of Bashir Video. She told her they had financial problems. Interview around noon. Janet wanted to start meeting with video of Mj and Gavin at Neverland. She says Janet didn't want anybody there to leave; she said they were her support and friends. They did leave the premises she says. Only people there were social workers and Janet and kids. Janet asked to be present with Gavin during his interview. All interviews took about 2 ½ hours. Janet told her Mj has been like a father to her children. Never said anything negative about Mj. She told her she's (Janet) very aware of what goes on at Neverland. Janet told her the kids were doing well in school.

May 17th

Janet denied all allegations of general neglect. Janet told her the kids never slept in bed with Mj. She says Janet was overly affectionate. She says Janet is witty? Children would interject things during mom's interview about Mj and they all said the same thing. No one was abused or held against their will. She says Janet wanted to have this interview at Neverland. **Gavin told her he never slept in bed with Mj**. 30 minute interviews. Gavin told her Mj never sexually abused him or touched him. She calls Gavin smart and very articulate. Gavin said his mother was by his side during the entire cancer ordeal. Starr never said anything negative about Mj. She says all the family's answers seemed spontaneous not thought out or scripted. Davellin never said anything negative about Mj. She says Janet called her at least every other day on her cell phone. She first called her on her cell phone between 14-20 of February. She got her cell number from her caller ID.

May 17th

Janet never asked her to call police in person or any phone call, before February 20th or after February 20th. She says Janet was trying to impress her with the stars that she knew. February 27th her decision was neglected by Janet and molestation by Mj were unfounded. People under investigation who call her or her agency those calls are supposed to have a record made. If she thought any abuse was going on, she would have called the police. Saw Janet April 1st, 2003 at Fat Burger in LA. Janet was taking the kids to tutoring. She told her kids missed too much school, they didn't have any money. Hadn't heard from Mj and Janet told her Mj (or his people) told them to go to Brazil but she said she didn't want to go to that dump. She, Janet, never told her to call police or anything else on April 1st, 2003. They know if there was a previous referral if they get another referral.

Cross-Examine

Her unit was formed in 1994 because of prior allegations that were leaked pertaining to Mj. Only if they deem allegations true then they call police.

May 17th

She says it can be difficult for a teenage boy to admit to sexual abuse by an adult. Difficult for a teenage boy to admit in front of his mother or other women that he was molested by an adult male. She talked to a counselor at the school. It was not the principal of the school who called in the allegation ; she says it was Dr. Tesh. Is he the principal? She knew from media shows not from watching Bashir Video what the allegations in this case were. She told her Jay Jackson was paying for the tutoring. She says the 2 men at the interview were "Big." She says she wasn't overly concerned about the bodyguard of Mj being there at the interview. If Janet insisted on someone staying for an interview they could have that is her right? Any tape recording is illegal of the interviews. She doesn't recall if Janet went into room 1 of the big guys, she never went into the bedroom with 1 of the big guys. She, Janet, may have gone into the bathroom. They usually like to interview kids alone without parents, but in this case, Janet wanted to be with Gavin.

May 17th

It did not concern her that each child answered the first question the same that Mj is like a father to them. Janet told her she would never put her children in harm's way, She didn't do any verification of anything Janet told her like Mj room being easy come easy go she says that's not her job? Starr told her that he was never left alone with Mj. Davellin told her, her mother knew everything that was going on at Neverland. She didn't use **unfounded** for Mj part of interview she just says the children **denied** any sexual abuse or molestation. It was her understanding that they visit Neverland quite often.

Re-Direct

She's had teenage boys report molestation to her before. She says Gavin appeared very open and not uncomfortable with any questions asked. They did, Gavin, Starr, maybe Davellin admit to sleeping in Mj bed and bedroom but Mj slept on floor if they were in there. She knew she was getting welfare. Janet or the kids never suggested these security guards were a threat to them.

May 17th

Janet never told her that she knew their interview was being recorded. No check into Jay Jackson background. Hiding from media made her, social worker, feel like Janet needed security. She said Mj room was open for her to go in and out of Mj bedroom any time she wanted. Counselor told her that Arvizo's were getting homework sent to them.

Re-Cross

Davellin told her that she takes a friend with her to Neverland. Coming from a broken home, no father at home. These are indicators of possible sexual abuse or molestation.

Re-Direct #2

They spoke highly of Jay Jackson. She didn't meet Jay Jackson. She says it didn't sound like a broken home.

27th Witness – Karen Walker

Works DCFS Supervisor LA for 13 years. She only needed 2 specific licenses for private practice no for what she does. They all went to the interview in the same car. She is usually not in the field; she's usually in the office. In her 7 years before supervision she did approximately 1,000 interviews. It's unusual for people to hug them who were being investigated.

May 17th

She says Arvizo seemed close to Aja. She says Jay Jackson was out of town to her understand. It was unusual to start interview with watching of video? **Janet wanted everybody in same room together not one on one interview**. Peter's took Janet into bedroom for a moment door was open. Janet and children said Mj like a father to them and one of them had anything bad to say about Mj. She, Janet, told them her and David were separated and she has a restraining order against him. Janet told her Gavin was being teased at school because of Bashir video. She was not upset at Mj just over media attention and that she didn't sign release for kids to be in video. She didn't have any contract with Arvizo's be 2-20-03. Had her sign language form on 2-21-03. She (Janet) wanted to know if Mj could pay for homeschool, private school, or tutoring because of media attention from Bashir video. Janet never told her she was being held against her will. She didn't notice any tension between Janet and man with her who worked for Mj?

May 17th

After interviewing her supervisor Brenda Blackburn got a call from Santa Barbara County Sheriff's. Last phone call was a month, 6 weeks after the interview, Janet or Jay didn't say anything inappropriate happened with Mj at this time or at any time?

Cross-Examine

She heard about the prior investigation in 93-94. The information in that case was leaked to the press. She got the impression that Janet had anything to hide. She says one of Mj people looked like he had makeup on. She did not know the interview was being tape recorded. Her mom heard it through the media. She didn't recall Janet going into another room with Mj security guard. This referral was generated by Bashir Video and the statement of Mj sleeping with little boys. She says they think they contacted Santa Barbara County CPS but they hadn't gone out there yet.

Re-Direct

Janet may have told her she needed to move and put boys in new school. Davellin told her she spent time at the theater with her friend. Her statement was that Mj visited with Gavin while he was in hospital, not necessarily that he went to hospital.

Juror Notebook 6

Chapter 6

May 17th

29th Witness Simone Jackson

Mj cousin. 16 years old. Lives in Lompoc. 8 or 9, the first time she went to Neverland. She met Arvizo kids in Feb 2003. There for Prince's B-Day. 10 kids at a B-Day party. She met Janet in March 2003. She went home after the party, somebody drove her home. Saw Arvizo kids March 2003. Rio and her brother were with her then also. They spent 3 nights there in the guest units. Rio stayed with Gavin and Starr and spent the night in the guest unit with them. She saw Gavin and Starr in the kitchen in the main house at 1:00 am in March 2003. She saw both of them take wine, 2 bottles. Starr got a wine glass and Gavin just took a bottle. She was in the corner playing the video game. After Gavin and Starr saw her, they told her to be quiet and not to tell anyone. She went into Janet's guest unit in March 2003. She went to the zoo 1 or 2 times with Davellin. They became friends. Her and Davellin would walk around Neverland. Spent 2 of the 3 with Davellin. She saw Rio hanging out with Gavin and Starr.

May 17th

She says Davellin told her mom (Janet) wanted to go to Brazil. She says Janet never looked scared or upset in March 2003. She was in Gavin and Starr's unit 1 time at night with Rio. She had meals with Davellin in the kitchen in March 2003. She would enter the main house through the back door with Davellin.

May 18th

<u>Cross-Examine</u>

She knew the Arvizo boys were friends of Mj. She made 2 visits to Neverland in March, and stayed a total of 5 nights. She didn't tell anybody about them stealing the wine from the kitchen till the next day, she told her mother. She has spent the night in Mj bedroom in his bed when she was 9. She spent the night in Mj bed with her brother when she was 14. She says the doors were locked to the main house while Janet was there.

<u>Re-Direct</u>

She says Janet could enter the main house if she wanted to, she thinks. She didn't have any passcodes for Mj bedroom or house.

May 18th

30th Witness Rio Jackson

Simone's brother. Mom goes to Neverland with them. Met Gavin and Starr at Neverland. He stayed in the guest unit for 1 night with Gavin and Starr. He says Gavin and Starr were watching naked girls on TV in the guest unit and he say's they were masturbating. He told his sister and she told him to go to Mj room. She says Gavin and Starr took wine from Chefs upstairs to Mj bedroom. He says he saw Gavin and Starr look through drawers and take money from Jesus's office and little crystals. Saw Gavin and Starr take money out of a drawer in Kitchen that he says was Angel's, the chef. He went to Toys R Us with Mj, Gavin, Starr and fans. They picked up boys and girls.

<u>Cross-Examine</u>

His father never went to Neverland with them. He didn't tell Mj about Gavin and Starr because he says he forgot about it. He told Mj about Gavin and Starr watching naked girls. He didn't believe they would do that. He didn't tell Mj about the masturbation because he was scared.

May 18th

The people he picked up on the way to Toys R Us were adults at Mj front gate, not kids. He told his mother about the show Arvizo's were watching and she called Chris Carter. Mj ordered the wine while Gavin, Starr and himself were in Mj room. Gavin and Starr took wine from the chef. Took it upstairs, about 10 minutes later they ran outside with no wine. He says they would stay up all night with Mj. He says Mj didn't ask him why there was wine missing from the bottle.

31st Witness Michelle Jackson

Mj is her nephew. Rio and Simone are her grandchildren. She has met the Arvizo children. Not Janet. She says the kids didn't want to go to Brazil, they told her Gavin and Starr? That their mother wanted to go to Brazil.

Cross-Examine

Went to Neverland 3 or 4 times or more in Feb and Mar. Met the kids only 1 time.

May 18th

32nd Witness Christian Robinson

Develops reality TV Shows. Post Production. TV Videography. 8 years. Operates video cameras professionally. 1st worked for Mj in Sept 2001 charity single "What More Can I Give". He interviewed all the artists on this project. Schaffel was the organizer because Mj wasn't always around. Next time I worked for Mj was Las Vegas? His role in Debbie Rowe was to prepare and ask questions, but he didn't do that. He ended up running a camera. Ian Drew did the interview. He says there was no script for this. There was a list of questions but that is a normal process for an interview. He read a transcript from the Bashir video before he saw it on TV. He says Debbie Rowe was very eager and excited to do an interview and was very angry about Bashir Video. Wasn't rehearsed at all, he says when the camera was on or off. Schaffel made deals, so the Debbie Rowe thing had to be done right away. He wrote questions and did interviews for Arvizo's. There was no script for the interview!!

May 18th

He knew this Arvizo interview was urgent and had to be done right away. He says Brad Miller had no intervention in the Arvizo interview, same for Vinnie. He says nobody had footage but Hamid. They weren't going to use his voice on TV shows. He says no answers were scripted or had any answers before the question was asked. He says all answers were spontaneous. He says kids were very comfortable in Hamid's house. He says Janet was very comfortable there too. She was eating, on her cell phone. No one was there doing makeup or hair. Janet looked that way when she got there. He says Janet was saying "a lot", eager to stand up for Mj and he says she was saying a lot of kooky stuff. She referred to her ex-husband as the kids biological father. A model release is required. She was eager to do an interview but wouldn't sign model releases? He didn't see anybody coercing her into signing releases. Nobody did anything to intimidate Janet or the kids. None of them indicated they were being extorted, held against their will or mistreated by anybody related to Mj.

May 18th

Cross-Examine

Talked business with Mj about 100 times. He says he's a public relations nightmare. He says he became King of Pop because he's a musical genius, not because he knows how to do good PR. Gary, Indiana Spring 2003. Britto Party Fall 2003. Both of these were Neverland Valley Entertainment productions. Met Brett Ratner Home Movies Shoot. Met Schaffel in 2000 or 2001. Schaffel admired and respected Mj a great deal, he says. Worked 15 different jobs for Schaffel, a total of 70-100 days. Never seen Schaffel intentionally do anything to hurt Mj. He says Schaffel is a friend and a good guy. He says the PR thing was more important than making money from Rebuttal. He knew it would be worth money though. He says Vinnie is his friend and a good guy. He knows Frank and Dieter. It was more convenient to do an interview at Hamid's, rather than Schaffel's because Hamid had all the gear in his garage. List of questions was formed by the committee and he says they were thematic.

May 18th

He said Mj helped Gavin with his cancer. He was instructed no to use words like sex or molest in the interview. He got information on Arvizo's on how Mj treated them by Vinnie, Frank, Stuart etc and his feelings of seeing Mj pushing Gavin in a wheelchair in a video he saw. He did show Janet the questions before the interview and gave the kids an idea of the questions he was going to ask them. Paul Hugo is someone who knows Schaffel. Seemed odd to him that there was a P.I. (Brad Miller) at the interview. He thought the whole Arvizo interview was odd. He says he felt some of Janet's answers were rehearsed. He says the kids parroted the mother.

Re-Direct

The Mother would answer some of the questions asked of the kids. He says he wouldn't necessarily ask the questions on the list if they were making good answers. It was implied to him that Arvizo's really loved Mj. He says he was getting a lot of good spontaneous answers from Arvizo's. He says Mj childhood house, 2 rooms maybe and eleven people lived there.

May 18th

He says Vinnie is not big in stature and very nice, and went to ivy league school. He couldn't believe Frank and Vinnie were best friends. Value of the interview would be, if used on TV. He says that maybe $8 million was made on "Footage You Weren't Supposed To See". Vinnie was agitated by having to do pointless chores. He had a business degree. He has seen Mj with his own kids. He had no reason to believe that it wasn't Arvizo 's answers for the interview.

Re-Cross

He left without tape that evening.

33rd Witness Vernee Watson Johnson

She has met Janet Arvizo at an acting school. Arvizo kids were in her acting class at her school. She says Janet and her husband brought and picked up the kids. Her and Carol Lemure were going to organize a fundraiser for Gavin. She didn't trust Janet. She told Janet she needed a separate account for Gavin for fundraiser money and Janet didn't want too. She wanted to put money in her account.

May 18th

She stopped fundraising once Janet wouldn't open an account in Gavin's name. Visited Gavin in the hospital. She saw Janet once at the hospital and David all the time. She gave them money. She doesn't recall if Janet asked her for money. She says Janet would give hints about how they didn't have things, no place to live etc. Starr has called her and she could hear Janet prompting him. She says the Arvizo kids were very disruptive and into all of her things at her house. Children would ask to spend the night but Starr was prompted by Janet. She helped set up Gavin going to Neverland. Carol Lemure helped with a little reluctancy. She says Davellin was at Carol's house all the time for a couple of months. She spoke to Davellin at Carol's house.

May 19th

34th Witness Aja Pryor

Chris Tucker is the father of her son. First went to Neverland in 1999. First met David Arvizo's kids, Oct 2000. First met Janet, July Aug 2001. Chris Tucker met Arvizo's at the Laugh Factory.

May 19th

The Arvizo kids would normally call her at home. Late in 2001, she felt she developed a relationship with Arvizo kids aside from Chris Tucker. She's seen David Arvizo 3 or 4 times. She says she really did love Arvizo children. She visited Gavin on New Year's 2001 in hospital. Saw Arvizo's, Janet and Jay on the bus to go to Neverland for her son's b-day party. Sept 14, 2002, Mj was not there that day. Davellin was by her side the entire day. Chris Tucker and Arvizo kids spent the night at Neverland. Doesn't know if Janet spent the night. Went to Neverland Feb 2003. Arvizo kids asked her to take them. Davellin has spent the night at her house. The boys never have but wanted to. She says Gavin and Starr were really rough and roughhoused a lot. She says David and Gavin spent the night at Chris Tucker's house. Janet never asked her for anything. She did give them a Christmas gift of $600. The mom and kids would tell her about their hardships and things they needed or didn't have. So a lot of hints without directly asking for money.

May 19th

She says Janet told her Gavin broke his arm playing baseball not from the JC Penney incident. She was never told about the JC Penney lawsuit. Feb 2003, Janet thanked her for a car that Aja knew nothing about. Chris Tucker said he would give it to them. They never got the car. She says if Janet didn't call her, Davellin would go to the car. Arvizo kids stopped calling her. 7-10 requests from Janet or Davellin for car Feb 2003. She says Gavin and Starr were very mischievous and they lacked discipline. She says she never saw David discipline the kids. Spoke to Davellin after she watched Bashir Video, Janet also. The only time she ever saw Jay was on a bus to Neverland for a b-day party. She says Janet was in over her head? That's why they talked so much in Feb 2003. **Janet told her they were going to Brazil for Carnival and Janet asked her to go. They had 3 discussions about them going to Brazil. Janet, Mj and his family were going with her and her family.** Janet didn't want to go in March because of unknowns.

May 19th

Janet never told her anything about Mj doing anything bad to her or her family. They talked all the time in Feb 2003?!!! Janet never told her she was being forced to go to Brazil. She says Janet would call her all hours of the day. Janet never told her that she or her kids were ever forced to do an interview. She says Janet was more than happy to do a rebuttal video. She (Janet) praised her and Chris so much that it made her uncomfortable. She told her that Mj helped cure Gavin. Janet was scared her children were going to be taken away from her. She walked in the same time the social workers did. Janet put up a fight when they asked her and her sons to leave. She says it was tense at first and when she came back, it was totally different. Everybody was hugging and the tenseness was gone. (She went to Janet's house to pray with her. Janet wasn't there but kids were there alone in 2001.) Janet put Hamid on the phone before the interview. She was happy, never asked for help or anything.

May 19th

Her and her son took Arvizo kids to Neverland after an interview with social workers. She says Janet was eager to get Birth Certificates for Passports to go to Brazil. She, Janet, never showed up at Neverland and she never saw Janet again. She left the Arvizo kids at Neverland. She did not see Mj there. Marie Nicole, Aldo and Frank? And Miko

Brando and his kids were there. Janet never complained to her about the media after Bashir but Davellin did. Davellin called her the next day from Neverland after she left Friday night. **Janet told her she didn't like the German people. She says they were keeping her and kids away from Mj.** Next time she talked to Janet, she, Janet, was at Neverland. JANET NEVER COMPLAINED TO HER ABOUT MJ at any time. She says Davellin talked about Marie Nicole a lot.

5090 Photos of Arvizo's
5091 With writing on back of them
5092 With writing on back of them
5093 With writing on back of them
5094 With writing on back of them

Children at No time ever complained about Mj for any reason. Arvizo kids asked to stay in Mj room in Feb when she took them. Mj was not there, Joe said no.

May 19th

She watched the Maury Povich Rebuttal show at Neverland with Arvizo kids, the Brando's and Cascio's. Janet did mention Mj was going to set up a college fund for Arvizo kids. "Janet said what good is college fund, he may not be alive". Janet told her she did not sign a release. Janet never mentioned anything about monitored phone calls at Neverland. Gavin did invite a female to Neverland. She says Starr opened the keypad combo on Dance Studio and Gavin and Starr, the main house. Janet said everyone is making millions off a Bashir Video. Janet told her David watched some white boys beat up her and her 2 sons.

5095 Letter from Davellin with Janet's driver's license info on it Feb 13, 2003.

She, Aja, didn't know she was going to send this to her.

Cross-Examine

She knew they were a religious family. Hugged everybody. Arvizo children went to Chris Tucker's brother's wedding. She says Davellin is very nurturing and loving. Davellin's graduation from Cadets, Janet had bruises on her. She didn't know the interview was secretly taped.

May 19th

Arvizo's went with Chris to pick out her new car. She may have said her family when talking about Arvizo's. Janet told her they all held hands and prayed to meet Mj and Chris Tucker. She was not aware Jay Jackson was in the picture at this time?

35th Witness Larry Nimmer

Legal graphics company. Been involved in multimedia and graphics for 30 years. He testified in Santa Barbara, Ventura, LA. Prepared 900 – 1,000 exhibits. Prepares charts and video documentation.

5096 Neverland Alarm Test. DVD May 2nd 2005
5089 Neverland Valley 2005 DVD Tour of Neverland

He went to Mj home to do these tests and make videos 15 feet from the front door to start the video. He made a walk through the hallway to trigger the alarm. 2nd test 2 or 3 feet behind the bed. Made walk through and triggered the alarm again. Door at the bottom of the stairway is open. He says these tapes are fairly accurate. Video of the ranch done over 3 days, some footage was done at night.

May 19th
Went to Neverland 4 or 5 times. There are clocks in the guest unit and you can see clocks from the guest unit #4. Basically, you can see clocks from wherever you are at Neverland.

Cross-Examine

First DVD of the alarm has all footage, nothing cut out or left out. Didn't photo speakers or sensors that set off alarms. Sony VX 2100 camera. He didn't use a decibel calibrator. His camera does have some type of device but he didn't document anything. He basically didn't investigate anything, he just made this video. He says the chimes are inconsistent and doesn't know why. He thinks it chimes softer when you exit, louder when you enter? Other noises could affect someone hearing those chimes.

May 20th

Joe Marcus and Grace were present during filming. Joe was standing behind him. He couldn't tell if the sound was from right or left. He had different instructions for the 1st scene and the 2 other scenes. He was not asked to film the wine cellar, bathroom next to the arcade, Mj office or ref in the kitchen.

May 20th

Re-Direct

Nobody prevented him from taking pictures of anything. There were other areas he didn't film also.

Re-Cross

They told him the room was set like in 2003. He didn't ask if the chime system was the same though.

37th Witness Mark Geragos

Brad Miller told him about the DCFS meeting Arvizo's were going to have. He didn't know it would be tape recorded. He learned from Brad or items from Mr. Sneddon about tape recording. He says Janet wanted somebody there, that's why Asaf was there, is what he thinks Brad told him. He didn't give Brad specific instructions about surveillance of Arvizo's. He was briefed before April about surveillance of Arvizo's by Brad Miller and his people. He didn't know of tape of phone call of Frank and Janet. He always had concerns of the Arvizo family. He didn't direct Brad to work directly with any of Mj's people. He didn't tell Brad to move Janet. He just told Brad to tape it if he was going to do that.

May 20th

#625 Collection of documents.

Letters sent from Dickerman to Geragos and Geragos to Dickerman. 2 of the letters, Geragos says he doesn't think are letters that were sent to him. He doesn't think he talked to Dickerman in March. Brad never told him he followed Arvizo's to any Federal building. Conversations with Dickerman were no to specific items, just the contents of the storage locker. He didn't know if passports were in storage. He says Asaf picked up passports from Vinnie and then dropped them at the Geragos office. He didn't know he ever had passports in his evidence lockup at his office. He doesn't know who received the passports in his office. He discussed with other lawyers before turning over passports to this court. He thought he,

Dickerman, wanted everything right away, that's why he tried to have them delivered to his office. He did tell Brad to find out what Hamid did with videotape. He didn't know who Johnny Megitich was in 2003, he now knows.

May 20th

#277 A note?

Left at Grandparent's house by Johnny to have Gavin and Starr contact Vinnie. He's not aware of any surveillance of Arvizo boys at school. He did not ask Mj if it were true if he slept with kids that weren't his own. Schaffel just told him he went to Brazil, nothing to do with Arvizo's. Mj never told him he was going to Brazil or Arvizo's were going to Brazil. He did tell Brad to talk to Frank or Vinnie. Listened to a taped phone call of Frank and Janet sometime after Feb March 2003. He says he probably called Brad after he listened to the taped phone call. He says Brad Miller would orally update him on Arvizo's. Doesn't remember any written reports.

<u>Re-Direct</u>

Janet wanted her items stored and wanted somebody else to pay for it. He says Brad said Janet wanted the rent paid for the Soto Street Apartment. He was aware that Janet and the kids were living with Jay. A private citizen can record phone calls if they feel they are going to be extorted.

May 20th

His concern was Arvizo's were going to extort Mj. He had knowledge of Janet trying to get money from other people. Brad checked criminal and civil history and found Arvizo name on criminal and civil cases as a complainant or plaintiff or witness? He knew Arvizo's wanted passports when he lodged them with the court.

Re-Cross

He wanted Brad Miller to videotape the move. He has never seen a videotape of Arvizo's movie. He believes there is a tape of the "things" that were moved. He probably told Ronald about his concerns with Janet Arvizo.

May 23rd

38th Witness Maria Gomez

Been at Neverland 11 years. She helped make a video of the alarm test. She first heard the alarm many years ago. Halfway down the hall the chimes begin. Stop for a few seconds and then start louder when you get to the door. She says it's the same chime alarm she's heard for years.

Cross-Examine

2 times up and downstairs do not appear in the

video.

May 23rd

She goes out of room counts to about 15 and comes back. She did not clean or go into Mj room for any reason. Feb, Mar 2003, but she does clean the bathroom in the hallway that leads to Mj room. She says the chimes at the first door were working on Nov 03 and Dec 04.

<u>Re-Direct</u>

Watched the Sheriff's video. She says it's the 2nd bell you hear in this video. You don't hear the first one has already gone off??

39th Witness Mike Radakovich

CPA for 30 years. Office in SLO.

#5105 Analysis chart. He prepared after reviewing a certain doc.
#5097 Washington Mutual Bank Statement.
#5098 Copy of a Washington Mutual Bank cashiers check. Nov 9, 2001. First 2 lines Palanker checks. Next 5 lines are deposit source fundraisers.
#5099 Copy of a check deposited 11-5-2001 $32,308 JC Penney lawsuit. Janet withdraws $29,000 in money order on 11-9-01 to Hollywood Ford.

Dec 2001 Aja Pryor $600 deposit in Janet's

Account. Jan 2nd #5100, #5104 Copies of Welfare checks. Mar 17 from Jay Jackson's account. Bank of America 4-4, 4-6 Expense reports. 2 entries for Janet Arvizo from Neverland Valley Entertainment. Several thousands of dollars spent on Janet and children. Feb 7 Lines of Expenses while at Neverland ranch. Feb 20 $2000. Hamid to Arvizo's Nov 2. Jay Jackson to present an unknown amount.

Cross-Examine

Janet signed her first Palanker check. David signed second. Given a book by the defense of transactions involving Arvizo's and Jay Jackson's accounts. Assumption is from a fundraiser but he has no proof that's true. Bank could have cashed a cashier's check? But would show a re-deposit, wouldn't it? Or she kept cash? Not necessarily cashed by Hollywood Ford.

Re-Direct

Never shows $29,000 going back into Janet's bank account. Payment from Jay Jackson's account for (Janet) Soto Apartment after depositing her welfare check. $7,000 in expenditures from Neverland Valley Entertainment.

May 23rd

#416 $4,800 in expenditure from Neverland Valley Entertainment. Account title is Janet

40th Witness Mercy Manrriquez

County of LA. Dept. of Social Services. Determines Welfare Eligibility. Opening sealed records. Subpoenaed from County of LA on records of Janet Arvizo.

#5106 The Records.

She does medical food stamps and Cal-Works Cash Assistance. They cannot verify everything in forms, they rely on people being truthful.

40 Forms are under penalty of perjury. **11-15-01 Application. 10-23-02 Application for Welfare.** CW7 monthly form filled out for welfare. Janet started receiving 11-01 and stopped 1-03.

Medi-Cal goes hand in hand with Cal-Works, Cash Assistance. She received checks in Feb and Mar 2003. 11-15-2001 started receiving food stamps. Doesn't show when or if it has ended. **Janet didn't disclose her part of the children's part of JC Penney settlement or David's.** They have to report any change on a monthly basis.

May 23rd

JANET LIES ON WELFARE FORM. SHE COMMITS Fraud on Applications. (Note of Gavin Cancer. Abused mother. Last worked 10-31-01 on disability. Foot Surgery. No Bank accounts, no cars. Applying for divorce because of Domestic Violence. Note written on bottom of the sheet.) **(Emergency) marked on forms to imply the right way. 11-2-01 Receives check from JC Penney Settlement. 11-05-01 Deposits into her bank account she doesn't have. Applies for Welfare, Food stamps, Medi-Cal 11-15-01.** Janet does not report any money she received or her living half the time with Jay Jackson. SHE LIES ON EVERY FORM. Janet writes a note to discontinue and be off Welfare 3-3-03. **In 2001, Janet indicated she did not want to go to a shelter because of domestic violence. She received disability benefits. Shows rent receipt but got free rent once or twice. Never reported that.**

Cross-Examine

She was afraid to go back home. She says she asked for an escort home.

May 23rd

Any trust would affect eligibility of Welfare.

Re-Direct

Over a month out of the house, has to be reported. Any form of money in any bank account, trust etc, has to be reported.

41st Witness Marian Arvizo

David's sister. Met Janet 18 years ago. She organized a blood drive at Vons in El Monte. Had a friend at Kaiser tell her how to set up a blood drive, Marie Triggs. She also works at Vons in store, David in warehouse. 25 or 30 at Blood Drive. 2nd Blood drive at Church. Her, her sister and Marie Triggs. She never contacted Janet about the blood drive. She says she didn't think Janet wanted to be involved. Janet told her, "she didn't need her fucking blood." She just needed money. She hung up on Janet. After separation, the kids went swimming at her house. No contact with Janet since she hung up on her. No contact with kids since the blood drive.

Cross-Examine

Connie Keenan met her today, never before that.

May 23rd

Hadn't spoken to her brother in 15 years.

42nd Witness Connie Keenan

Editor for Mid Valley News. June 1999. Office in El Monte. Never met Janet. Spoke to her. Janet wanted another story because the first one didn't make enough money. Year 2000, assigned story to Christy Kauser. She questioned some amounts of things, the cost of injection. Janet was to have money sent directly to her house. She couldn't allow that. She says that's unethical. Article appeared 1 time. She found out Gavin in fact did have insurance coverage. She told Christy, Janet Arvizo had to have a Bank Trust Fund set up to receive money for Gavin. Can't be sent to Janet's house.

Cross-Examine

She's not acquainted with any Arvizo. A picture accompanied the article. She is sure the phone call between Janet and Christy Kauser was tape recorded. Contacted Kaiser before she learned of allegations in this case. She doesn't mention David or contact any stars.

May 23rd

She authorized information on the trust account to be put in the story.

Re-Direct

She says Janet never called and said there was a type error. It wasn't $12,000 it was $1,200. Article was not to raise money for repossessed cars. Article was just to raise money for medical costs in her eyes. Her newspaper had a staff of 3. No articles ever dealt with a family in need until this one.

Re-Cross

3 months later, she talked to Christy Kauser.

May 24th

43rd Witness Jay Leno

Deals with a lot of kid's organizations. At least 13 years. He's known Jaime Masada for a while, and doesn't go to Laugh factory very often. I Have known Louise Palanker for a long time. He got a lot of voicemails from Gavin. He called the hospital room he thinks he talked to Starr and Janet. He says listening to Gavin was like listening to adults, not a 10-13 year old. He says Gavin sounded scripted to him.

May 24th

He told Louise Palanker he was getting too many calls from Gavin and he wanted them to stop. He says he wasn't asked for any money, nor did he give money.

<u>Cross-Examine</u>

He has seen Bashir Documentary. He knows of Comedy Camp and has never been involved in it.

<u>Re-Direct</u>

Police called him at the studio, secretly recorded the conversation. He told police then he thought they were looking for money, even though they never asked him for anything.

Re-Cross

He got no more calls from Gavin after he talked to Louise Palanker.

44th Witness Suli McCullough

Actor, comedian. Regular at Laugh Factory since 1989. Visited Gavin at the hospital 3 or 4 times. He invited the family to a taping of Jaimie Foxx Show and they went. Jaimie Masada told him the purpose of Fundraisers was to **pay for medical expenses**.

Cross-Examine

He was not aware the Arvizo's had insurance at Kaiser from the dad's work.

45th Witness Monica Wakefield

Client Services Advocate. Works for Kaiser Permanente in Hollywood. Talked to Sheriffs in Spring 2004. Looked into records to see if creatinine clearance test was done. She says it was done, but she says there was not enough specimen to complete the test (she thinks). March 10, 2003 Date of Collection. She does remember saying to Sgt. Robel it couldn't be completed because they needed blood and urine. She says you need at least 10 ml of urine for the test. Apparently, there were 90 ml. She told Sgt. The test was not completed because they didn't have blood.

Cross-Examine

From the document neither specimen was sufficient to do that test, blood or urine.

Re-Direct

She told Scott Ross, Defense Investigator 4 days ago that the test couldn't be completed because of a lack of blood not urine?

46th Witness Mary Holzer

Paralegal. Office manager for Feldman and Rothstein. Started work there in 1985. She met Janet Arvizo in 1999, maybe.

May 24th

Her firm represented Arvizo's in the JC Penney lawsuit. Janet would call for her several times a day. She says Janet was a client, not a friend. Arvizo children would come into the office and sit on her lap and tell her how great she was. She says Janet threw herself down the driveway and said the doctor and nurses were the devil, she was told to leave. She was told by Janet that she was a victim of domestic abuse and told her the children were mistreated by David. Photos of Janet. Injuries shown to her by Anthony Reneri. **Janet told her that the bruises were inflicted on her the night of the JC Penney incident by David. She was threatened by Janet**

<u>if she told anyone she and her daughter would be killed by David's brother. Janet threatened her and her daughter 8 or 9 times. Janet would tell her how great Mj was and would invite her and her daughter to Neverland. Janet told her kids went to acting classes. So she could tell her kids what to say. Janet never told her to tell JC Penney or their lawyers she lied !!!</u>

May 24th

She never asked how children left JC Penney because David and Janet were arrested. She says Janet showed her injuries 3 years after the JC Penney incident that looked to her to be the same. She went with Janet to her family law lawyer, if he would file a restraining order.

<u>Re-Direct</u>

Booking photo's day of the JC Penney ordeal shows no injuries. Her firm got involved with Arvizo's 9 months after the JC Penney incident. Janet went to the bank with her to set up accounts for Starr and Gavin. Her name is on the account as legal guardian. Statements were sent to her mother's house in El Monte. Janet called her 3 or 4 months ago and said she wanted to be friends and have a girls weekend and she told her Mj was the devil and no longer her savior.

47th Witness Anthony Raneri

Met Janet in 1998. Personal Injury Attorney. 2 weeks after JC Penney, he had a meeting with Janet. Janet denied under oath her husband ever beat her.

May 24th

Janet had not told him about her supposedly being fondled in the previous 25 meetings?, but she said that under oath in a deposition. Janet asked him for money directly.

48th Witness Karen Brando

Marlon Brando's daughter in-law. Been to Neverland 10-15 times. Met Janet 2003 at Neverland in the kitchen. Prudence was 7, Shane 14. Husband Miko was at the ranch. Janet told her she was going home with her. She told her husband she didn't want Janet going home with her. She says Janet was hyper demanding and someone she wouldn't trust. Later, when Janet told her she wasn't going home with her, she was much calmer she said.

49th Witness Prudence Brando

His dad is Miko, mother Karen. Goes to Neverland a lot. Friend of Mj. He says Starr and Gavin were crashing the golf carts on purpose. He says Starr and Gavin would throw candy off the rides. He doesn't recall Davellin telling Starr and Gavin to stop doing anything.

May 24th

50th Witness Phillipp Esplin

Forensic Psychologist. Office in Phoenix, AZ. Interested in how children learn. Brain injury – Congenital runs in family disease. Studies in children 3-14 years of age who have been a victim or witnessed a crime. Has dealt with a lot of sexually abused children. Did a conference in Italy on the study of sexually abused kids and not sexually abused children. Would train sex crime investigators. He's developing techniques to get the truth from children. Been licensed in Arizona since 1978. Has written 25 articles on child witnesses that have been published. Published 1st article 1991. He does speak at seminars. Sent a transcript of the testimony of Dr. Anthony Urquiza. Child Accommodation syndrome has little effect on determining real or false allegations. Delay in reporting is the only one that's been validated. None of the 5 factors have been used in studies. Delay in reporting abuse doesn't mean it didn't happen. He says 10 and up have good memories of what happened.

May 24th

Contradictions of key details would be uncommon with what the studies show. Studies 2% to 40% of false allegations. Intentional false claims happen most in 10 and up. Parents pushing a child for gain could cause false claims. Children come to realize the power of some of their statements. He says you would have to look at the environment of a child. The make-up of the parents etc.

Cross-Examine

Child Abuse Neglect 1994 study. He says there are a lot of people who wait a long time to come forward. He says 10 and up less capable of deciding what's important to tell? He believes older kids would tell a friend not a parent.

Re-Direct

Not every loving caring adult who takes kids fun places does fun things etc is not necessarily a molester.

51st Witness Julio Avila

I Worked at Neverland for 4 years, 6 months. Park operator now security. He met the Arvizo family in Jan 2001. Accommodated Gavin, Starr and Davellin almost every time they wanted to get on a ride.

May 24th

He says Gavin and Starr would spit and throw things at him and his co-workers from tops of rides. Gavin and Starr did operate one of the rides themselves. Davellin was on the ride Starr was operating. Found Starr in the control room writing on the wall "You Suck Dick". **Saw Starr with an adult magazine that he says he brought from home.** Happened in 2003. He says Gavin would try to start rides also. He says Gavin and Starr were very destructive on quad runners. He hardly ever saw the mother.

Cross-Examine

Arvizo boys became more and more rowdy the longer they were at Neverland. He had a hard time with determining Arvizo and Cascio, but then he says Cascio kids were not rowdy at all. He says he didn't tell the Sheriff he knew Mj had nude magazines. Why was he operating a zipper on it when Starr operated swings with Davellin on it?

May 24th

52nd Witness Lessie Wraggs

Has met Janet Arvizo in 1998 at Universal Dance with her kids. Janet wanted free classes for her kids. Owners decided to let them have free classes, they went for 3 years. She says Janet asked the owner for money. She says Arvizo kids were not well behaved and always talked smart. She says the mom had more control of kids than the dad did. She saw them arrive in a new SUV 3 or 4 times. Janet told her JC Penney security guards were black and after that incident the kids were afraid of black people and the family hated black people now.

Cross-Examine

She was present during Janet's talk with the owners of dance school. She says Janet was wrong, the kids didn't hate black people.

53rd Witness Arlene Kennedy

She runs Universal Dance School. She says her brother gave Arvizo kids a scholarship (free classes). She doesn't think the mother worked.

May 24th

She never charged them a dime to go to her school. **Janet told her a different story about JC Penney than David Arvizo.** Janet told her they got a lot of money from JC Penny but all they had to show for it was these bicycles.

Cross-Examine

Janet used to go to church with her. She has given scholarships to children before.

54th Witness Chris Tucker

Known Mj for 4 years. He met Mj through Gavin Arvizo. Met Gavin and David Arvizo at Laugh

Factory. First time was a benefit to raise money. He wired some money because Gavin told him they didn't make money from the fundraiser. Met Janet for the first time in Las Vegas on the set of a movie. Next time he saw them was at his house before his trip to Miami. Janet always said he was the kid's brother and he remembers Janet crying on the phone a lot on 1 occasion. He says Gavin used to call him all the time. Starr would call sometimes.

May 24th

They've been to his house 3 times. He gave Gavin a pair of Nike's after fundraiser.

May 25th

Gavin and his father were at his house when Gavin asked for money because no money was made from the fundraiser. Janet went to his house 1 time, Feb 2003. He told his fiancée not to give Arvizo's keys to the vehicle because he got nervous and suspicious. He met Mj in New York after a phone conversation with him. Been to Neverland 5 or 6 times before 2003. Mj was there once or twice. He spoke to Gavin after Bashir Video. Gavin told him it was hard to get around without a car and the media followed them everywhere. His brother and a few of his assistants told him to be careful. Everybody was telling him it was time for them to leave. He says Janet or David did not discipline the kids while they were on set. He didn't expect Arvizo's to stay for weeks in Las Vegas. Janet told him he was part of the family and he was like a brother to kids.

May 25th

Gavin told him he wanted to be around Mj, so he helped them go to Miami to be with Mj and get away from the media because of Bashir Video. He says Gavin and Starr were very cunning. He says something mentally wasn't right with Janet. He says Janet and kids were very excited to go see Mj in Florida. He told Mj to watch out for Janet when he saw him in Florida, be careful. He doesn't remember paying for massages for Arvizo boys. Janet told him Mj was the father and he was the brother. That's when he became even more suspicious. He never got the keys to the truck back from Janet. After the Florida trip, Gavin did call him and continued to call him. He says he was getting sick of them calling for the truck. Last talked to Gavin a year ago. He called to see if the number worked. Gavin answered, his mother Janet screamed at him, Gavin, to get off the phone now.

May 25th

<u>Cross-Examine</u>

He says he or his attorney did not decline to talk to Law Enforcement. He knows Al Malnik. He was in a photo with Mj and Malnik from a birthday party in Miami after the charges were filed in this case? He says the only start Gavin mentioned to him was Mj. He was not aware of how medical bills were being paid. He says it was Gavin asking for money a second time and he thought his father was part of it but he says it was Gavin asking. He says the Arvizo's basically invited themselves to his brother's wedding in Pasadena. Gavin gave him the paper with all the information of the bank to wire money too. He never said the vehicle was going to be a gift for Christmas. He doesn't know if Brett Ratner is married to Al Malnik's daughter. He says Janet kept interrupting him when he was trying to talk to Mj alone. He knows who Evvy Tavasci is. He says he did not call XtraJet the day of the Florida Trip.

May 25th

He didn't know if Mj called Gavin the morning of the Florida trip. He doesn't know who Gary Hearn is. Mj limo driver?

<u>Re-Direct</u>

He says Aja was entangled with this family. He did warn Aja to get away from his family. He says Arvizo kids were ashamed to talk about their mothers. Got info on Arvizo's from Aja. He knew nothing of the finances of the Arvizo's.

Defense Rests

Prosecution Rebuttal

May 25th

1st Witness – Tim Rooney

He was responsible for searching the filing cabinet in the security office. He found no records 2003 of Arvizo's.

Cross-Examination

He was never told the records for 2003 were in fact in the filing cabinet. He says he searched that cabinet very carefully and thoroughly. HE doesn't know if any other officers searched there before he got there.

Re-Direct

He says he is certain those records were not in there when he searched.

2nd Witness – Shane Meredith

February 17-20 during his work hours. He never saw anybody driving one of the ranch cars.

Cross-Examine

He says he could have been doing any of the jobs that relate to security. If doing a perimeter check he couldn't have seen anybody driving a car. He says it wouldn't be unusual for some incident to not get logged.

May 25th

Supervision discretion to log an incident.

Re-Direct

He says underage drivers of ranch vehicles would definitely be logged in.

3rd Witness – Jesus Salas

House manager 2003. Weeks of February and March worked almost every day. Spent night a few times, never witnessed or head of underage children driving ranch vehicles. **Never kept money in his desk or office at Neverland.** Says nothing from his office ever came up missing when Arvizo's there. Never told about money being taken from Kitchen, nor was knife incident with Starr and Chef Angel Vivanco. Never told Joe Marcus he was leaving with Arvizo's. He was aware of locations of guests in main house. He says Arvizo boys, the spent 90% of February – March in Mj bedroom. He saw Mj intoxicated quite a few times, 3 times in front of his children.

Cross-Examine

There was almost always a nanny around if MJ was drinking or drunk. He was never in Mj room when Arvizo's were in there.

May 25th

He was not aware of the knife incident with Kiki Fournier. He was not aware of Starr having adult magazine writing suck dick on wall, Gavin and Starr found in Wine Cellar, Milkshake incident etc. NOTHING talked about was ever reported to him.

He doesn't know who called Joe's number at 12:55am on February 12th. If he was working all day and all night in the house how would he know if someone underage was driving a ranch vehicle if it wasn't reported. And he's driving people every other day off the ranch to LA, Burbank, etc.. So he wasn't always there. No door on the office he used anybody has access to that office.

<u>Re-Direct</u>

He says it got to the point in 2003 Mj was intoxicated 4 times a week he says. He says a child asking for alcohol would have been reported.

May 25th

4th Witness – Det Alvarez

Interviewed Avila about Starr operating ride. He says Avila told him he was operating Zipper ride doesn't know for who because all Arvizo's were at the ride Starr was operating. Avila told him that kids pretty much ran amuck here. He says Avila was confusing Arvizo and Cascio families when talking about kids. Avila never told him about Arvizo's kids driving the quads recklessly. He tried to contact Chris Tucker 3 times. He never made contact with him. He says he did get to Chris Tucker's front door left a card with his numbers, never received a call from Chris Tucker or his lawyer. He called his lawyer and said he would like to interview Chris Tucker, his lawyer said Chris Tucker has nothing to say. After this is when he went to Chris Tucker's house 3 times. Avila said Arvizo's are destructive more often than the other children who come to ranch. He never asked Avila about the quads.

May 26th

5th Witness – Gina Villegas

Hollywood Ford Office Manager. Searched records for evidence. Janet bought a car 2000-2004. She says Janet never bought a car from there.

Cross-Examine

He did not ask her if a money order was ever presented as a money order during this period. She was never asked to check the deposits of the dealership during that time. Never asked her to see if a check was made out to Janet or someone she designated from Hollywood Ford. She says no vehicle was ever sold to Janet Arvizo or Janet Ventura.

6th Witness – Donna Aggers

Record Supervisor. West Covina Police August 28, 1998.
Arrested – August 27 – 18:18. Booked 21:45
Released – 12:03 am

#5109 – David's records
#5110 – Janet's Records

Janet 1800 – Arrested
1948 – Booked
2115 – Released

No indication in record Janet was beaten up.

May 26th

She says you would want to know if someone was severely beaten up when being booked. Head photo taken during booking shows no signs of injury to the face , head or neck.

Re-Direct

Wouldn't change into jail clothes for a misdemeanor. Still a crime.

7th Witness – George Erwin

Owner Dino's Moving and Storage. North Hollywood. Has a storage facility at the office. Records of storage of Brad Miller.

#904 – Those records. Move took place on 3-1-03. Another bill of lading 3-5-03 (02). Even though it says 2nd pick up was on 3-5-93. Even though it says 3-4-00
#905 – Document showing what was picked up the 1st pickup on 3-1-03. X shows the release of items from storage.

10-1-03 the date these items were released to Jay Jackson and Janet Arvizo.

Cross – Examine

Licensed by the state of California, obtained in 1984. Items 1-19 were picked up on 3-1-03. They charge for packing, 3-1-03, show no packing or use of packing materials.

May 26th

He does not know Brad Miller personally. If the people moving have their own materials, they would use those, but if they had to pack, they would still show a charge for that wouldn't it? Everything was already packed? Materials were not tampered with from time of storage to time of pick up. They generally do not do cleaning of house, apartment, etc. but he says it's possible but it's not a service they generally offer.

<u>Re-Direct</u>

There were 4 boxes and a roll of tape used on the 2nd move that shows charges for.

8th Witness – Theresa Marquez

Custodian of records. Kaiser Permanente. Baldwin Park. Emergency room visit. 8-29-98 for Janet Arvizo.

#906 – Records of that visit. Time 1:11 am, Registration time.

<u>Re-Direct</u>

She was released at 4:15 am? She had x rays all come back negative.

May 26th

9th Witness Bill Dickerman

#903 Letters between him and Mark Geragos

3-26-03 Letter that refers to passport and visas of Arvizo's
4-3-03 Letter that references the 3-26-03 letter from Geragos to him
4-6-03 Letter from Geragos to him
4-8-03 Letter to Geragos that refers to passport, visa's and birth certificates.
4-9-03 Letter to Geragos again refers to visa passports, birth certificates
4-11-03 Letter to Geragos
4-15-03 Letter from Geragos to him, advising him he has things from storage and where does he want them delivered
4-22-03 Letter to Geragos refer to passports, visa's, birth certificates
5-12-03 Letter to Geragos
5-15-03 Letter from Geragos to him. No reference of passports
5-15-03 Letter from Geragos from him to immediately return these items.
5-17-03 Letter to him from Geragos
5-20-03 Letter to Geragos from him.

May 26th

5-29-03 Letter to Geragos
6-6-03 Letter to Dickerman
6-12-03 Brad Miller to him

<u>Re-Cross</u>

He says he always signs his letters. Doesn't have the signed letter from 3-26-03. He didn't immediately advise Geragos where to deliver items like Geragos asked for? He says Geragos knew where he wanted things delivered and what he wanted delivered. He says he doesn't remember if he was told the address off Soto St. Apartment. He says he wasn't necessarily going to sue Mj on behalf of Arvizo's. Geragos letter offers for him or Janet to take over the storage unit for $100 a month. He does respond to that request by saying if he returns other things, they could work the other things out.

Re-Direct

He says Geragos never told him where the items were stored. He says he knew nothing of delivery of Arvizo things before the attempt of delivery.

May 26th

10th Witness – Christie Causer

Rose Hills Mortuary. Visitation person. Used to work at Mid-Valley News with Connie Keenan. She delivered 9 uncooked turkey and $5.00 to the Arvizo's. She says she got in trouble for that. Wrote an article on Arvizo's. Everything she told Keenan was pretty everything Kenan testified to.

Cross-Examine

Janet told her; her car was repossessed. She did tape record the interview

11th Witness – Maria Ventura

August 27th, 1998 went to the mall to pick up grandchildren after Janet and David were arrested.

The kids stayed with her until the next day. Janet and David picked them up the next day.

12th Witness – Det Bonner

#448 Brad Miller Cellular phone records. January, February, March, 2003.
#449 Geragos and Geragos phone records
#460 Link charts of phone call for rebuttal part of this case

May 26th

60 Calls Brad Miller, Frank Casio
50 Calls Brad Miller and Geragos and Geragos
15 Brad Miller and Marc Schaffel
1, 3 way call Geragos, Miller, Schaffel
2-12-03 Geragos, Miller, Schaffel.
2-19-03 1, 3 way call. Went back to Neverland
12-4 Heard Chimes
11-18-03 Hear Chimes

#157 Photo
#159 Photo
#160 Photo

He observed sensors that start chime. He also tested or was part of the test of the chime system. 2 sensors located outside of Mj bedroom. He says the 1st sensor did not activate in November 2003 or December 2004.

1 Chime in bathroom with Jacuzzi (Works)
1 Under chair was not working (Didn't work)

May 27th

#909 Photo showing where the chime speakers were. These have been in the same location since November 2003 – December 2004.
#908 DVD of search warrant December 2004.
#907 Diagram.

Cross-Examine

He is not an expert on certain sensors or annunciators. He says the camera guy was right close to where the cabinet speaker is.

May 27th

Volume setting at 1 for this DVD. They had no decibel test. Did not analyze Geragos and Geragos office phones that ended in 3900. Just his cell phone 21000. He says he found out yesterday that Brad Miller was working on a different case for Geragos during February, March 2003. So he doesn't know for sure, all or any calls between Miller and Geragos pertain to this case.

#5108 – Page from Neverland Valley phone bill 688-1679.
February 13 2003 – 12:55am call from Ranch phone to #805?

Re-Direct

He says chime is consistent when he was at Neverland and DVD heard in court.

#419 $500,000 check from Mj Cash
#418 $1,000,000 check from Mj for Fox TV Shows

#417 Pg. 12 – Letter to David Legrand terminating his services for Mj
#410 Pg. 10 – Note recorder for phone Janet and Gavin, P.I. Brad Miller
Long letter about disbursement of money
#405 Statement by Janet issued through Bell-Yard represents Mjj Production but does not act for Janet Arvizo.

May 27th

13th Witness – Sgt Robel

He interviewed Gavin for 1st time July 6th, 2003 at SART Building, Sexual Assault Response Team. Det. Paul Zellis was also there. Original VHS transferred to DVD

#900 – Playing of DVD – 1 hour and 4 minutes

He doesn't say "Biological Father" every time when talking about David. They asked to fix Gavin's computer and the car Mj gave them, why would you ask the person who gave you this stuff for free to fix it if it breaks? He says Mj doesn't like the internet because the government can monitor the internet. He says Mj told him to keep drinking the wine out of coke can even in front of Janet. Gavin says Janet didn't know there was wine in it?? He, Gavin, says he doesn't know if he ejaculated or not when MJ masturbated him? He says Mj masturbated him 5 or less times. He says he, Gavin slept in Mj room every night after the Miami trip.

May 27th

He says Mj never threatened him, Frank did. He says his mother Janet always wanted to leave Neverland. Mj never showed him videos, but he says he did show him black suitcase with adult magazines in it. He says Mj gave him the watch and told him not to say anything about "anything." He says he could tell Mj was naked, but it was too dark to see his penis and genitals?? How do they know he was naked then? He makes a good description and details of MJ room but other things he doesn't.

Cross-Examine

He Sgt Robel didn't ever challenge anything Gavin said.

Prosecution Rebuttal Rests

No Defense Rebuttal

June 2nd

Prosecution Closing Arguments

George Lopez – Janet never asked for money?
Fritz Coleman – Janet never asked for money?
Jay Leno – Janet never asked for money?

Didn't testify who defense say Janet asked for money

Adam Sandler
Jim Carey

Janet was not at Laugh Factory for either or any fundraiser.

No celebrity was brought to Soto St. Apartment. Fritz Coleman and Louise Palanker went on their own.

Janet never told Law Enforcement she needed money?

Mj never interrupted his career to help Gavin?

She, Janet, did commit fraud against welfare.

Head licking of Gavin? Was the same 10 years ago of Jordan Chandler.

NOTES

Quantitative Models

"An Analytical Approach to Efficiently Structuring Data"

A Quantitative Model with use of Qualitative Variables Applied to Situational Behaviors and to Structure data in a manner that is meaningful to the observer.

A Model relating to an individual, event or pattern.

(1)
$qa = x_1 y_1 + x_2 y_2 + x_3 y_3 + x_4 y_4 + x_5 y_5 + x_z y_z$ (2)
$x_1 y_1 = a_1 b_1 + a_2 b_2 + a_3 b_3 + a_z b_z x_2$
$y_2 = a_1 b_1 + a_2 b_2 + a_3 b_3 + a_z b_z x_3 y_3$
$= a_1 b_1 + a_2 b_2 + a_3 b_3 + a_z b_z x_4 y_4 =$
$a_1 b_1 + a_2 b_2 + a_3 b_3 + a_z b_z x_5 y_5 = a_1$
$b_1 + a_2 b_2 + a_3 b_3 + a_z b_z x_z y_z = a_z b_z$

(1) Main function quantitative model exploring qualitative equilibrium points
(2) Subfunction quantitative model exploring qualitative equilibrium points
(3) Quantitative model with qualitative equilibrium points to exhibit an equilibrium between qualitative variables
(4) Use of a multi-dimensional equation of mathematical programming combined with a subfunction multi-dimensional equation. Use of mathematical programming methods, to model situational behaviors or patterns
(5) The model accounts for unknown and additional variables with data stored in corresponding variables
(6) Derived meaning and understanding from the model can be exhibited
(7) Structuring data or information in this manner can elicit greater clarity as the model brings one towards equilibrium
(8) The model can be applied to a diverse amount of fields with a similar method to determine equilibrium

Conspiracy Charge: OVERT ACT NUMBER 26

On or about March 9, 2003, MICHAEL JOE JACKSON was told by John Doe that John Doe had a medical appointment the following day, at which time he was to give the medical staff a 24-hour long urine collection specimen for laboratory analysis. MICHAEL JOE JACKSON, in Santa Barbara County, did tell John Doe to cancel the appointment, because the sample would reveal that John Doe had been consuming alcoholic beverages while staying at Neverland Ranch. On or about March 10, 2003, in Los Angeles County, after Jane Doe refused to cancel the medical appointment and while on the way to the medical appointment, VINNIE AMEN did destroy most of John Doe's collected urine specimen, intended for laboratory analysis in connection with John Doe's follow-up treatment for the disease of cancer.

The Account

For a period of time, Gavin Arvizo had to urinate in a large bottle to keep a record of it. Janet Arvizo, his mother, was the individual monitoring the urine preparation. The urine would then be brought to Gavin's doctor for Analysis the next day. The Analysis was to determine how Gavin's kidneys were functioning due to his prior illness of cancer which limited his kidney function. In the morning, prior to leaving Michael Jackson's Ranch by car, the sample was collected, Gavin, Star and Janet Arvizo entered the car to leave for Gavin's doctor

appointment at Kaiser Permanente Hospital in Los Angeles.
Vincent Amen drove the car with the family to bring them to Gavin's doctor with the urine sample. The kids sat in the back seats of the car with Janet Arvizo in the front with the urine sample. Everyone left the ranch in the morning and would arrive in Los Angeles several hours later. The children had fallen asleep in the back seat of the car while in route to the hospital.

Account in Contention

Vincent Amen's Account

Closer to Santa Barbara than L.A., the urine sample spilled in the car in the front passenger seat floor where Janet was holding the bottle. Janet asked for the car to be pulled over so the urine could be cleaned up. The car pulled over at the next rest stop where there was a gas station. Janet exited the car to get paper towels. She then came back, cleaned the spilled urine and then everyone proceeded to the hospital.

Janet Arvizo's Account (from media/Santa Barbara DA)

Closer to Santa Barbara than L.A., Janet asked Vincent to pull the car over since she needed to use the rest area. Janet alleges she exited the car, went into the rest area and left the urine sample in the car. Janet alleges that when she returned the urine sample bottle was nearly empty. Janet alleges when she asked Vincent what happened, he said it spilled. Everyone then proceeded to the hospital.
On arriving at the hospital, the car was parked and everyone exited the car with Janet bringing the

bottle with the urine sample. Everyone went up several floors of the hospital to the floor of Gavin's doctor. Upon this arrival, Vincent left the building to have lunch. The appointment would take some time due to a kidney dye test needed to be performed on Gavin. Janet called Vincent roughly 1 1/2 hours later when she was finished with the appointment to pick her and the kids up.

On return, Janet told Vincent that the urine sample was not enough to run the test and would have to be retaken at some point in the future.
Let's take a look at the quantitative model and see if we can determine equilibrium points and motive.
A Model relating to the individuals and events surrounding the Urine Story.
$qa = x_1\, jf_1 + x_2\, jf_2 + x_z\, jf_z$
$x_1\, jf_1 = a_1 b_1 + a_z b_z$
$x_2\, jf_2 = a_1 b_1 + a_z b_z$
$x_z\, jf_z = a_z b_z$
(3)
qa = urinesample$_1$ jf_1 + car$_2$ jf_2 + seatingincar$_3$ jf_3 + placement$_4$ jf_4 + samplespilled$_5$ jf_5 + reststop$_6$ jf_6 + hospital$_7$ jf_7 + appointments$_8$ jf_8 + departed$_9$ jf_9 + return$_{10}$ jf_{10} + sampleinsufficient$_{11}$ jf_{11} + $x_z\, jf_z$
urinesample$_1$ jf_1 = (Gavin's urine sample collected for future test)$_1$ $b_1 + a_z b_z$
car$_2$ jf_2 = (Everyone entered car to leave for the appointment)$_1$ $b_1 + a_z b_z$
seatingincar$_3$ jf_3 = (Vincent drove, Janet in passenger seat, kids in backseat)$_1$ $b_1 + a_z b_z$
placement$_4$ jf_4 = (Urine sample on floor of passenger seat, Janet holding)$_1$ $b_1 + a_z b_z$

samplespilled$_5$ $jf_5(1)$ = (Janet spilled urine in car)$_1$ $b_1 + a_z b_z$
reststop$_6$ jf_6 = (Car pulled over to rest stop)$_1$ $b_1 + a_z b_z$
samplespilled$_5$ $jf_5(2)$ = (Vincent alleged spilled urine sample when Janet left car)$_1$ $b_1 + a_z b_z$
hospital$_7$ jf_7 = (Car left for Kaiser Permanente Hospital)$_1$ $b_1 + a_z b_z$
appointments$_8$ jf_8 = (Doctor Appointment, dye test for Gavin's Kidney)$_1$ $b_1 + a_z b_z$
departed$_9$ jf_9 = (Vincent left and went downstairs, Janet and kids at appointment)$_1$ $b_1 + a_z b_z$
return$_{10}$ jf_{10} = (Janet called Vincent to come back to pick the family up)$_1$ $b_1 + a_z b_z$
sampleinsufficient$_{11}$ jf_{11} = (Janet disclosed the urine test could not be determined due to insufficient sample)$_1$ $b_1 + a_z b_z$

---

(3)
a variable can be verbal, written description, picture or video
b variable can be verbal, written description, picture or video

---

Motive can be determined by analyzing the model and asking a question of interest between each or summation of equilibrium points.

Motives for Janet spilling urine |

1. Accidentally
2. Knowledge of Gavin drinking alcohol and it might show up in test
3. Delay Brazil Trip
4. Unknown Motive Variable

Motives for Vincent allegedly spilling urine |

1. Knowledge of Gavin drinking alcohol and it might show up in test
2. Unknown Motive Variable

Credibility is another factor that needs to be accounted for to bolster witness statements about occurrence and action

Credibility

1. Vincent Amen's Credibility
2. Janet Arvizo's Credibility

Conclusion

The equilibrium point in question is the account of who spilled the urine and why. Based on the model, it can be determined that Vincent and Janet wanted to bring Gavin to the doctor for kidney tests. This is due to Vincent driving the family to the hospital and Janet keeping the appointment. The person who spilled the urine may be stored in an unknown variable. These variables are absent from the model that can be added.

Unknown Variables

Drinking$_{12}$ jf$_{12}$

jf$_{12}$ = Gavin drinking with Michael and being seen by witnesses.

Delay$_{13}$ jf$_{13}$

jf$_{13}$ = Janet delaying Brazil trip after rescheduling Gavin's doctor appointment for some time in the future.

A plausible explanation is that Janet Arvizo's children told her Gavin was drinking prior to the test with Michael since they witnessed this behavior. This is apparent from Janet's and the children's witness statements known to prosecutors.

Another plausible explanation is that Janet did not want to go to Brazil at the time. Gavin would have to go to the Doctor for a kidney test. Janet knew the urine sample would not be sufficient and would need to repeat the urine test and Doctor's appointment in the future.

The overt act of the conspiracy charge states that Vincent Amen destroyed the urine sample. This is untrue since Vincent Amen did not destroy the sample and had no knowledge Gavin was drinking. If this knowledge was not present to Vincent, there would be no motive for him to spill the urine when allegedly Janet left the car. During witness testimony, not one witness said Vincent was a witness to Gavin drinking. The urine spilled in the front passenger seat by Janet Arvizo.

Lastly, it is plausible that Janet accidentally spilled the urine and motives were derived from the equilibrium point in contention.

Based on the model it can be determined Janet had knowledge Gavin was drinking and intentionally spilled the urine with the introduction of the drinking variable.

For further determination of the person of interest who spilled the urine, credibility can be accounted for.

Application to the law can be made by prosecutors and attorneys by creating this model, determining pattern and motive. Motives can be also closer to equilibrium or truth.

Last Point of Interest not included within this model

This was the day the Brazil trip was cancelled by Vincent Amen.

INDEX

Witness List - Prosecution

Martin Bashir 1st pg 3
Ann Marie Kite (Gabriel) 2nd pg 4
Albert Lafferty 3rd pg 8
Davellin Arvizo 4th pg 8
Star Arvizo 5th pg 17
Gavin Arvizo 6th pg 28
Terry Flaa 7th pg 45
Lieutenant Jeff Klapakis 8th pg 47, 42nd pg 122, 68th pg 217, 70th pg 222, 74th pg 228, 94th pg 258
Detective Steve Robel 9th pg 48, 96th pg 260
Paul Zellis 10th pg 52, 92nd pg 256
Detective Victor Alvarez 11th pg 55, 72nd pg 224
Karen Shepard 12th pg 56
Fritz Coleman 13th pg 58
Kiki Fournier 14th pg 60
Detective Wolff 15th pg 64
Shawn O'Grady 16th pg 65
Jeffrey Ellis 17th pg 65
Con Abel 18th pg66
Dr. Anthony Urquizo 19th pg 69
Lauren Wallace 20th pg 74
Louise Palanker 21st pg 75
Robert Cooley 22nd pg 80
Deputy Freddy Padilla 23rd pg 82
Det Craig Bonner 24th pg 83, 71st pg 222, 87th pg 248, 91st pg 252, 95th pg 259
Dr. Antonio Cantu 25th pg 85
Lisa Susan Roote Hemmen 26th pg 88
Charlene Marie 27th pg 91
Heriberto Martinez Jr. 28th pg 92

Alicia Romero 29th pg 92, 31st pg 95

Detective Tim Sutcliffe 30th pg 92, 65th pg 216
Nancy Torres 32nd pg 97
Michelle Shelley 33rd pg 97
Detective Tim Wittenbrock 34th pg 98
Robert Spinner 35th pg 99, pg 112
George Lopez 36th pg 102
Ann Lopez 37th pg 105
Jamie Masada 38th pg 109
Cynthia Bell 39th pg 113
Stan Katz 40th pg 116
William Dickerman 41st pg 119
Jack Green 43rd pg 124
Larry Feldman 44th pg 126
Jesus Salas 45th pg 130
Jason Francia 46th pg 136
Kris Kallman 47th pg 141
Blanca Francia 48th pg 141
Ralph Chacon 49th pg 147
Adrian McManus 50th pg 151
Phillip Lamarque 51st pg 157
Bob Jones 52nd pg 159
Stacy Brown 53rd pg 161
June Chandler 54th pg 163
Dwayne Swingler 55th pg 168
Jay Jackson 56th pg 169
Janet Arvizo 57th pg 174
Detective Alvarez 58th pg 201
Maria Ventura 59th pg 202
William F. Caldwell 60th pg 202
Rod Forney 61st pg 203
Michael Davy 62nd pg 204
Janet Williams 63rd pg 206

Brian Barron 64th pg 208
Stephen Cleaves 64th pg 215
Tim Rooney 66th pg 216
Steven Moeller 67th pg 217
Kassim Abdool 69th pg 218
Cynthia Montgomery 73rd pg 225
Hamid Moslehi 75th pg 229
Gabriel Dominguez 76th pg 237
Ann-Marie Sims 77th pg 238
Joseph Shebroe 78th pg 239
Jeanne Mulcahy 79th pg 240
Deborah Rowe Jackson 80th pg 240
Iris Joan Finsilver 81st pg 244
Andrew Dietz 82nd pg 244
Jeffery Schwartz 83rd pg 246
Crystalee Danko 84th pg 246
Jennifer Simmons 85th pg 247
Joe Corral Jr. 86th pg 248
Dr. Harry Koons 88th pg 249
Detective Rose Smith 89th pg 250
Beverly Wagner 90th pg 251
David Saunders 93rd pg 257
John Duross O'Bryan 97th pg 260
Rudy Provencio 98th pg 264
Witness List – Defense
Wade Robson 1st pg 275
Brett Barnes 2nd pg 277
Joy Robson 3rd pg 278
Chantal Robson 4th pg 281
Marie Lizzete Barnes 5th pg 283
Karlee Barnes 6th pg 284
Francine Contreras 7th pg 285
Gayle Goforth 8th pg 285

Violet Silva 9th pg 286
Ramon Velasco 10th pg 291
Joe Marcus 11th pg 292
Macaulay Culkin 12th pg 296
James Van Norman 13th pg 298
Carlos Velasco 14th pg 302
David LeGrand 15th pg 303
Mark Geragos 16th pg 311
Jean Seamont 17th pf 314
Tiffany Hayness 18th pg 315
Carol McCoy 19th pg 315
Kathryne Bernard 20th pg 316
Maria Gomez 21st pg 317
Shane Merideth 22nd pg 318
Brian Salce 23rd pg 320
Russel Birchum 24th pg 320
Angel Vivanco 25th pg 322
Irene Peters 26th pg 323
Karen Walker 27th pg 328
Simone Jackson 29th pg 331
Rio Jackson 30th pg 332
Michelle Jackson 31st pg 334
Christian Robinson 32nd pg 334
Vernee Watson Johnson 33rd pg 338
Aja Pryor 34th pg 339
Larry Nimmer 35th pg 343
Mark Geragos 37th pg 345
Maria Gomez 38th pg 348
Mike Radakovich 39th pg 349
Mercy Manrriquez 40th pg 351
Marian Arvizo 41st pg 352
Connie Keenan 42nd pg 353
Jay Leno 43rd pg 355

Suli McCullough 44th pg 356
Monica Wakefield 45th pg 356
Mary Holzer 46th pg 357
Anthony Raneri 47th pg 359
Karen Brando 48th pg 359
Prudence Brando 49th pg 359
Phillip Esplin 50th pg 360
Julio Avila 51st pg 361
Lessie Wraggs 52nd pg 362
Arlene Kennedy 53rd pg 363
Chris Tucker 54th pg 363

Witness List – Prosecution Rebuttal

Tim Rooney 1st pg 367
Shane Meredith 2nd pg 367
Jesus Salas 3rd pg 368
Detective Alvarez 4th pg 369
Gina Villegas 5th pg 370
Donna Aggers 6th pg 370
George Erwin 7th pg 371
Theresa Marquez 8th pg 372
Bill Dickerman 9th pg 372
Christie Causer 10th pg 374
Maria Ventura 11th pg 374
Detective Bonner 12th pg 375
Sergeant Steve Robel 13th pg 377

Biography

Vincent Amen attended Carnegie Mellon University and graduated with Honors with a BS in Business Administration in 2002. He is a CEO of a restaurant and real estate group. His expertise is in finance, accounting, operations and management information systems. Vincent worked for Michael Jackson from 2002 – 2003 and then took part in the Michael Jackson Trial from 2003 – 2005. Notable projects included Fox's the Michael Jackson Interview:
The Footage You Were Never Meant to See, Fox's Michael Jackson's Private Home Videos, The Neverland Valley Ranch Romero Britto Celebrity Charity Event, Video Montage of What More Can I Give for the Michael Jackson Bambi Award Ceremony. Vincent resides in New Jersey and has a passion for travel to Europe where his family is from, Austria and Italy.
Vincent, in his spare time, enjoys developing business models as well as creating other quantitative models and its application in diversified fields.

The Michael Jackson

Trial Juror Notebooks

The investigation and Trial of Michael Jackson lasted from November 2003 to June 2005. Leading up to the trial was jury selection. A man named Jeffrey Welbaum was selected as a juror, more specifically an alternate juror. Jeffrey is a controversial juror due to the fact his mother in-law worked at Michael Jackson's Neverland Ranch and he was still selected as a juror. Jeffrey was able to keep his notebooks after the trial since he was an alternate juror. There were only several alternate jurors that had notebooks that fully documented the trial. This book is one of them which is a summary or shortened version of the trial that documents what Jeffrey found meaningful from trial testimony documented witness by witness. In 2006, Vincent Amen purchased the notebooks from Jeffrey Welbaum and later the rights to publish them as a book. There is a great value to the notebooks with positive implications. What does a juror note from Trial testimony to ultimately render a verdict? This question may have never been explored before prior to publishing these notebooks. For prosecutors and defense attorneys alike, these notebooks can be helpful in determining how to try cases. Based on all evidence shown and witness testimony, what a juror finds meaningful to note can provide a means to being more effective in organizing and trying a case.
Enjoy reading the notebooks and based on what is documented, try to come to your own conclusion or verdict.

By Vincent F. Amen

Made in the USA
Monee, IL
04 November 2026

67382288R00223